JAMES FOSTER,

His Book.

1744.

Getty Research Institute
Issues & Debates

PROVENANCE

AN ALTERNATE HISTORY OF ART

Edited by
GAIL FEIGENBAUM
and INGE REIST

THE GETTY RESEARCH INSTITUTE PUBLICATIONS PROGRAM
Thomas W. Gaehtgens, *Director, Getty Research Institute*
Gail Feigenbaum, *Associate Director*

Published by the Getty Research Institute, Los Angeles
Getty Publications
1200 Getty Center Drive, Suite 500
Los Angeles, California 90049-1682
www.getty.edu/publications

Tobi Kaplan, Diane Mark-Walker, and Michele Ciaccio, *Manuscript Editors*
Tobi Kaplan, *Production Editor*
Jeffrey Cohen, *Designer*
Amita Molloy, *Production Coordinator*
Diane Franco, *Typesetter*
Stuart Smith, *Series Designer*

Type composed in Minion and Trade Gothic
Printed in China

16 15 14 13 12 5 4 3 2 1

Library of Congress Cataloging-in-Publication Data
Provenance : an alternate history of art / edited by Gail Feigenbaum and Inge Reist.
p. cm. (Issues & debates)
"This volume evolved from the session "Provenance: The Transformative Power," held at the 96th annual College Art Association conference in Dallas, 21 February 2008."
Includes bibliographical references and index.
ISBN 978-1-60606-112-0
1. Art — Provenance. I. Feigenbaum, Gail. II. Reist, Inge Jackson.
N3999.P76 2013
702.8'8 — dc23

2012029355

Front cover: "Eleanor" crystal vase (detail). See p. 24, fig. 6.
Back cover: Zhao Mengfu, *Four Anecdotes from the Life of Wang Xizhi* (detail). See p. 38, fig. 6.
Frontispiece: Unrecorded typographic bookplate in *A Hymn of St. Bernard's to the Holy Jesus*. See p. 158, fig. 1.

This volume evolved from the session "Provenance: The Transformative Power," held at the 96th annual College Art Association conference in Dallas, 21 February 2008.

CONTENTS

ACKNOWLEDGMENTS

For their unflagging support of this project, we thank Thomas W. Gaehtgens, director of the Getty Research Institute, and Anne Poulet, director emerita of the Frick Collection. At the Getty Research Institute, the invaluable efforts of Galina Tirnanić, Lisa Cherkerzian, and David Mather helped get the manuscript into shape, and Melanie Lazar coordinated the translations. We are especially grateful to our editors, Tobi Kaplan, Michele Ciaccio, and Diane Mark-Walker.

—Gail Feigenbaum and Inge Reist

GAIL FEIGENBAUM AND INGE REIST

INTRODUCTION

Provenance, firmly entrenched though it may be as a standard part of art-historical research today, is neither stable as a concept nor constant as an instrument. Not everyone in the course of history or in every part of the world has cared about who used to own something, even something precious. In fact, it may be fair to claim that it is an interest in how something moved from hand to hand that is noteworthy and prompts our examination, not the absence of such an interest. Sometimes information about provenance has been deliberately suppressed. The role of provenance is contingent on the societies, disciplines, and institutions that make use of its focus of inquiry, tools, and records. Provenance offers an alternative way of narrating a history of art, and the essays in this volume make a strong case for recuperating this narrative for art history.

On the face of it, we all know what *provenance* means: *Merriam-Webster's Collegiate Dictionary*, eleventh edition, defines it quite simply as "the history of ownership of a valued object or work of art or literature," tracing its derivation from the French *provenir* (to come forth), and dating the first known use to 1785.[1] Moreover, information about the procession of ownership has traditionally been understood to be essential to any art-historical examination of a work of art, even if that inquiry was not regarded as a subject worthy of study in its own right. The literature of art history has passed with little reflection on this category of information, favoring other kinds of analysis—stylistic, iconographical, or theoretical—and questions of connoisseurship. Patronage and collecting, which are related to but not quite the same as provenance, have garnered more attention, especially of late. Provenance research has been left to the experts in the art market and to the advisers, collectors, and curators who actively play a role in the transfer of art from one owner to another. For those outside and even inside this latter group, *provenance* might mean little more than a listing of the owners, auctions, and art dealers to which an object has been attached through time. A work's provenance might be mined for clues that contribute to fundamental art-historical knowledge. For example, provenance might reveal that a panel painting in one museum was once in the same collection as one in another museum, and prompt research to discover whether both were once part of the same dismantled polyptych. Or provenance research might suggest that a particular object was commissioned by a patron in whose inventories it appears early on.

In this volume, however, we expand our scope beyond the narrow definition of the term *provenance,* which attends only to the facts of ownership and transfer, to explore ideas and narratives about the origins and itineraries of objects, consider the historical uses of provenance information, and draw attention to the transformative power of ownership. Regarding the last of these points, the essays in this volume demonstrate in myriad ways how the relationship of an owner with a work of art or, in varying degrees, with the work's previous owners, may change irrevocably the way that work will be perceived and understood by future generations.

It is useful to situate the particular concern with provenance within the recent history of Western art history; obviously, this requires that we work with a very broad brush. Half a century ago, art historians tended to understand their primary task to be the recovery of the circumstances attending to a given work of art's origins—its attribution, style, patronage, function, iconography, social context, physical state, and setting. Consequently, an account of a work's subsequent ownership was deemed useful mainly to establish a chain reaching back to the moment of creation and thereby provide evidence to help substantiate authenticity or attribution.

An interest in provenance per se was associated primarily with the art market—not least because a work that had been in a distinguished collection tended to gain value from that association alone—and with writers of the entries that fueled the great age of museum collection catalogs and catalogues raisonnés. Researchers needed to look up evidence to discover and reconstruct the provenance of a given object. The impetus to gather and publish vast quantities of auction and inventory records to support such research drove projects such as the Getty Provenance Index®, to which scores of researchers in at least ten countries have contributed.[2] Provenance is, of course, especially relevant to the history of collecting, and in the early twentieth century classificatory reference tools were created, such as Frits Lugt's monumental dictionary of marks on drawings and prints, *Les marques de collections de dessins & d'estampes* (first published in 1921). More recently, students of the history of collecting found their own uses for the kind of evidence produced through object-by-object provenance research, often aggregating it to reconstruct a collection. Throughout, provenance tended to be circumscribed as a specialized subcategory within the broader scope of the history of collecting.

In the last quarter of the twentieth century, however, lightning struck what had seemed a quiet, essentially antiquarian pursuit. Revelations about systematic and extensive Nazi-era looting and forced sales ignited heated discourse around disputed claims of ownership; these claims posed real-life ethical dilemmas and held legal consequences for prominent stakeholders. Museums felt the pressure to investigate the provenance of works in their collections that could have been implicated in the compromised circulation of art during this period. A large investment had to be made in the research necessary to "clear" (the term that was often used) the provenance of each work. Specialists trained in provenance research were in demand, and guides to help people conduct such research were published.[3]

In parallel with this development, the international archaeological community forcefully articulated a position against the looting and illegal importation of antiquities from sites around the world. New legislation, a heated discourse, and claims for restitution prompted a surge of provenance research targeting traffic in such artifacts. Ethnographic collections likewise came under scrutiny, and questions of what constituted legitimate ownership were hotly debated. Many museums responded by attempting to formulate acquisition policies that were more ethical. Now a number of museums—as well as some scholars—will have nothing to do with an artifact that does not have a known provenance, even if there is no evidence of illegitimate traffic.

Today, the word *provenance* is likely to conjure these kinds of issues, with their complicated interests battled out by attorneys, museum directors, organizations devoted to protecting cultural property, and diplomats, and it is an indication of the power of provenance that it can engender newsworthy drama. Although that story plays in the background of some of the essays in this volume, it is not the focus of the book. Rather, the authors' critical approaches are aligned with interdisciplinary developments in the academy: a conversation among anthropologists, sociologists, economic historians, and cultural historians about the social life of things has suggested new ways for art historians to think about the transmission of the categories of objects that interest them. Marcel Mauss's seminal study on gift exchange (1923), for example, was widely read by art historians in the later twentieth century who were then prepared to take on the models of object biography outlined in Arjun Appadurai's important volume, *The Social Life of Things* (1986).[4] Art historians could also connect such reflections to earlier writings of the Frankfurt school. Walter Benjamin, in "Unpacking My Library," for example, famously remarked how, for its owner, an object's value was affected by its itinerary through history, its provenance.[5] In the wake of such thinking, even provenance research that was of an antiquarian, scientific, and practical character became more susceptible to interpretation.

This book traces its genesis to a conference, in which the editors of this volume participated, held in Paris in 2004 and jointly sponsored by the Getty

Research Institute and the Institut National d'Histoire de l'Art. That conference and a subsequent book, *The Circulation of Works of Art in the Revolutionary Era, 1789–1848,* considered the sheer number of works that changed hands—and the velocity of their transfer—as a direct consequence of revolutions and other political and economic upheavals.[6] Three years later, at a conference in Rome co-organized by the Getty Research Institute and the Bibliotheca Hertziana, the editors again found themselves circling issues relating to the impact that changes in ownership can have on works of art; the resulting publication, *Sacred Possessions: Collecting Italian Religious Art, 1500–1900,* was published in 2011.[7] Here the focus was on how the passage of time and changing possession—as, for example, from a church to private hands or a museum—reconfigured the reception of religious art in the age of collecting, forcing a recalibration of the commingled aesthetic and religious meanings. The two conferences strongly indicated that the moment was ripe to undertake an analysis of the concept of provenance, transnationally and over the long term. Limiting the scope of provenance to only the highly charged context of international legal custody battles or a mere list of names and dates that are painstakingly researched in personal and institutional archives, auction catalogs, and dealers' account books seemed entirely insufficient to the richness of the subject. Engaged in the study of the history of collecting as we are (one of us at the Getty Research Institute's Project for the Study of Collecting and Provenance and the other at the Frick Collection and Frick Art Reference Library's Center for the History of Collecting), we have become convinced that scholars who embrace a broader view of provenance stand to enrich and change their understanding of the works of art that drive their larger research projects.

With that aim, we organized a session on provenance at the College Art Association's annual conference in 2008. The presenters, whose papers are included in this volume, testified to ways that provenance constituted a kind of shadow social history of art. Encouraged by Thomas W. Gaehtgens, director of the Getty Research Institute, to present a broader view of the issue in a publication, we invited additional distinguished scholars to consider the topic from other historical and cultural perspectives. The result is a volume that extends chronologically from ancient archaeology to conceptual art, encompasses Europe, Asia, and the Americas, and includes a variety of media. We see it not as a comprehensive treatment of the topic but as a way to open a discussion and encourage reflection on the more tacit or sublimated concerns of art history.

The book is organized into four thematic parts. The first, "Inscribing Provenance," considers the ways the story of an object's itinerary adheres to that object and why collectors quite literally put their marks on a work of art. "The Time and Place of Provenance" offers a disciplined analysis of the conditions over the *longue durée* of an object's life: how to parse the place of manufacture, subsequent ownership, findspot, and postdiscovery history, and how provenience and provenance inform the conception of cultural patrimony. The essays in "Provenance and Commerce" examine how provenance translates into market value and status. Part four, "Provenance Research Instrumentalized," takes a hard look both at what can be and has been learned through such research and at how such knowledge has been utilized by the art market, political actors, art history, and artists. Finally, in an afterword, Anne Higonnet compellingly argues that art historians would be wise to attend to those "epic tales compressed into such dry lists" and to reclaim the alternate narrative of provenance for the history of art.

Notes

1. *The Oxford English Dictionary* extends the definition to the "documented record" of such history.
2. Founded at the Getty Museum by Burton Fredericksen, established as a separate department in 1983, and now overseen by the Getty Research Institute, the Getty Provenance Index databases were created in order to assemble and make accessible research information related to provenance and the history of collecting. The Provenance Index now contains the records of more than a million paintings from auction sales catalogs and inventories, and it has been expanded to include sculptures, drawings, miniatures, and decorative arts. www.getty.edu/research/tools/provenance/search.html.
3. This phenomenon has been addressed in the press far more than in the literature of art history, and it has produced more instruction manuals than analyses; see, for example, Nancy Yeide, Konstantin Akinsha, and Amy Walsh, *The AAM Guide to Provenance Research* (Washington, D.C.: American Association of Museums, 2001).
4. Marcel Mauss, *Essai sur le don: Forme et raison de l'echange dans les societies archaiques* (Paris: L'année socialogique, 1923); Arjun Appadurai, ed., *The Social Life of Things: Commodities in Cultural Perspective* (Cambridge: Cambridge University Press, 1986). Chris Gosden and Yvonne Marshall, "The Cultural Biography of Objects," *World Archaeology* 31 (1999): 169–78.
5. Walter Benjamin, "Unpacking My Library: A Talk about Book Collecting," in idem, *Illuminations,* trans. Harry Zohn (New York: Schocken, 2007), 66.
6. Roberta Panzanelli and Monica Preti-Hamard, eds., *La circulation des oeuvres d'art=The Circulation of Works of Art in the Revolutionary Era, 1789–1848* (Rennes: Presses Universitaires de Rennes, 2007).
7. Gail Feigenbaum and Sybille Ebert-Schifferer, eds., *Sacred Possessions: Collecting Italian Religious Art, 1500–1900* (Los Angeles: Getty Research Institute, 2011).

PART ONE

Inscribing Provenance

GAIL FEIGENBAUM

MANIFEST PROVENANCE

As a bride, Eleanor gave this vase to King Louis, Mitadolus to her grandfather, the King to me, and Suger to the Saints.

— Abbot Suger's inscription on the mount of the so-called Eleanor of Aquitaine vase[1]

I, Giovanni Andrea Donduzzi, snatched this drawing out of the hand of Signor Agostino Carracci, who wanted to clean the frying pan and light the fire with it.

— Inscribed (according to Carlo Cesare Malvasia) on the back of a pen drawing by Agostino Carracci belonging to Duke Altemps in Rome[2]

Paintings move around... it is up to the experienced dilettante to inquire as to their previous whereabouts.

— Padre Sebastiano Resta[3]

The most distinguished trait of a collection will always be its transmissibility.

— Walter Benjamin[4]

Signs and Codes

With some of the more fascinating voices in the history of art criticism—Abbot Suger, Carlo Cesare Malvasia, Padre Sebastiano Resta, and Walter Benjamin—lighting the way, my essay inspects what might seem to be the most obvious, even banal, attributes of provenance.[5] My interest lies in how the narrative of provenance is made manifest, and how an object's history adheres to it. How is provenance materialized, made visible, reified, expressed? What triggered Walter Benjamin's reveries about past histories of each volume while he was unpacking his library? What was Padre Resta after when, on his visit to Queen Christina's palace, he and Cardinal Azzolini took the pictures off the walls to search their backs for signs of their previous owner? The inscription by Malvasia (quoted above) on the verso of a drawing by Agostino Carracci gives the drawing's provenience—its findspot—which provides a point of departure for the object's provenance as it landed in Altemps's collection.[4] The repertoire of visible marks of ownership such as coats of arms, seals, collectors' stamps, paraphs, and inscriptions is so conventional and ubiquitous as to seem almost natural; the marks tell us, of course, who once owned the thing they are affixed to. Considered in aggregate and over time, however, their patterns of deployment raise essential historical questions. The same holds true for what we might call the literary genre of provenance: the terse, densely formatted listing of owners, in which entries are separated by colons and interspersed with "his sale" or "by descent," that is de rigueur in auction and collection catalogs. Formulaic demonstrations of provenance may be an especially desiccated expression of history—codes to be deciphered by specialists that are of the narrowest interest—yet they are saturated with information and significance, revealing not only taste but also attitudes, events, politics, and social relations that would otherwise go unnoticed. The very fact that provenance slips so easily into an analogy with pedigree, and that genealogy, studbooks, and provenance records employ such similar conventions of expression and have been often associated with the same aristocratic social groups, raises questions worth looking into. Forms and codes of provenance—so straightforward and technical, so scientific—are at the same time indispensable indicators in the exploration of the concept of provenance as it affects the reception and meaning of works of art.[5] Indeed, that is the point of this entire volume. Scholars can confront the ideas underlying the process of ownership and transmission, and recognize transformative effects. But in the end, such analysis depends upon physical evidence, on the ways that information about an object's itinerary attaches to it, on the system of marks, codes, and records of provenance.

Asserting Ownership, Obscuring Provenance

Marking a movable object with a visible sign of ownership is characteristic of many, but by no means all, societies. Ownership marks range from cattle brands to monograms on linens, and so they are hardly peculiar to works of art. The fields of anthropology, sociology, and economic history have traditionally been better equipped than art history to analyze the freight of significance embodied in such a gesture of marking[6]—designating individual or corporate property, assigning particular value to such property, signaling a concern with rightful ownership or theft, and so on. However, for the kinds of *things* conventionally encompassed by the category of art, whether an illuminated manuscript, a drawing by Raphael, or a Chinese scroll, marks of ownership have tended to become elaborate and conventionalized. Marks are often placed on works of art that are portable and easily transmissible. In a sense, this enacts in miniature the kind of self-identifying gesture associated with real property, such as placing coats of arms above the entrance of noble houses. On movable property, one function of marks of ownership is to discourage theft, which has, throughout the history of valuable objects, been a common challenge. This explains in part why museums long continued the tradition of putting their stamp of ownership on drawings, often prominently, often on the recto, and sometimes even on unmounted drawings where the verso was exposed and available for marking.[7] Until recently, the practice was widespread, even though its effect can be disfiguring and can interfere with artistic intention.[8] Marks that discourage theft are, like a cattle brand, meant to be visible and indelible. Such is their raison d'être.

In practice, marks of ownership fulfill functions that are more varied than mere security. They are a means to *display* ownership.[9] This can be useful when an object is deployed in social circulation—when, for example, it is given as a gift or is loaned—in which case a mark prominently declares the owner of the thing. On the occasion of a sumptuous banquet in Renaissance Italy, the host might borrow silver from another prominent family. Silver engraved with a monogram or arms is, of course, more likely to be returned safely to its owner afterward. But the mark could also serve a representational function: guests who recognize the monogram would understand that the host enjoys a relationship with the tableware's important owner. The mark would act as signifier of politics, status, and power.[10] Conversely, someone in possession of previously owned silver might want to obliterate the original owner's mark and thereby erase its identification with that person. Taking this to an extreme, the provenance, and even the object itself, might be of little value to a new owner. Evidently, the Marquis de Marigny had no use for the monogrammed silver tableware he inherited from his sister Madame de Pompadour. Whatever sentimental value it may have had was outweighed by the value of the silver content; he had it melted down and made into a spectacular toilette service in the new style, turning it into a wedding gift for his new wife.[11]

Heraldry was widespread in medieval and early modern Europe and functioned as a way of marking ownership. Coats of arms very frequently appear on the covers and pages of books and on medieval manuscripts. Arms can identify the patron of the manuscript or, if the object was commissioned as a gift, the intended recipient. In the case of a manuscript by Jean de Courcy, *La Bouquechardière,* the arms of the patron are incorporated into an illumination.[12] They appear on folio 133v in the corner of the cheerfully decorated margins of a page illuminated with a miniature, *Dido Directs the Building of Carthage.* The arms of Jacques d'Armagnac, the bibliophile and Duke of Nemours, who commissioned the work, are painted in the lower left corner. Banderoles extending from the arms are inscribed with his motto, creating a highly personalized page. Soon after the book was made, in 1476, Jacques d'Armagnac was arrested for joining a revolt against the king. *La Bouquechardière* was seized and became the property of Tanguy du Chastel, who had his coat of arms painted over the original one; however, it must have been important to make manifest the superimposition of the new over the old, and Jacques d'Armagnac's motto was left prominently visible. It was the coat of arms per se that functioned as an explicit mark of ownership and that had to be supplanted. The superimposition of Tanguy du Chastel's arms can be interpreted as a gesture of *damnatio memoriae,* or a cautionary sign (in light of the original owner's treason), but this kind of obliteration is widespread enough to suggest that this was not such a special case.

It would be worth conducting a more systematic investigation, but many owners of medieval manuscripts seemed to have been disinclined to preserve the marks of previous owners. For example, in a Boccaccio manuscript of circa 1413–15, the ex libris of the original owner, Girard Blanchet, was scraped off so effectively by its subsequent owner that it can now be seen only with ultraviolet light.[13] Simon de Varie's book of hours includes a frontispiece miniature of a woman holding an escutcheon by Jean Fouquet (fig. 1). Originally, the shield displayed the heraldry of the recently ennobled commissioner, but it was overpainted with the arms of Bourbon-Condé, representing its later owner, while once again the motto was allowed to remain visible.[14] The conventions of marking ownership on luxury manuscripts were highly developed and artful, and they contributed to creating a personalized object. A few examples hardly suffice to establish a trend, but the evidence suggests that in the case of continental medieval manuscripts a new owner was often inclined to erase or paint over the mark identifying an old owner and thus disinclined to preserve the visible marks of the history of the manuscript.

English Renaissance books of hours, which were often passed down within families for generations or bequeathed to a close friend or associate, offer useful evidence of provenance being recorded and effaced. Changes in ownership would typically be recorded in the books in the form of inscriptions, obituary entries, and coats of arms. If a book definitively left the circle of family and friends, usually moving to an owner lower down on the social scale, the old marks of elite ownership evidently were regarded as an undesirable sign of secondhand goods. For someone who was not in a position to commission a new book, the next best thing was to erase all signs of earlier owners and start fresh with his own marks of ownership, thereby establishing his own provenance. A late-fourteenth-century book of hours in the Bodleian Library made for minor gentry, for example, is filled with inscriptions added as it passed by marriage

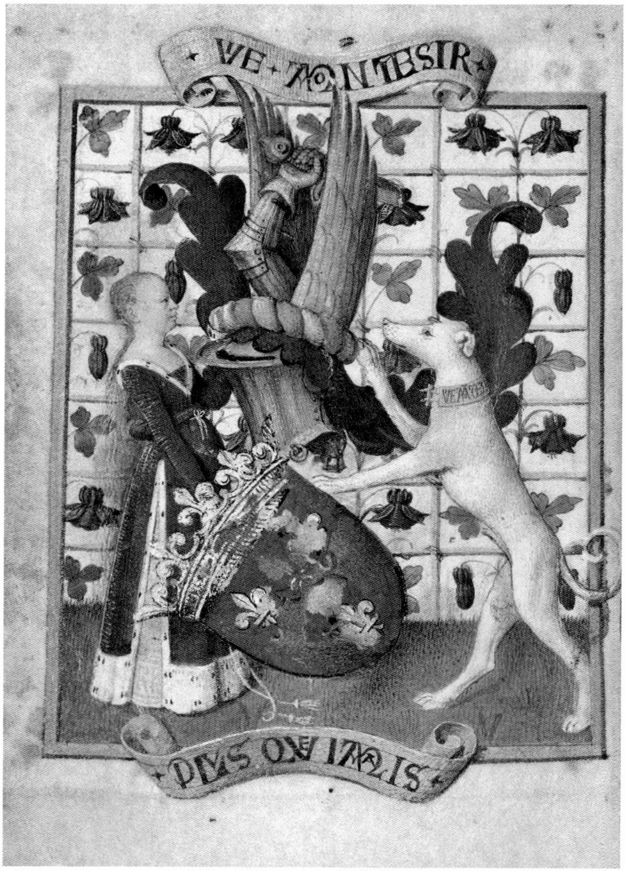

Fig. 1.
Jean Fouquet (French, ca. 1415–81).
Coat of Arms Held by a Woman and a Greyhound, 1455, tempera colors, gold paint, gold leaf, and ink on parchment, leaf: 11.4 × 8.3 cm (4½ × 3¼ in.). Los Angeles, J. Paul Getty Museum, Partial gift of Gerald F. Borrmann, Ms. 7, fol. 2v, 85.ML.27.2v.

and inheritance. Eventually, it seems to have been sold, and either the seller or the new owner made sure to have all traces of the previous family's ownership (now readable under ultraviolet illumination) carefully pumiced from the vellum, whereupon the new owner's family started fresh with a long litany of their own births and deaths.[15] On the other hand, when Henry VII gave his mother a book of hours seized from the defeated Richard III, she took it as a trophy, scratching through Richard's name so that it could still be seen while marking her proprietorship with her own name, Margaret Richmonde—only to have her name eventually scratched out by a subsequent owner.[16] These examples indicate both that the recording of family history, a manifestation of ownership, in the English books of hours was a widespread practice and that such traces of the identity of previous owners—including elite proprietors—could become unwelcome marks that would need to be erased. In the case of something confiscated from a defeated enemy, a message could be conveyed by the very gesture of crossing out the visible marks of ownership—name and coats of arms—in such a way that they could still be detected.

Collectors' Marks on Drawings

Drawings have been a prime locus for the notation of provenance in the Western tradition. Systems of marking drawings grew so elaborate, and have been so meticulously researched, that they are especially useful to a discussion on how provenance is made manifest. A medieval manuscript was marked as a unique possession; for drawings, the mark of ownership seems to originate in, and be linked specifically to, the practice of collecting a quantity of similar objects. The owner of a single sheet is not as likely as the owner of many drawings to have given it a mark. There is a fine distinction between what can properly be called a collector's mark and a broader category of marks of ownership; collectors did not necessarily mark every object they owned. The practice of forming a collection of drawings originated as early as the fifteenth century, and collectors' marks date back to these beginnings. The earliest example in the great drawings expert Frits Lugt's repertory was that of a fifteenth-century Veronese signatory named Felixo.[17] By the mid-sixteenth century, the collecting of drawings as a practice had taken hold, and the tendency was for such collections to grow fascinatingly large: Giorgio Vasari's famous albums may have contained as many as 2,000 drawings. In the seventeenth century, Padre Sebastiano Resta amassed a collection of 3,500 drawings, and Queen Christina of Sweden's numbered more than 5,000. These seem almost modest compared with the megacollections of the eighteenth century, such as those of Lambert Krahe, who sold some 15,000 of his drawings, and Pierre Crozat, who left 19,201 drawings in

202 portfolios at the time of his death in 1774. These, however, were dwarfed by some of the great print collections, which grew even more immense.[18]

Vasari was the first in a distinguished line of writers—including Malvasia, Pierre-Jean Mariette, Giovanni Pietro Bellori, Francesco Maria Niccolò Gabburri, Roger de Piles, and Joshua Reynolds, among many others—who avidly collected drawings and used their collections as a means to work out the history of art. Such collector-*amateurs* conducted serious research on their drawings, trying to figure out their attributions, linking them with a finished commission, and working out the characteristics of regional styles. Often, they recorded their findings on the mount, on the page of an album, or on the verso of the drawing itself. As part of their research, they paid attention to provenance. Jonathan Richardson Sr., among the most avid and important collectors of the eighteenth century, was interested in provenance and made frequent notations of it. Sometimes he recorded simple information about provenance, writing on the mount of one drawing, "given me by Mr. Frankland,"[19] and on another, "Brought from Florence by Sr. Andrew Fountayne."[20] Provenance is an integral part of the information he inscribed on another sheet: "Bought at Rome by Mr. Andrew Hayes of Sigr Anto Crecolini, a painter." He goes on to say that this head of Saint Peter is by the same artist as the one who painted this apostle "on one side of an Altar in a Church in Rome (Mr. Hayes has forgotten the name of it) S. Paul stands on the other side," adding later "the Ch: of San Giacomo delli Spagnoli, going to the Piazza Navona, the first altar on the Lefthand."[21] The great Italian drawings collector Padre Sebastiano Resta had a particular concern with provenance. He made use of it, for example, in figuring out the attribution of one of his drawings considered by many to be by Annibale Carracci. Padre Resta thought it was more likely by Peter Paul Rubens, his opinion bolstered by the fact that it had been acquired from Monsù Habbè, from whom he had gotten other Rubens drawings.[22] Writing such provenance information on the verso of a drawing or on its mount was one of the most efficient ways to attach a story to an object.

Organizing and administering collections of drawings that ran into the thousands presented a challenge. Drawings, even whole albums of drawings, were prone to circulate rather too easily. Anecdotes abound about collectors who lent a drawing or an album to someone, whether to interest them in buying it or in response to a request, only to find that getting it back from the borrower proves to be a struggle. Outright thefts were a problem. In the late eighteenth century, the Roman sculptor and dealer Bartolomeo Cavaceppi had an enormous collection of drawings that he kept in numbered order in ninety albums; after he died, but just before an inventory could be made, fourteen of those albums were stolen. Later, many of the drawings missing from the

Cavaceppi collection found their way into the collection of artist Johann Martin von Wagner, agent of King Ludwig I, where they could be identified by the numbering that tied them to gaps in the inventoried albums.[23] Inscribing inventory numbers on drawings or their mounts, or adding folios to album leaves, was one method for keeping track of a collection, either by the owner or, after his death, by the executor, when a collection was inventoried for purposes of an inheritance or a sale. These inventory numbers can be regarded as marks of ownership intended to record the identity of objects in a particular set, and experts have learned to recognize them as evidence of provenance.

As part of their collection's organization and presentation, many owners put their drawings in special mounts, both to preserve them and to enhance their display. Specialists can recognize the characteristic mounts of certain collectors, and the mat itself can become a sign that carries forward information about the previous owner of the drawing. The mounts of renowned eighteenth-century collector and dealer Pierre-Jean Mariette are perhaps the most famous example in this regard.[24] It was common for collectors to inscribe their paraph or to impose a personalized stamp on drawings or on their mounts, though not every collector did so. In some major collections, for example that of Peter Lely, stamps were added not by the collector but by his executors, after the owner's death in 1680, as part of the process of preparing the collection for transfer or sale.[25] An object coming out of such a famous collection would have gained a special cachet rendered visible by the mark, hence adding to its desirability and market value. In fact, the use of the word *cachet* to designate prestige is a metonymic figure of speech deriving from the French word for an official seal or stamp.

It is important to note that in some collections not every sheet would be marked. A collector might place his mark only on selected groups of his finest drawings, which were often the same ones provided with elegant mounts. In such cases, the marking can be understood as the exercise of a collector culling masses of drawings, filtering out those of highest quality. It was the ordering and marking process that created a collection out of what had been merely an accumulation.[26] In the seventeenth and eighteenth centuries, an age of spectacular drawings collections, the markings become more elaborate, evolving into a system of signs by which an "amateur communes with his colleagues of the past and the present."[27] As a drawing changed hands in this tradition, its new owner added his mark in proximity to that of his predecessor and so inscribed himself in a visible chain of ownership. Marks can be on the drawing itself (recto or verso), on the mount, or on both the drawing and the mount; as a drawing changes ownership, the marks can add up. One sees venerable old-master drawings marked with a flurry of stamps, paraphs, and inventory

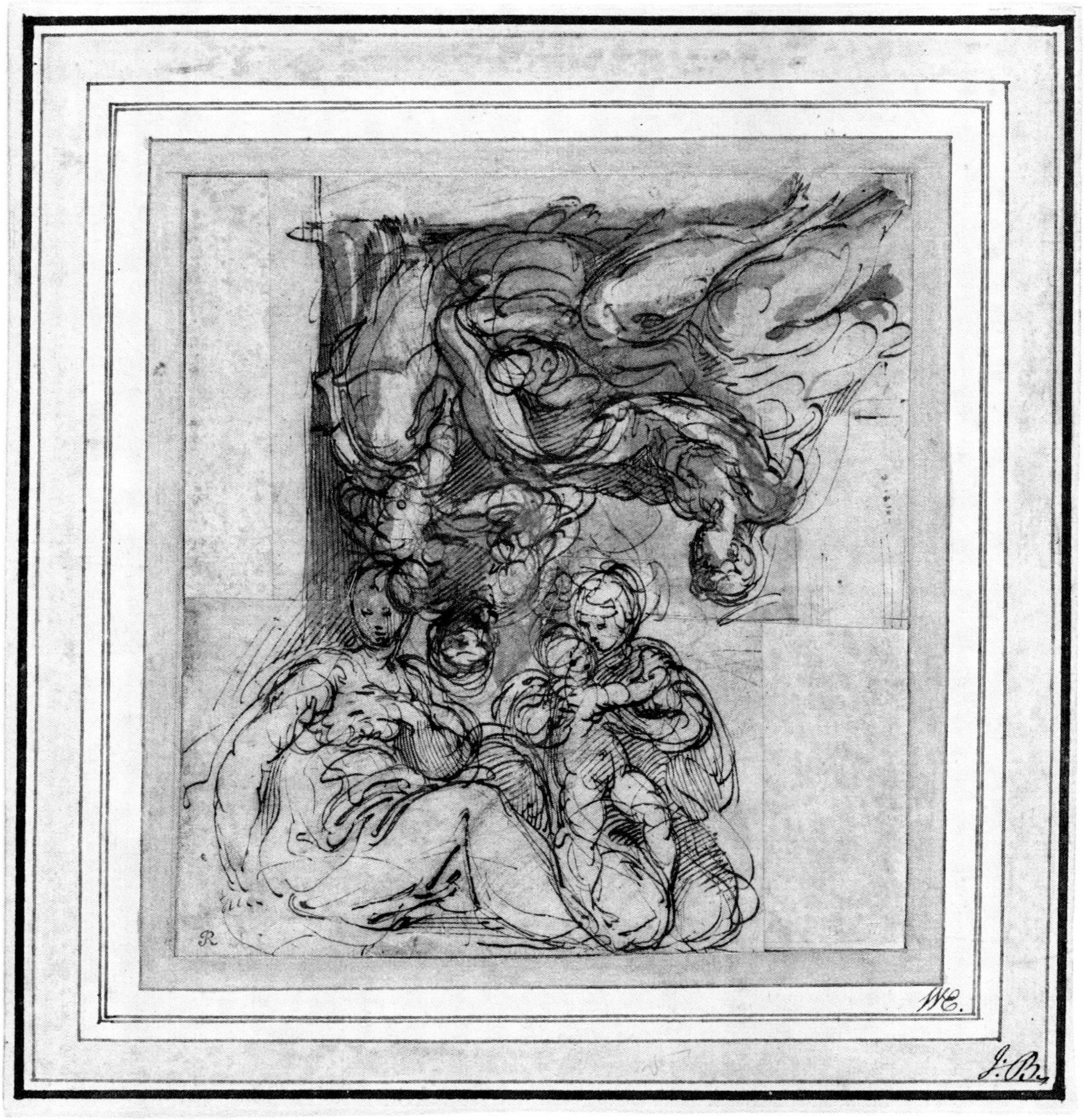

Fig. 2a.
Parmigianino (Italian, 1503–40).
Two Studies for a Holy Family, 1526, pen and brown ink, brush with brown wash over red chalk, heightened with white gouache, incised line separating the two studies at the center of the sheet, 14.9 × 13.7 cm (5⅞ × 5⁵⁄₁₆ in.). Los Angeles, J. Paul Getty Museum, 96.GB.317.

numbers that, depending upon one's eye, embellish a drawing with its distinguished history or interfere with the artist's aesthetic intention. A sheet at the Getty with two lively sketches by Parmigianino of a Holy Family contains rich evidence for tracking provenance (figs. 2a, 2b). Laid down on what is evidently a Jonathan Richardson Sr. mat, with his characteristic ruled border banded with pink wash, the drawing includes a mark (by Richardson) on the recto of the drawing and a plethora of marks on the recto and verso of the mat and mount: William Esdaile's monograph in brown ink, Benjamin West's dry stamp, John Barnard's monograms on the front and back of the mat, John Thane's mark

Fig. 2b.
Verso of fig. 2a.
Los Angeles, J. Paul Getty Museum, 96.GB.317.

(J. Th) in graphite, the marks of Charles Sackville Bale, and a note indicating the Charles Fairfax Murray collection.[28] From other records comes the information that the drawing also had been in the collection first of Thomas Howard, Earl of Arundel, and then Sir Peter Lely.[29] It is no accident that the desire to have visible signs of its itinerary displayed on an object coincides with the new practice of including provenance information in auction catalogs of paintings (see the essay by Raux, this volume). The information about an object's earlier owners constitutes both historical value and market value, wherein cachet is commodified.

Some marks on drawings signify historical episodes of great drama: deaths, spectacular sales, politics, and reversals of fortune. The unsurpassed holdings of the Musée du Louvre's Cabinet de Dessins had their origins in the drawings owned by the French kings. Curators of this vast collection have combed the archives and meticulously studied its formation, much aided by the copious markings on the drawings and the characteristic mounts of the contributing collectors.[30] The royal collection was formed mainly of large collections of drawings assembled by others, such as Everhard Jabach or Pierre Crozat, sometimes acquired for the express purpose of selling them to the king but other times acquired in a more peremptory fashion. For example, after the death of Charles Le Brun, Louis XIV's court painter, all of his productions and his collection of drawings were seized by the crown, and, as part of the accession process, the sheets (at least the finest of them) were marked with the paraph of Jean Prioux, chief examiner of the Châtelet de Paris.[31]

Such marks attest to a remarkable episode in French history: the transfer of ownership, in the aftermath of the Revolution, of the French royal collections and property seized from the Church and from émigrés. The politics of transferring royal property to the revolutionary government just when power was being centralized in the Committee of Public Safety, and of moving the property into a newly created museum, were intensely charged. The transfer of the drawings collection was orchestrated with great ceremony: on the appointed day, 20 February 1794, the entire Conservatoire traveled to the home of Citizen Vincent, who had custody of the drawings, to begin the process. On this occasion, the drawings' reception was effected by impressing on the recto the mark of the French Republic (a small "RF" stamped on one corner by Citizen Vincent) and the mark of the Commission of the National Museum ("MN" in a circle).[32] These are marks of a new beginning; the state itself is under new ownership, and the stamps enlist the drawings in the establishment of the new order. One can see evidence of this deployment in the case of a composite of three drawings by Domenico Beccafumi in the Louvre that consists of a study of Hercules flanked by two sketches of Venus, laid down and framed with elegant volutes and cartouches that place it in Giorgio Vasari's *Libro de disegni,* which was in turn laid down on Mariette's characteristic mount (fig. 3). To the cartouche, Mariette added the inscription "olim ex Collectione Georgii Vasari, nunc P.J. Mariette." The work was acquired by King Louis XVI in 1775 during the posthumous sale of the collection of Pierre-Jean Mariette. Nineteen years later, on the occasion of the French Republic and its national museum taking possession, the marks of the Conservatoire and the Commission of the Museum were stamped on each of these three studies on the lower left and right corners of the recto, respectively.

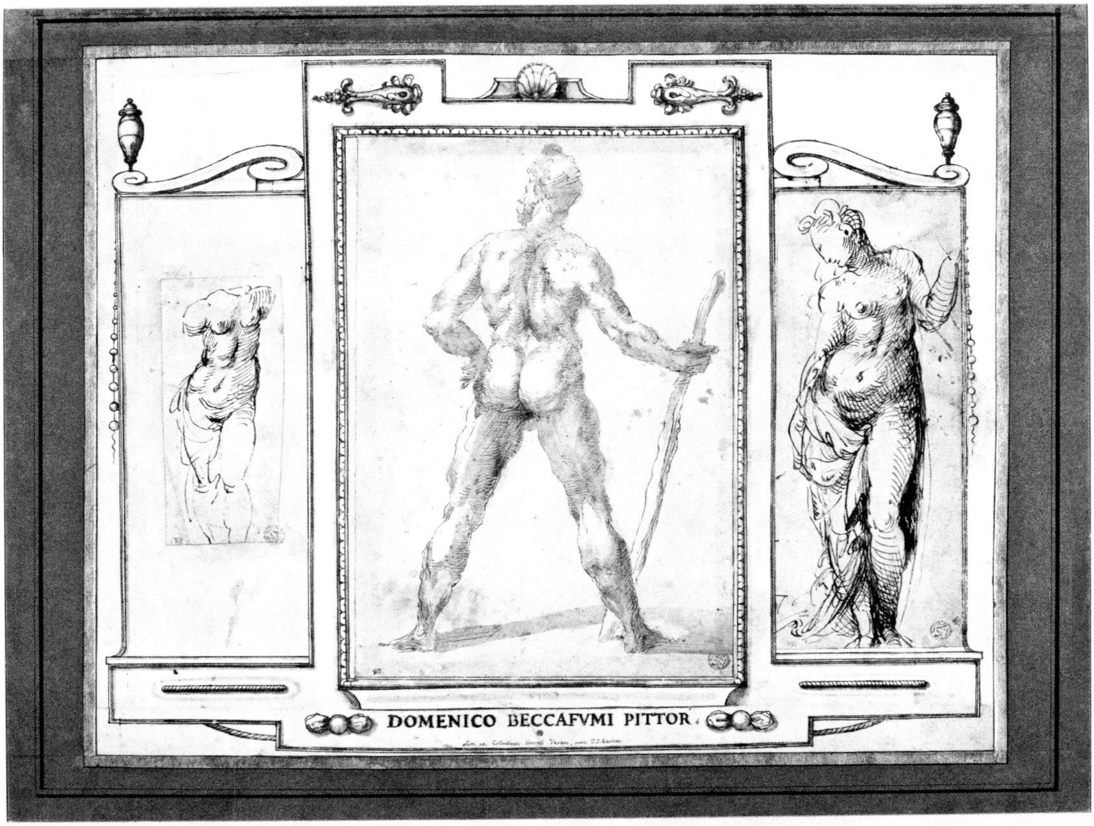

Fig. 3.
Domenico Beccafumi (Italian, 1486–1551).
Torso of Woman without Arms or a Head Viewed from the Front (Venus); Standing Nude Man Viewed from the Back, Legs Apart, Holding a Stick (Hercules); Standing Woman Viewed from the Front (Venus), ca. 1530s, pen and brown ink with brown wash, drawing: 34.4 × 43 cm (13⅝ × 17 in.), mount: 40.2 × 52 cm (15⅞ × 20½ in.).
Paris, Musée du Louvre, Département des Arts graphiques, 255.BIS.

Marks on Paintings

Old-master paintings are also frequently marked by their owners, though not as systematically as drawings are. Paintings belonging to some major collections, such as the Giustiniani, have wax seals with the owner's arms on the back of the canvas, panel, or stretcher; occasionally, they have the seals of a succession of prominent owners (fig. 4).[33] Marks are often put on pictures when they enter royal or state collections, or when the collections are moved or reinstalled. Typically, such marks are a form of aristocratic, royal, or state insignia—a simplified coat of arms—often a wax seal impressed on the back of the canvas or panel, or branded on the wood of the stretcher. Presumably, it was this kind of evidence that Padre Resta was seeking when he visited the palace of Queen Christina after her death, in 1689, in the company of her heir, Cardinal Azzolini, and they took the pictures off the walls to search the backs for information about their provenance.[34]

In a gesture analogous to giving personalized mounts to drawings, many collectors, like the Giustiniani in Rome, the Niccolini in Florence, or the Elector Palatine, Karl Theodor, in Düsseldorf, had their prized pictures put into

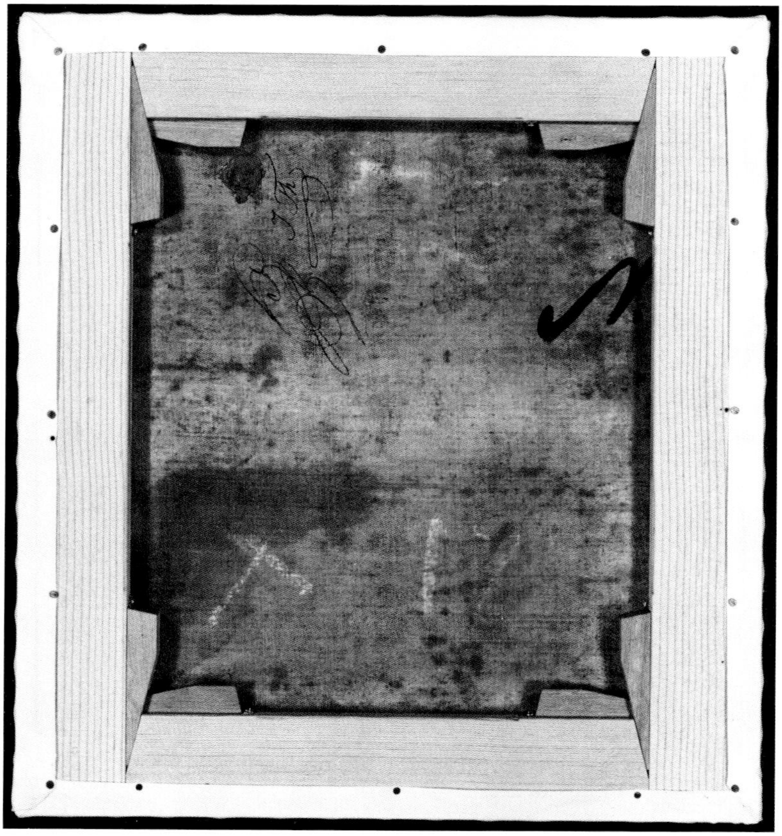

Fig. 4.
The back of Lorenzo Lotto (Italian, 1480–1556). *Portrait of a Young Man,* ca. 1526–30, oil on canvas, 47.5 × 37.5 cm (18¾ × 14¾ in.). Berlin, Staatliche Museen zu Berlin, Gemäldegalerie, inv. 320.

specially designed frames that made the works immediately recognizable as belonging to their collection.[35] Both marks and frames are specifically intended to identify an owner's possession of an object, but the frames can also serve to indicate that the object belongs to a collection. When King Charles I engaged Abraham van der Doort as surveyor of his collection in May 1625, his duties included marking the works of art and giving them inventory numbers; the king commanded him "to prevent and keepe them . . . from being spoiled or defaced, to order marke and number them, and to keepe a Register of them, to receive and deliver them, and likewise to take order for the makeing and coppying of Pictures." Under Van der Doort, the king's pictures were branded on the stretchers with a distinctive monogram.[36]

Placing an inventory number on a painting, quite often on the front, was on the one hand a tool for managing movable property and on the other a means of indicating that an object had been incorporated into a collection. Inventory numbers can serve as evidence to restore the link between an object and its history of ownership. This was recently demonstrated by searching the Getty Research Institute's Provenance Index® database for information about

Rubens's *The Entombment* (ca. 1612), a painting in the collection of the J. Paul Getty Museum. Searching "Rubens" and "146," the number inscribed on the front of the canvas, retrieved a record describing the painting in the inventory of Gaspar de Haro y Guzmán Carpio (1629–87), revealing the previously unknown identity of the painting's first owner.

One can compare the European early modern practices and systems of provenance marks and recordkeeping to those described in Zaixin Hong's essay in this volume. That essay considers the most highly developed tradition of imposing the marks of owners on works of art: the seals impressed on Chinese handscrolls and the poetic inscriptions (colophons) recording the reception of these works. The seals and colophons rest on the surface plane of a scroll as if occupying a dimension of time and space independent from that of the painting as representation. In these marks and inscriptions, the record of provenance is visually cast to capture a cultural conversation that takes place over the *longue durée* of history, in which each owner responds to the ones who came before and addresses the ones who will come after. The self-conscious gesture of an owner situating himself in this historical chain creates an insistent visual commentary that not merely affixes the narrative of provenance to the object but also inheres in the work itself.

Provenance and Bloodlines

The expression of provenance in words has developed into a formula to articulate systematically and "scientifically" the litany of past owners and record the means by which an object passed from one to the next. Over time, this set piece has grown conventionalized and standardized, although without quite attaining a thoroughgoing consistency. Provenances reified in this way can even exist independently of an object, as, for example, the provenance of a portrait of Sir Thomas More by Hans Holbein the younger. This portrait had a remarkable early history; it was commissioned in 1526 by King Henry VIII and purportedly thrown out the window by an angry Anne Boleyn. An entry in Giuseppe Gualdi's unpublished Roman diary from the years 1651 to 1655 in the Getty Research Institute records such a portrait displayed in 1652 in the annual exhibition of paintings at San Giovanni Decollato in Rome, where it is described in terms of this dramatic episode of its provenance rather than any other features.[37] Yet today there exist three versions of such a portrait, and we are not at all certain which one was so dramatically defenestrated. Here, provenance has become detached from its object.

On occasion, an object has what could be regarded as a perfect provenance tightly bonded to it, as might be said of Sébastian Bourdon's *Portrait of Countess*

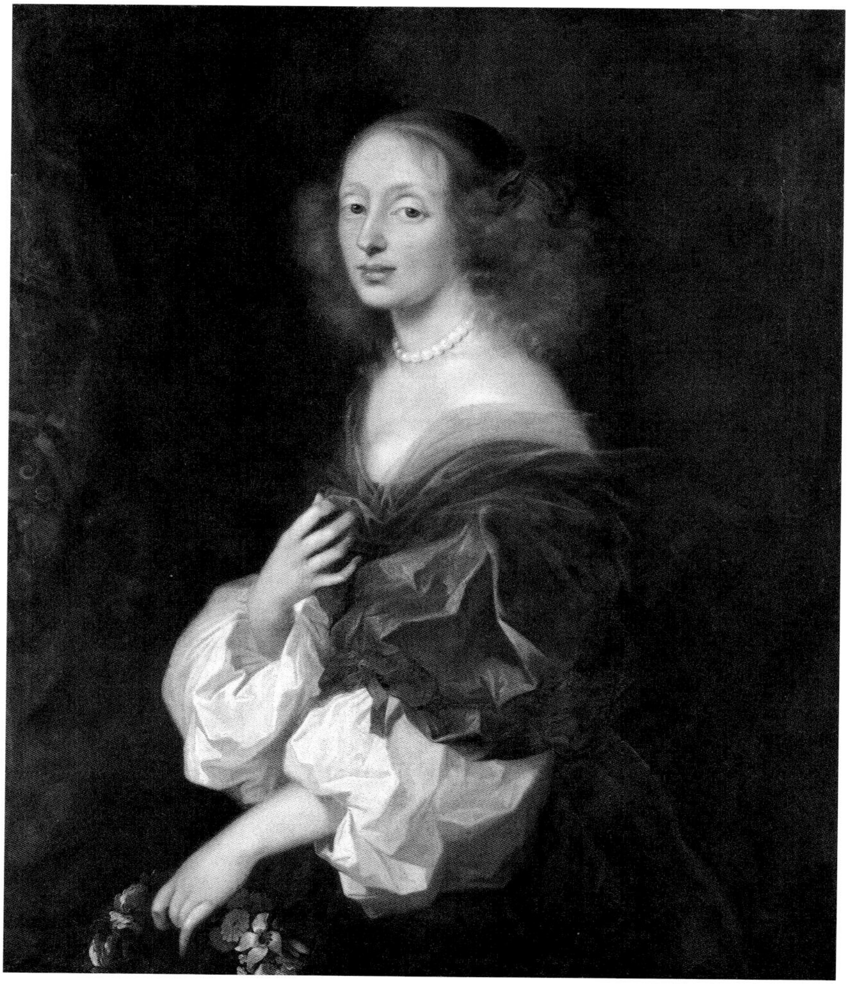

Fig. 5.
Sébastian Bourdon (French, 1616–71).
Portrait of Countess Ebba Sparre, 1652–53, oil on canvas, 106.1 × 90.2 cm (41¾ × 35½ in.). Washington, D.C., National Gallery of Art, Samuel H. Kress Collection, 1952.5.34

Ebba Sparre (1652–53), the beautiful lady-in-waiting to Queen Christina (fig. 5). This is a case where the painting's ownership and whereabouts can be tracked at virtually every moment in its three-hundred-year history, from the artist's easel in Stockholm to the walls of the National Gallery of Art in Washington, D.C. Here is the statement of its provenance as it was commissioned, sent, sold, bought, consigned, given, and inherited by queens, cardinals, princes, dukes, counts, auctioneers, dealers, businessmen, and a museum, all impeccably recorded in the National Gallery's recent *Catalogue of French Paintings:*

> Probably commissioned by Christina, queen of Sweden [1626–1689], Stockholm, Antwerp, and inventoried 1656 among her goods to be sent to Rome; by inheritance to Cardinal Decio Azzolini [1623–1689], Rome; by

inheritance to his nephew, Marchese Pompeo Azzolini [d. 1696], Rome; sold to Principe Livio Odescalchi, Duke Bracciano [1652–1713], Rome; by inheritance to his nephew, Baldassare Odescalchi-Erba [d. 1746]; sold 1721 through Pierre Crozat [1665–1740] to Philippe II, duc d'Orléans [1703–1752], Paris; by inheritance to his son, Louis Philippe Joseph, duc d'Orléans [1747–1793], Paris; sold 1791 with the French and Italian paintings of the Orléans collection, which figure as a group in the next three sales, to Edouard, vicomte Walkuers [or Walquers], Brussels; sold 1792 to his cousin, François Louis-Joseph, comte Laborde de Méréville [d. 1801], Paris and London; on consignment until 1798 with (Jeremiah Harman, London); sold 1798 through (Michal Bryan, London) to a consortium of Francis Egerton, 3rd Duke of Bridgewater [1736–1803], London and Worsley Hall, Lancashire, Frederick Howard, 5th Earl of Carlisle [1748–1825], Castle Howard, North Yorkshire, and George Granville Leveson-Gower, 1st Duke of Sutherland [1758–1833], London, Trentham Hall, Stafford, and Dunrobin Castle, Highland, Scotland; (Orléans Collection sale [French and Italian paintings], Coxe, Burrell and Foster, London, February 14, 1800, no. 11, as *The Portrait of the Queen of Sweden*). John Maitland [d. 1831], London, Loughton Hall, Essex, and Woodford Hall, Essex; (his estate sale, Christie & Manson, London, July 30, 1831, no. 14, as *Portrait of Christina, Queen of Sweden*); Joseph Neeld [d. 1856], Grittleton House, near Chippenham, Wiltshire; by inheritance to his brother, Sir John Neeld, 1st bt. [1805–1891], Grittleton House; by inheritance to his son, Sir Algernon William Neeld, 2nd bt. [1846–1900], Grittelton House; by inheritance to his brother, Sir Audley Dallas Neeld, 3rd bt. [1849–1941], Grittleton House; by inheritance to Joseph Neeld's descendant through an illegitimate daughter, Lionel William [Inigo-Jones] Neeld [d. 1956], Grittleton House; (Neeld sale, Christie, Manson & Woods, London, July 13, 1945, no. 52, as *Portrait of Christina of Sweden*); purchased by Kaye. (Wildenstein & Co., Inc., Paris, New York, and London); sold 1947 to the Samuel H. Kress Foundation, New York.[38]

The form of notation is a marvel of clear, efficient communication of a detailed narrative. The densely concentrated provenance also informs us that at some point in the century after Queen Christina's death, the queen, rather than Ebba Sparre, becomes named as the sitter, a misidentification that persisted consistently until the mid-twentieth century. As the countess's portrait traveled—from Stockholm to Rome, then to Paris and the Orléans collection, then to London, New York, and, finally, Washington, D.C.—its provenance remained firmly attached to it, even when it passed for a queen.

A work of art that comes down to us without its history of ownership has often been considered as somehow diminished, missing something important. Frits Lugt compares fine drawings that bear no mark of their provenance to foundlings—*enfants trouvés*. He believed that fine pieces, conversely, carry the indications of their provenance like "*titres de noblesse*" that ensure them a worthy reception in society.[39] Lugt slips easily into the ubiquitous analogy of provenance and genealogy or pedigree. He makes the claim that the quality of provenance can be judged by a set of criteria that have nothing to do with aesthetic quality or the character of an object but rather constitute a parallel narrative of the history of that art object. In this, Lugt takes a position opposite that of such writers as Antoine-Joseph Dézallier d'Argenville, or Jonathan Richardson Sr., or Eugène Piot, who are careful to separate the judgment of artistic merit from distinguished pedigree. D'Argenville claims that the history of a drawing and its association with the names of amateurs, the fact of its belonging to grand collections, is useful only for *marchands* who are interested in this sterile knowledge for the market advantage it affords them;[40] Richardson was especially skeptical of the good provenance that purportedly guaranteed authenticity of a drawing.

Lugt was only one of countless writers to embrace the metaphor of pedigree or genealogy and provenance. One often reads of an object possessing an impeccable or an impressive pedigree. This usually means either that it has arrived in our time with an exceptionally well documented history of ownership or that it has passed through the hands of someone important or famous, or who is an especially discerning collector. If an object's itinerary of previous owners is actually quite different from the ancestry of a person or animal, the elision of this difference reveals a curious habit of thought in which things gain luster by association, like a touch relic. Like provenance, a pedigree confers value and can be used as proof of superior qualities. It is about noble bloodlines for people and champions for animals. In fact, the conventions for expressing bloodlines are very close to the conventions for expressing provenance. In Weatherby's studbook of 1791, for example, which supplies this information for Thoroughbred horses, words like *begat* or *out of* are substituted for *bequest* or *by descent*.[41] The people likely to be most keenly interested in exalted bloodlines of Thoroughbred horses, or in titled prospective mates for their daughters, were frequently the same sort of people who acquired works of art. It is easy to see how this slippage could be exploited in the art market. Elizabeth Pergam's essay in this volume examines a fascinating instance: what might be called portraits of provenance and pedigree in the American market for British portraits of the aristocracy.

Thereby Hangs a Tale

I will conclude by invoking the words that Suger, abbot of Saint-Denis monastery near Paris, had engraved on the mount of the so-called Eleanor vase, now in the Louvre (fig. 6). He thought the vase's provenance was so crucial to the meaning of the object that in the 1140s he not only recorded it in detail in a document but also used a robust means—a new mount he had fabricated with an inscription—to attach it sturdily and make it integral with the piece. The mount is a parerga that holds the vessel in its embrace and transforms it into a new work, one that also takes on the task of conveying the object's biography. As Suger expresses with such poetic economy in the inscription, the provenance of this object embodies an extraordinary historical narrative of conversion. The rock-crystal vessel is of Sasanian origin and probably dates to the seventh century, but its first identified owner is Mitadolus, the twelfth-century Muslim king of Saragossa. Mitadolus gave the vase to William the Troubadour, his ally in the reconquest of Spain; in a Christian-Muslim collaboration, the two had fought side by side and had emerged victorious at the Battle of Cutanda in 1120.[42] William took the vase back to his capital in Poitiers and bequeathed it to his granddaughter Eleanor, who brought it as a wedding gift in her marriage to Louis VII of France in 1137, symbolizing the short-lived unification of the Duchy of Aquitaine and the French crown. It likely came to Suger when Eleanor's marriage was dissolved, and in the 1140s Suger "converted" the object by offering it to the saints.[43] This is a perfect instance of an object that has been transformed and must make its provenance manifest, must testify and memorialize its history as it is transferred from one owner to the next—in this case as it was transformed from its Muslim origins into first a symbol of state and political alliance and finally into an object dedicated to the Christian saints. The course of the vase's provenance was drastically altered yet again at the time of the French Revolution, when the goods belonging to the saints at Saint-Denis were seized by the French Republic; those goods, including the Eleanor vase, entered the National Museum on 5 December 1793.

Perhaps one can think about the visible sign or mark of provenance as a sort of parerga, an accessory that carries the freight of the memory and history of an object. It can take the form of an integral inscription pertaining to origin or reaching back to the provenience, as defined in Rosemary Joyce's essay in this volume. Engraving such an "autobiographical" message is an old and widespread practice, as evidenced by the text on an ancient Chinese set of bronze bells dating to the Warring States period indicating that the bells were given by King Hui of Chu to Marquis Yi. It can take the form of heraldry or insignia

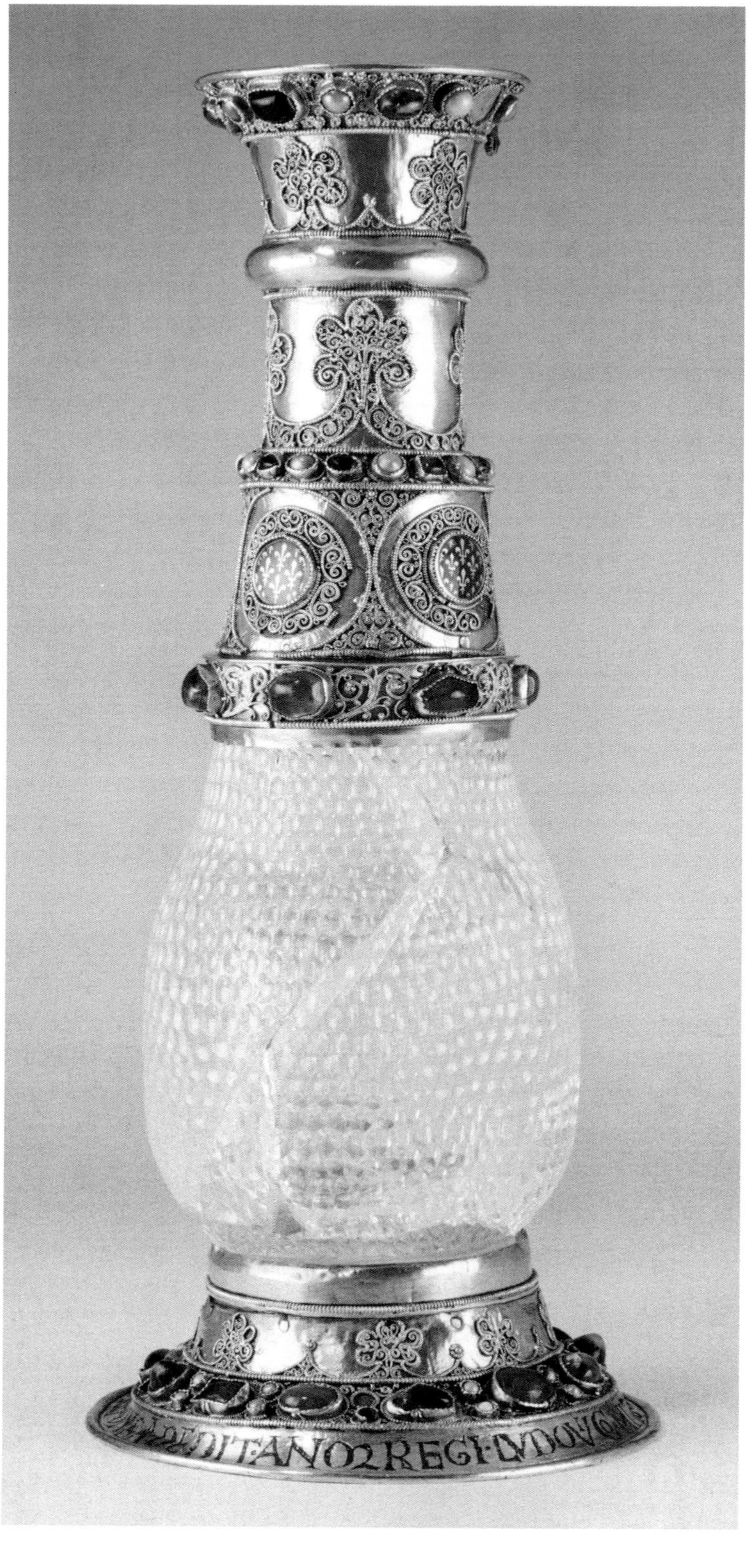

Fig. 6.
"Eleanor" crystal vase.
Crystal: Sasanian, 6th or 7th century; mount: French, before 1147, 13th and 14th centuries; rock crystal, gilded and filigreed silver, niello, gemstones, pearl, champlevé enamel, height: 33.7 cm (13¼ in.), diameter: 15.9 cm (6¼ in.). Paris, Musée du Louvre, MR 340.

of the commissioner or subsequent owner. Or, in the early modern age of collecting, it can be imposed on an object to designate it as part of a collection. We cannot always know if an object was marked in this way with the expectation that it would remain forever part of a collection, or if the consciousness of previous transfer and future transmissibility was embodied in the very act of imposing the mark.

Notes

1. Inscription on the mount of the so-called Eleanor of Aquitaine vase (see fig. 6, this essay); mount and inscription added by Abbot Suger in the 1140s: "HOC VAS SPONSA. DEDIT. ANOR REGI. LUDOVICO. MITADOL[us]. AVO MIHI REX. S[an]C[TIS] Q[ue] SUGER[ius]." See George T. Beech, "The Eleanor of Aquitaine Vase: Its Origins and History to the Early Twelfth Century," *Ars Orientalis* 22 (1992): 69–79; Daniel Alcouffe et al., *Le Trésor de Saint-Denis*, exh. cat. (Paris: Réunion des Musées Nationaux, 1991), 168–72.
2. Anne Summerscale, ed. and trans., *Malvasia's Life of the Carracci: Commentary and Translation* (University Park: Pennsylvania State University Press, 2000), 265.
3. "Girano le pitture... resta l'arbitrio al dilettante e sperimentato d'inquirere dove altre volte si trovassero," quoted in Genevieve Warwick, "Connoisseurship and the Collection of Drawings in Italy c. 1700: The Case of Padre Sebastiano Resta," in *Collecting Prints & Drawings in Europe c. 1500–1750*, ed. Christopher Baker, Caroline Elam, and Genevieve Warwick (Aldershot, U.K.: Ashgate, 2003), 148–49.
4. Walter Benjamin, "Unpacking My Library: A Talk about Book Collecting," in idem, *Illuminations*, trans. Harry Zohn (New York: Schocken, 2007), 66.
5. I am grateful to Peter Fuhring for his helpful comments on this essay.
6. Arjun Appadurai, "Introduction: Commodities and the Politics of Value," in *The Social Life of Things*, ed. Arjun Appadurai (Cambridge: Cambridge University Press, 1988), 3–59. In the same volume, see Igor Kopytoff, "The Cultural Biography of Things: Commoditization as Process," 64–90, and Patrick Geary, "Sacred Commodities: The Circulation of Medieval Relics," 169–90. Also see Michael Thompson, *Rubbish Theory: The Creation and Destruction of Value* (Oxford: Oxford University Press, 1979); and Mary Douglas and Baron Isherwood, *The World of Goods: Towards an Anthropology of Consumption* (London: Routledge, 1996).
7. Although the new French Republic embraced this practice, institutional stamping seems to have started systematically in France only under Louis Philippe during the July Monarchy, as a reaction to a certain *désordre*, when the following line was added to the rules governing libraries, dated 26 March 1833: "Every book, every manuscript, every piece of music, printed sheet, that enters the royal library must be stamped without delay" (translation mine). See P. Josserand and J. Bruno, "Les estampilles du département des imprimés de la BN," in *Mélanges d'histoire du livre et des bibliothèques offerts à Monsieur Frantz Calot* (Paris: Librairie d'Argences, 1960), 261–98, particularly 283. I thank Peter Fuhring for this information.

8. Laurence Lhinares, "Vers une nouvelle édition du Lugt," *Revue de l'Art,* no. 143 (2004): 80. Lhinares notes that Joseph Maberly (1783–1860) considered the practice of collectors stamping the recto of drawings to be "barbare" and "vaniteux" and recommended that amateurs put their marks discreetly on the verso of their drawings.
9. See Barbara Furlotti, *A Renaissance Baron and His Possessions: Paolo Giordano I Orsini, Duke of Bracciano (1541–1585)* (Turnhout, Belgium: Brepols, 2012), for an excellent discussion of this.
10. Barbara Furlotti, "Consumption and Baronial Identity in Sixteenth-Century Rome: Paolo Giordano I Orsini and His Possessions, 1541–1585" (PhD diss., Queen Mary College, University of London, 2009).
11. Alden R. Gordon, "Breathing Life into Inventories Made after Death: Strategies for Decrypting and Correlating Archival Sources with Social Practices of Daily Life" (paper presented at the symposium Taste and the Senses: Aesthetic Formation and Material Experience in Eighteenth-Century France, Getty Research Institute, Los Angeles, 3 June 2011).
12. Elizabeth Morrison and Anne D. Hedeman, *Imagining the Past in France: History in Manuscript Painting, 1250–1500* (Los Angeles: J. Paul Getty Museum, 2010), 253–55. My thanks to Elizabeth Morrison and Thomas Kren for their generous help with questions of provenance on manuscripts.
13. Morrison and Hedeman, *Imagining the Past in France,* 220, 222n2.
14. James H. Marrow, *The Hours of Simon de Varie* (Malibu: J. Paul Getty Museum, 1994), 5.
15. Eamon Duffy, *Marking the Hours: English People and Their Prayers, 1240–1570* (New Haven, Conn.: Yale University Press, 2006), 24–25; and John Barron, "The St. George's Hours," *Bodleian Library Record* 20, nos. 1–2 (2007): 30–33.
16. Duffy, *Marking the Hours,* 33.
17. Frits Lugt, *Les marques de collections de dessins & d'estampes... supplement* (The Hague: Martinus Nijhoff, 1956), L. 2999a, 422. Formerly identified as Felice Feliciano, see Lhinares, "Vers une nouvelle édition du Lugt," 76, and 76, fig. 4. Lugt is available online at http://www.marquesdecollections.fr.
18. For this topic in general, see Christopher Baker, Caroline Elam, and Genevieve Warwick, eds., *Collecting Prints & Drawings in Europe c. 1500–1750* (Aldershot, U.K.: Ashgate, 2003); especially see therein Antony Griffiths, "The Archaeology of the Print," 9–27.
19. Carol Gibson-Wood, "'A Judiciously Disposed Collection': Jonathan Richardson Senior's Cabinet of Drawings," in *Collecting Prints & Drawings in Europe c. 1500–1750,* ed. Christopher Baker, Caroline Elam, and Genevieve Warwick (Aldershot, U.K.: Ashgate, 2003), 156.
20. Gibson-Wood, "'A Judiciously Disposed Collection,'" 163.
21. Gibson-Wood, "'A Judiciously Disposed Collection,'" 156.
22. Warwick, "Connoisseurship and the Collection of Drawings in Italy c. 1700," 152.
23. Stefan Morét, "Johann Martin von Wagner as a Collector of Drawings," in *L'Artiste collectionneur de dessin: De Giorgio Vasari à aujourd'hui,* Rencontres internationales du Salon du Dessin 2, ed. Catherine Monbeig Goguel and Cordélia Hattori (Milan: 5 Continents, 2007), 103–4.

24. For a description of Mariette's characteristic mount, see Carlo James et al., *Old Master Prints and Drawings: A Guide to Preservation and Conservation,* trans. and ed. Marjorie B. Cohn (Amsterdam: Amsterdam University Press, 1997), 19–21.
25. Diana Dethloff, "Sir Peter Lely's Collection of Prints and Drawings," in *Collecting Prints & Drawings in Europe c. 1500–1750,* ed. Christopher Baker, Caroline Elam, and Genevieve Warwick (Aldershot, U.K.: Ashgate, 2003), 123.
26. The very large drawings collections were built not sheet by sheet but by the acquisition of caches of drawings, sometimes from other collectors, sometimes from artists' studios where they had been preserved as a working archive. See, for example, Jeremy Wood, "Nicholas Lanier (1588–1666) and the Origins of Drawings Collecting in Stuart England," in *Collecting Prints & Drawings in Europe c. 1500–1750,* ed. Christopher Baker, Caroline Elam, and Genevieve Warwick (Aldershot, U.K.: Ashgate, 2003), 85–122.
27. Frits Lugt, "Introduction," in idem, *Les marques de collections de dessins & d'estampes...* (Amsterdam: Vereenigde drukkerijen, 1921), vi; available online at http://www.marquesdecollections.fr/introduction.cfm.
28. Nicholas Turner, *European Drawings 4: Catalogue of the Collections* (Los Angeles: J. Paul Getty Museum, 1988), 75–76, cat. no. 26.
29. *Catalogue of the Valuable Collection of Ancient and Modern Drawings, of Mr. William Benoni White,* Christie, Manson & Woods, London, 29 January 1880, lot no. 4.
30. For an excellent study and bibliography of the history and administration of the Louvre's drawings collection, see Lina Propeck and Laurence Lhinares, "Signatures, marques et paraphes administratifs des dessins du Louvre, 1671–1796," *Revue du Louvre* 2 (2003): 45–55.
31. Frits Lugt, *Les marques de collections de dessins & d'estampes...* (Amsterdam: Vereenigde drukkerijen, 1921), L.2953, 549; see http://www.marquesdecollec tions.fr/detail.cfm/marque/10293/total/1. This entry reads in part: "Jean Prioult [*sic*] was charged in 1690, probably on the occasion of the death of Lebrun, to verify the inventories of drawings acquired by Jabach (no. 2959) for the cabinet of the king in 1672. He did this with great care, renumbering again each of the drawings and countersigning them with his monogrammed initials beside those of Jabach."
32. Lugt, *Les marques de collections de dessins & d'estampes* (1921), L.1899, 348; see http://www.marquesdecollections.fr/detail.cfm/marque/8538/total/1#. Propeck and Lhinares, "Signatures," 50–51. This process is recorded, by the Conservatoire's President Fragonard and Secretary Le Sueur, in "Les Procès-verbaux des séances du conservatoire," published in Yveline Cantarel-Besson, ed., *La naissance du musée du Louvre,* vol. 1, *La politique muséologique sous la Révolution d'après les archives des musées nationaux* (Paris: Éditions de la Réunion des Musées Nationaux, 1981), 15–17.
33. Silvia Danesi Squarzina, *La Collezione Giustiniani* (Turin: Giulio Einaudi, 2003).
34. Genevieve Warwick, *The Arts of Collecting: Padre Sebastiano Resta and the Market for Drawings in Early Modern Europe* (Cambridge: Cambridge University Press, 2000), 79–80.

35. It is interesting to see that in the eighteenth century several paintings by particularly famous artists were selectively culled from the Giustiniani collection and given elaborate new gilded frames that also featured the name of the painter.
36. Oliver Millar, *The Queen's Pictures* (New York: Macmillan, 1977), 44–46. Thank you to Giles Waterfield for this reference.
37. Gioseffe [Giuseppe] Gualdi, "Diario del Gualdi: Tome II, 1651–1655," 1651–55, Getty Research Institute, Los Angeles (850961). Ingo Herklotz has published important selections pertaining to art from Gualdi's day. Ingo Herklotz, "Fabriche di Roma nel 1651, 1652, 1653: Kunst- und baugeschichtliche Nachrichten aus dem *Diario* des Giuseppe Gualdi," *Analecta Romana Instituti Danici* 29 (2003): 216n27. The painting described here is identified as the version formerly in the Crescenzi collection and now in the Frick Collection, New York.
38. Philip Conisbee et al., *French Paintings of the Fifteenth through the Eighteenth Century* (Washington, D.C.: National Gallery of Art, 2009), 40.
39. Lugt, "Introduction," vi.
40. Antoine-Joseph Dézallier d'Argenville, quoted in Lugt, "Introduction," vi.
41. Weatherby and Sons, *An Introduction to a General Stud Book* (London: Weatherby and Sons, 1791). My thanks to Faya Causey for this reference.
42. Beech, "The Eleanor of Aquitaine Vase," 69, 74–76, and Alcouffe et al., *Le Trésor de Saint-Denis,* 168–71.
43. Philippe Buc, "Conversion of Objects," *Viator* 28 (1997): 99–143. In discussing the "Eleanor" vase as a converted object, Buc notes that that the older identity had to be recognizable and memorialized, and that the "converted object should display its itinerary," 100.

ZAIXIN HONG

ISSUES OF PROVENANCE IN THE LAST EMPEROR'S ART COLLECTING

One of the most controversial cases involving provenance in China over the past centuries concerns the last emperor's collection of antique calligraphy and painting. Over the course of more than three decades, the Xuantong emperor Aisin-Gioro Puyi (1906–67, r. 1909–11) started to dismantle the Chinese imperial art collection that his Manchu forefathers had amassed.[1] Puyi's career as a collector can be tracked in three stages: first, during his time as the deposed emperor, when he still had a court in Beijing (1912–24); next, during his court's exile, partially under Japanese protection in Tianjin (1925–32); and, finally, as the puppet ruler of Japanese-controlled Manchukuo in Changchun (1932–45). Throughout these stages, he devoted a great deal of attention to his Manchu forefathers' art collection; it was a symbol of his imperial identity as he undertook a sustained effort to restore and reclaim his authority after being forced to abdicate in 1912.[2] From 1922 to 1923, he secretly arranged to have more than a thousand important scrolls of calligraphy and painting taken from the former palace. This action became the focal point of a major controversy about the last emperor's art collecting, especially after the Palace Museum was established in 1925, because the collection that Puyi considered to be his imperial family's property was seen by the Republican governments as national patrimony, even as national treasures.[3]

The dispersal of Puyi's collection of ancient calligraphy and painting during and after his stay in Tianjin, and especially after the collapse of Japan and Manchukuo in August 1945, has attracted the attention of collectors, dealers, and museum experts from all over the world. Among a number of studies of the dispersed collection,[4] of particular interest is *Guobao chenfu lu: Gugong sanyi shuhua jianwen kaolüe* (Record of the vicissitudes of national treasures: Investigation of the dispersed and lost calligraphies and paintings from the former palace that I have seen and heard about) by the former museum director Yang Renkai (1915–2008).[5] His investigations, which extended over a half century, have provided a comprehensive reference guide to these cultural properties.[6] His findings, as well as his biases concerning evidence of provenance, became widely available to Western audiences in a 2008 exhibition at the China

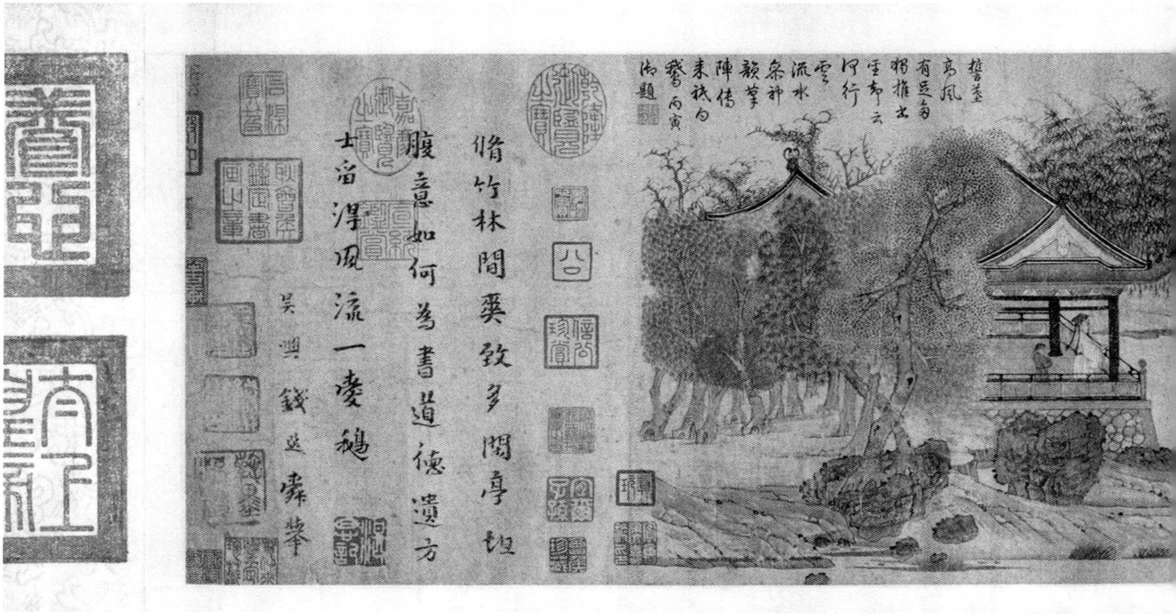

Fig. 1.
Qian Xuan (Chinese, ca. 1235–ca. 1307).
Wang Xizhi Watching Geese (detail), ca. 1295, ink, color, and gold on paper, this image: 23.2 × 92.7 cm (9⅛ × 36½ in.); overall handscroll with mounting: 27.9 × 1,063.8 cm (11 × 418 13/16 in.). New York, Metropolitan Museum of Art, Ex coll.: C.C. Wang Family, Gift of The Dillon Fund, 1973 (1973.120.6).

Institute in New York.[7] Coincidentally, another exhibition involving Puyi's dispersed collection (though it was not acknowledged as such) opened in New York at about the same time at the Metropolitan Museum of Art. One of Puyi's favorite handscroll paintings in the imperial collection, Qian Xuan's (ca. 1235–ca. 1307) *Wang Xizhi Watching Geese* (hereafter referred to as the Qian Xuan scroll) was among the highlights of the Metropolitan Museum of Art's exhibition (fig. 1).[8]

Unlike the exhibition at the China Institute, which addressed issues of provenance in its presentation of masterpieces of calligraphy and painting originally in the former Qing imperial collection (on loan from the Liaoning Provincial Museum), the exhibition at the Metropolitan Museum—which aimed to educate an American audience about the aesthetic and thematic qualities of Chinese painting—left the issue of the scroll's provenance outside the discussion. It is, however, this very issue that my essay considers. Focusing on Puyi and the last phase of the Chinese imperial collection, I examine the special characteristics of provenance in Chinese scroll painting and look at how notions of provenance shifted with the emergence of the idea of national treasures in China. The discussion will, I hope, shed new light on our understanding of provenance through "the cultural biography of objects"[9] such as the Qian Xuan scroll.

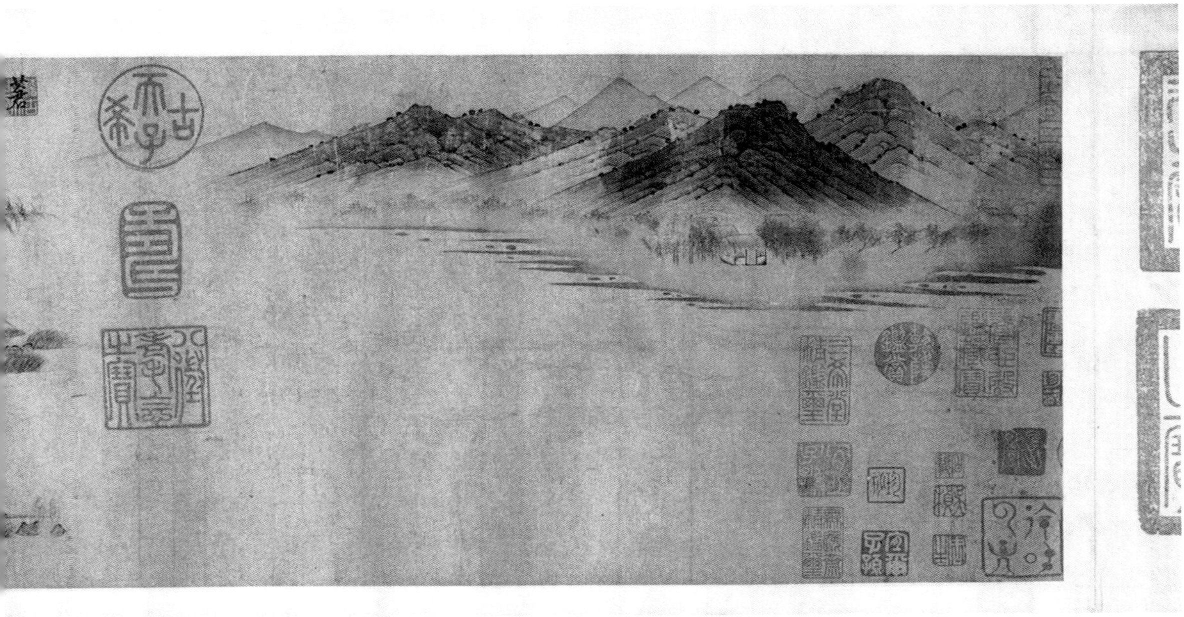

I

Before beginning our inquiry into Puyi's collection of antique calligraphies and paintings, let us first consider the format of the artworks that he removed from the palace during the years after his abdication in February 1912. According to the earliest catalog of the 1,353 items that he took,[10] 19.9 percent were in album leaf format and the rest were handscrolls.[11] Handscrolls and album leaves are both easily portable.[12] In fact, a nickname for a portable scroll is *xingkanzi*, meaning, figuratively, "an object to be viewed in motion."[13]

Because of the way it is read—by holding it in both hands and unrolling it horizontally—the handscroll is well suited for private viewing. As Robert Hans van Gulik observed, a handscroll "can unfold [its] beauty only when passing through the loving hands of the observer: while his left hand unrolls it he loosely rolls it up with his right. Thus one never sees more than one section at a time, a part only a few feet in length."[14] Compared with a vertical hanging scroll, a fan, or a screen,[15] a handscroll affords its owners the largest surface area for recording the work's provenance: collectors may add (or subtract) as many colophons (in either prose or verse), seals, or both as they wish.

The Qian Xuan scroll is a good example in this regard because it includes all three major sections found in traditional Chinese handscrolls (fig. 2). Each handscroll has a label ("L" in fig. 2). The first section, called the *yinshou* ("a" in fig. 2), opens the scroll with an inscription highlighting the theme of the painting; it functions something like a title page. In the Qian Xuan scroll, the

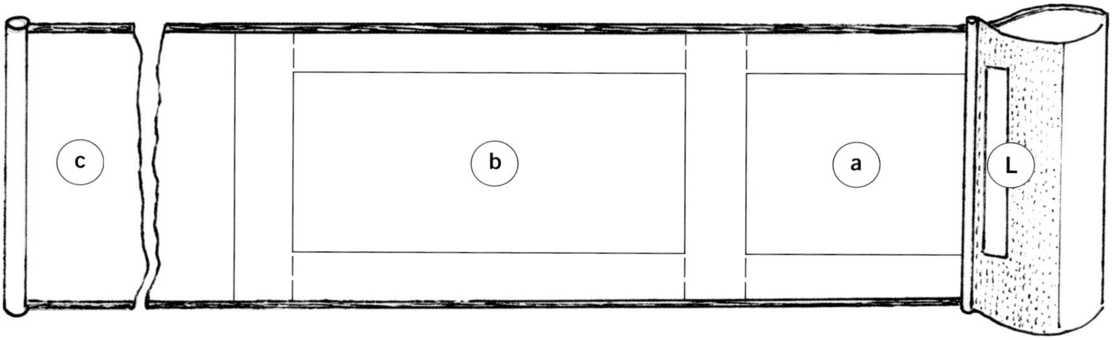

Fig. 2.
Diagram of a Chinese handscroll showing (L) *tiqian* (the label), (a) *yinshou* (the title sheet), (b) *huaxin* (the main body of the painting), and (c) *tuowei* (the last section, a long strip of blank paper).

sheet of ornamental paper ("a" in fig. 2) used for the *yinshou* is inscribed by the Qianlong emperor (1711–99, r. 1736–95), who added three of his seals—one applied in 1746 and other two in the 1790s. The next section, called the *huaxin* ("b" in fig. 2), comprises the body of the painting and can include the painter's handwritten poem or inscription, signature, and seals, along with various indications of those who collected or viewed the scroll, such as colophons, catalog-ing marks, and seals. The last section is called the *tuowei* ("c" in fig. 2). In the Qian Xuan scroll, it is a very long strip of ordinary blank paper that provides both the scroll's physical backing and an additional area for more commentary and information about provenance. Thus, a Chinese scroll can present a wealth of provenance information, all on its front surface. In contrast, a Western work on paper typically presents only a few inscriptions, collectors' seals, inventory marks, and so forth, and these are often placed on the reverse of the work because they may be regarded as visually disruptive.[16] In China, however, such marks can be welcome, especially from a collector's perspective; they often supplement and enrich the viewer's experience of a painting.

The three sections of the Qian Xuan scroll form a veritable archive, with their dense accumulation of a total of 52 colophons by the painter, the imperial collectors, and their courtiers, plus a total of 132 seals of the painter, collectors, and inscribers, ranging in date from the early thirteenth century to the 1970s.[17] The scroll is impressive not only for its high artistic quality but also for its valuable archival evidence.

Before leaving the Forbidden City, Puyi had his seals added to most of the calligraphies and paintings from the Qing imperial house, thereby declaring his ownership. The Qian Xuan scroll bears two of his seals, together with 21 colophons and 34 seals of his courtiers and loyalists—a large number that indicates the scroll was probably the masterpiece he most admired. Of all the works he took from Beijing, it has, as the only piece we know of so far, the greatest number of colophons (23 added after leaving Beijing, making 44 altogether) and seals (23 added later, making 57 altogether) by his followers. From 1918 to 1940, Puyi arranged for these colophons and seals to be added in three separate places on the scroll.

The attention Puyi paid to this single handscroll painting was unparalleled for him. Yang Renkai describes these activities in a distinctly negative way:[18]

> After the puppet Manchukuo emperor Puyi found his political position relatively secure, he began to think of those treasures that he had kept in Tianjin. The same treasures also caught the attention of the Japanese militarists. Both parties had their own plans [for their usefulness]. Puyi wanted to use them to parade his wealth. Pretentiously imitating the "elegant and gallant style" of his ancestor the Qianlong emperor, he sometimes summoned his subjects Zheng Xiaoxu [1860–1938], Hu Siyuan [1869–?], and Luo Zhenyu [1866–1940] to his "court," displaying the paintings in private viewings and having them inscribe them, as in such famous examples as the early Yuan painter Qian Xuan's *Watching Geese* scroll. Its *yinshou* [i.e., the title sheet] bears Qianlong's inscription of four characters "shanyin yixing" (Wang Xizhi's untrammeled inspiration) in regular script, and its *tuowei* [i.e., last section] has verses written by six [actually seven] of Qianlong's courtiers, such as Liang Shizheng [1697-1763], Wang Youdun [1692-1759], and so forth. Not wanting to be left behind, Puyi strove to follow exactly what his ancestor had done. Following the six [actually seven] poems by Liang Shizheng [and six other courtiers], there are forty more, by such figures as Chen Baochen [1848–1935] and Shang Liuyan [1869–1960], who were gathered together to inscribe new poems [on the scroll] using Qianlong's poetic rhyme. The event assembled nearly all the major servants of the puppet cabinet of Manchukuo, a special gathering that did no more than add a dog tail to a mink coat [i.e., added a wretched sequel to a fine work].

Yang's dismissive tone in this account will be discussed later, but here we may note that in describing the Qian Xuan scroll he offers both external and internal evidence, in traditional Chinese fashion. The external evidence is provided by the Qing dynasty inventories.[19] These are similar to but not nearly as numerous as the external documentation frequently available in the West, where there are often extensive archives or published inventories, sale and auction catalogs (usually with annotations), visitor reports kept in museum records, and so forth. Scholars of Western art can consult all of these resources when investigating provenance. While scholars of Chinese art may not have the benefit of those same resources, they can utilize provenance data visible on the surface of a painting itself, which can be extremely rich, as the Qian Xuan scroll demonstrates.

To better understand the last phase of the history of imperial art collecting, we should first note that Puyi must have regarded the Qianlong emperor as the most illustrious of all his Manchu Qing dynasty predecessors. Nearly contemporary with the Russian empire's Catherine the Great (1729–96), Qianlong initiated a comparable golden age of art patronage.

When we examine the Qian Xuan scroll more closely, we can see that the scroll's provenance while in the hands of both the Qianlong emperor and Puyi is more complicated than Yang's summary indicates. Though the second catalog of his collection of calligraphies and paintings, compiled in 1791, does not mention Qianlong's later interactions with the scroll,[20] it is evident that forty years after the first gathering, in 1746, when his followers had embellished the scroll with their colophons and seals, Qianlong added more seals to the *yinshou* (the title sheet) and the *huaxin* (the main body of the painting).[21] Furthermore, a close inspection of Yang's characterization of the scroll's history during Puyi's time—a history that is clearly visible on the scroll's surface[22]—shows that Yang's description contains historical inaccuracies in at least three places, related to three periods:

1. Although Shang Liuyan was the last inscriber of the scroll, he should not be juxtaposed with Chen Baochen, who did not follow Puyi to Manchukuo but died from an illness in Tianjin in 1935. As Puyi's mentor, however, Chen initiated the commemorative gathering inside the Forbidden City after the young emperor was forced to step down for the second time, the attempt to restore him to the throne having failed in July 1917.[23] On the *tuowei* section of the Qian Xuan scroll, twenty-one subjects contributed colophons between 17 February 1918 and February 1922.
2. Puyi summoned Zheng Xiaoxu, Hu Siyuan, Luo Zhenyu, and fifteen other loyalists to gather in his "court" not when he was in Changchun (from 1932 to 1940) but when he was in Tianjin, which was between February 1926 and sometime in 1927, and thus well before he was enthroned in 1932 as the puppet emperor of Manchukuo in northeast China. Figure 3 shows a section of the Qian Xuan scroll with the seal that Puyi added in 1926.[24]
3. In Changchun, only five, not forty, of Puyi's loyalists added colophons with their seals, dating from 13 February 1936 to 30 September 1940.

For the Qian Xuan scroll, a few external records of provenance, such as the Qianlong emperor's catalog and modern catalogs and writings, provide the kind of external evidence familiar to provenance researchers in the West; the

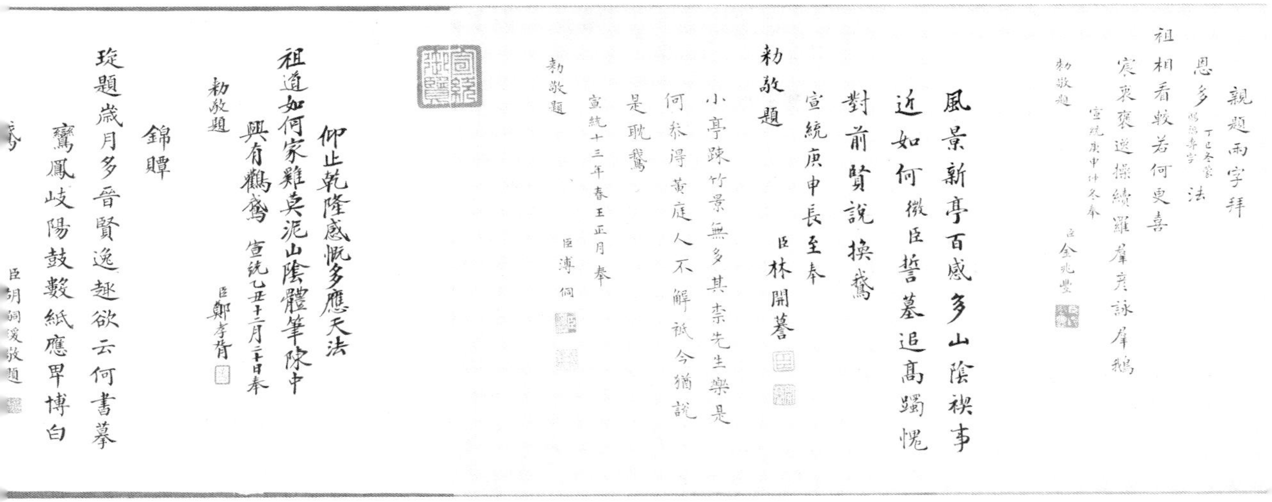

Fig. 3.
Detail of Qian Xuan, *Wang Xizhi Watching Geese* (see fig. 1), showing Puyi's seal, *Xuantong yulan* (Inspected by Xuantong), at the top, where one sheet attaches to another; seal added in 1926.
New York, Metropolitan Museum of Art, Ex coll.: C. C. Wang Family, Gift of The Dillon Fund, 1973 (1973.120.6).

bulk of the evidence—what I call the internal evidence—is visible on the surface of the scroll itself. As was the case for his Qing predecessors, the colophons added under Puyi's auspices to a prized work in the imperial collection were visible to all he invited to a viewing. For him and his court, such displays helped to affirm the continuity of his imperial status, even while he was forced to relocate from Beijing to Tianjin and then to Changchun.

The evidence of provenance recorded on the Qian Xuan scroll does not end with Puyi but continues from the late 1940s to the early 1970s. The scroll bears two seals of Jiang Zuyi (1902–73), a collector from Wuxing, Zhejiang, who moved to Taiwan before 1949, and seven seals of Wang Jiqian (Chi-Ch'ien Wang in Wade-Giles, well known as C. C. Wang [1907–2003]), a collector and artist from Suzhou, Jiangsu, who immigrated to America in 1948.[25]

What will a fuller account reveal?

II

According to Yang Renkai, Puyi wanted to match the Qianlong emperor's "mink coat" [i.e., fine work], though all he managed to do was attach "a dog tail" [i.e., a wretched sequel]. Why was Puyi so struck by Qianlong's "mink coat"? The Qianlong emperor's embellishments consist of the *tiqian* (label; "L" in fig. 2) written by Qianlong himself,[26] his four-character inscription on the *yinshou,* a colophon and a cataloging mark that he wrote in 1746 in the painting's upper left-hand corner, eighteen of his seals, and the colophons and seals added by seven of his courtiers during his long and glorious reign.

These embellishments were what inspired Puyi to add his three seals on the scroll and to enlist forty-four loyalists from his court to contribute their own

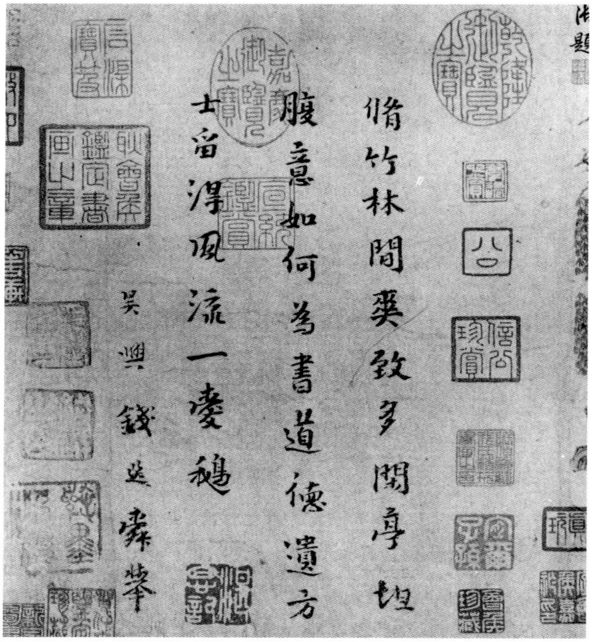

Fig. 4.
Detail of Qian Xuan, *Wang Xizhi Watching Geese* (see fig. 1) showing Qian Xuan's poem, ca. 1295.
New York, Metropolitan Museum of Art, Ex coll.: C.C. Wang Family, Gift of The Dillon Fund, 1973, acc. no. 1973.120.6.

colophons. In the Qian Xuan scroll, we can see the significance of all these embellishments; they demonstrate the three ways that imperial connoisseurs conducted an ongoing "conversation" with the painting.

The first mechanism was through their commentaries on the painter's excellence in combining painting and poetry. In practicing his art, Qian Xuan, who lived in the difficult period of dynastic transition from the Song (960–1279) to the Yuan (1279–1368), combined both professional painting skills and literati talents as a poet and calligrapher.[27] The several paintings by or attributed to him that entered the Qianlong emperor's collection in the mid-eighteenth century all include a poetic commentary.[28] In the Qian Xuan scroll, for example, the painter addresses the viewer with a poem (fig. 4):[29]

> How pleasant are the elegant bamboo and trees!
> In a peaceful pavilion, relaxing with bare stomach, how wonderful it must feel!
> Writing the Daodejing [The Way and Its Power] for a Daoist friend,
> He leaves behind a romantic image—a man who loves geese.[30]

The poem reinforces the theme of Qian Xuan's painting, which shows Wang Xizhi (307–65), "the sage of calligraphy" known for his supreme cursive style, "gazing at swimming geese from a lakeside pavilion, finding in their sinuous necks a gracefulness of line worthy of imitation in his calligraphy."[31] To this

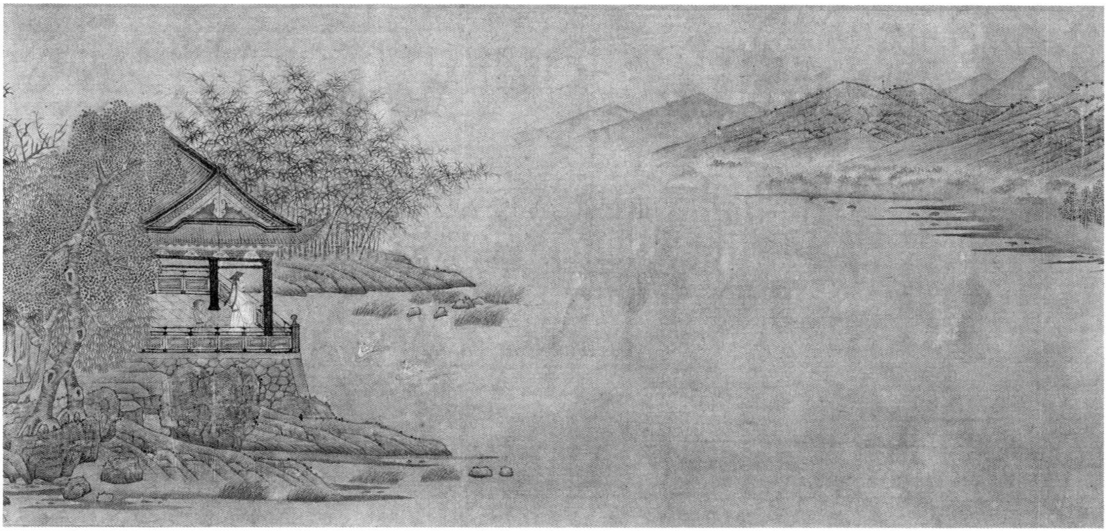

Fig. 5.
Qian Xuan (attributed) (Chinese, ca. 1235–ca. 1307).
Wang Xizhi Watching Geese,
a Ming copy, ink and color on paper, 24.7 × 82.1 cm (9⅔ × 32⅓ in.).
Taipei, National Palace Museum.

poem, Qianlong added his own echoing response, as did his courtiers and, later, Puyi's entourage. Modern scholars, however, have devoted little attention to the relationship between the painter's poem and the Qing additions as they relate to issues of provenance.[32] Conventionally, a requirement of colophon embellishments written at "elegant gatherings" was that all inscribers, here some fifty-two in all, should employ the original artist's poetic rhyme.

To understand the handscroll fully, we need to look at the Qianlong emperor's large collection of Qian Xuan's paintings. Among them is a second version of *Wang Xizhi Watching Geese,* a copy now in the collection of the National Palace Museum, Taipei (fig. 5). Like the original, it entered the Qing imperial collection sometime during the 1740s. Executed with color and ink on paper, the copy has a composition very nearly identical to that of the genuine painting, though its dimensions are slightly different (24.7 × 82.1 cm instead of 23.2 × 92.7 cm) and—more importantly—it has no poetic inscription.[33] The Qianlong emperor added only five of his seals to the copy and then seems to have paid no more attention to it.[34] From this we can infer that he considered it inferior to the Qian Xuan scroll, to which he devoted a great deal of attention—and thus we can further infer which of the two scrolls he considered to be the original.

The Qianlong emperor's 1746 gathering occurred toward the beginning of a period that saw the last great imperial assemblage of art. Initiating a veritable golden age of collecting, Qianlong acquired an enormous number of calligraphies and paintings. These were acquired by gift or by purchase, one after another, from the great collections of his time, such as those of Liang Qingbiao (1620–91), Geng Zhaozhong (1640–86), Geng Jiazuo,[35] and An Qi

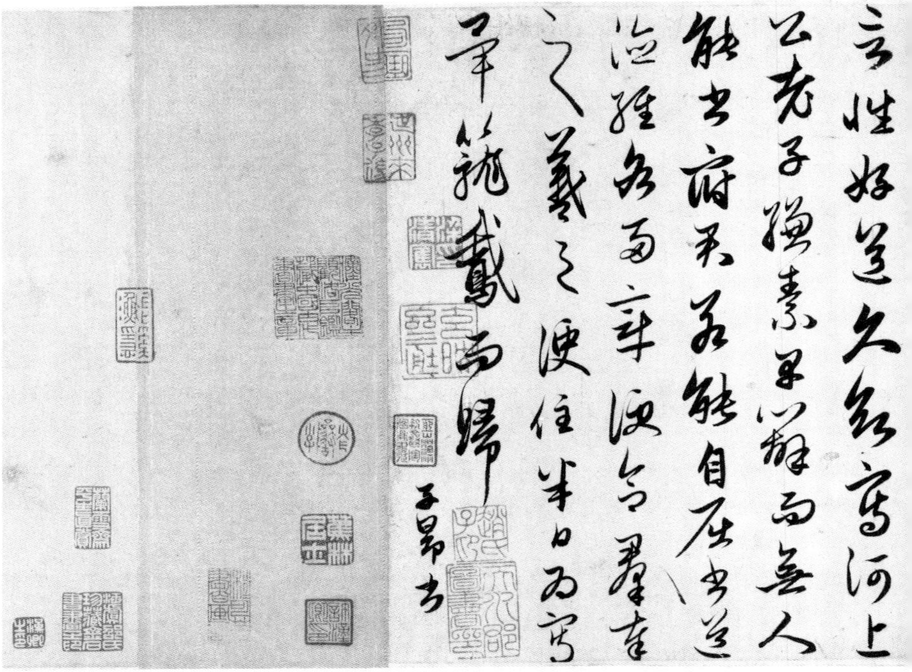

Fig. 6.
Zhao Mengfu (Chinese, 1254–1322).
Four Anecdotes from the Life of Wang Xizhi (detail, part four), ca. 1310, ink on paper, image: 24.4 × 117 cm (9 5/8 × 46 1/16 in.), overall with mounting: 26.5 × 851.2 cm (10 7/16 in. × 27 ft. 1 1/8 in.). New York, Metropolitan Museum of Art, Bequest of John M. Crawford Jr., 1988, acc. no. 1989.363.30.

(1683–after 1742); they supplemented a small number of works inherited from previous dynasties. It was a high point of imperial art collecting, recalling that of Emperor Huizong (r. 1100–1125) of the Song dynasty,[36] and the collection became one of the crowning glories of a vast and unprecedented empire integrating the Han Chinese and Manchurian cultures. Though he was a Manchu ruler, the Qianlong emperor showed extraordinary pride and confidence in his Chineseness, in effect declaring himself one of China's great legitimate monarchs. Puyi, whom Yang disparaged for fastening his "tail" onto his illustrious predecessor's "mink coat," must have wanted to convey his continuity with that tradition, whenever he brought out what he considered his special "family treasure"—the Qian Xuan scroll.

The second way that an imperial owner could establish a connection to the original painter of a handscroll was through the shared interest in a calligraphic practice of their poems. This is evident in the Qian Xuan scroll. The calligraphic style of Qian Xuan's poem (see fig. 4) held special aesthetic value for the Qianlong emperor. The poem, which does not appear in the Taipei copy, provided the emperor with confirmation of the painting's authenticity. It also inspired the emperor to write his poem in the calligraphic style of Zhao Mengfu (1254–1322) (fig. 6), who was from Qian Xuan's hometown and was a fellow art student and friend.[37] Indeed, the Zhao style was Qianlong's personal favorite,

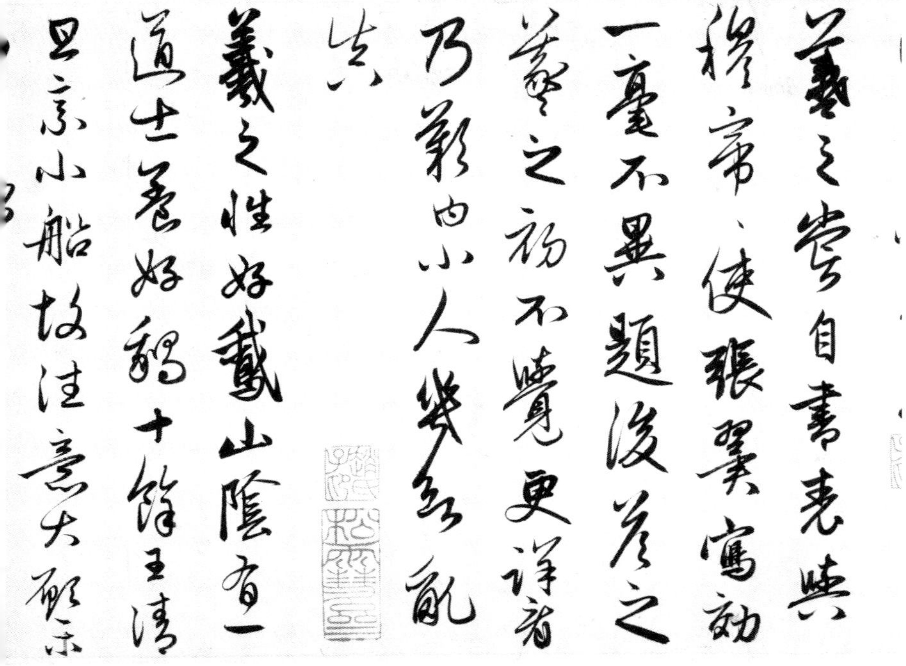

though different from that of the scroll maker. Each time the Qianlong emperor unrolled the handscroll, he must have been comforted not only by the serenity of the image but also by the homage he paid to the artist through his use of Zhao-style semicursive script at the top of the picture. By imitating the Zhao style in the inscription here, the Qianlong emperor showed his strong admiration for the painting.

Although Puyi did not himself contribute a poem to the Qian Xuan scroll, he commanded forty-four of his courtiers and loyalists to add colophons in the form of poems to the scroll, reaffirming his imperial right of ownership. Puyi's contributors, regardless of their loyalist positions,[38] were among the best calligraphers of the Republican era; his court was by no means a group of negligible functionaries without literary or artistic talents.[39]

In addition to the Qianlong emperor's poem echoing the artist's verses and the emperor's use of his favorite Zhao style to pay homage to the painter, there is a third form of continuity in the Qian Xuan scroll: the seals affixed by imperial collectors and connoisseurs. These seals aid us in tracing the extended cultural history of the painting. For example, the Qianlong emperor's seals impressed on the Qian Xuan scroll should not be seen in isolation. On the right side of the picture, directly below the Qianlong seal reading *Yi zisun* (Good for sons and grandsons) there is a seal belonging to Puyi (fig. 7).[40] Similarly, below the seal of

Fig. 7.
Detail of the Qian Xuan scroll (see fig. 1) showing Emperor Qianlong's seal *Yi zisun* (Good for sons and grandsons) at top with Puyi's seal *Wuyizhai jingjian xi* (Seal of authentication of the Diligent Studio) directly below it.
New York, Metropolitan Museum of Art, Ex coll.: C.C. Wang Family, Gift of The Dillon Fund, 1973, acc. no. 1973.120.6.

the Jiaqing emperor (r. 1796–1820) at the upper center of the painter's poem is another of Puyi's seals.[41] All of these were put on the scroll inside the Forbidden City; they give visual expression to the connectedness of the fourth, fifth, and the last emperor of the Qing empire, from its zenith to the end.

During the Qing dynasty, the Qian Xuan scroll, with its accumulated seals and inscriptions—"dialogues," as it were, with the original artist—was a star witness to Manchu-Han Chinese imperial continuity. It was a "family treasure," highly valued first by the Qianlong emperor in 1746, then revisited by him in the 1790s, later screened by his successor the Jiaqing emperor, and finally inspected by Puyi between 1918 and 1940. During all this time, the scroll was viewed and appreciated in private, remaining within the imperial collection and under the emperor's personal control.

III

Provenance issues in the history of Chinese art have been at least as thorny as those in the West.[42] As demonstrated here, the evidence of provenance preserved on Puyi's prized Qian Xuan scroll exemplifies practices unique to the format of the Chinese handscroll; together, that evidence creates a visible archive of ownership, reveals a network of relationships, and documents appreciative responses by usually very important individuals over several centuries. The circumstances that permitted accumulated evidence of this kind ceased after the fall of the Qing empire and the collapse of Manchukuo, when the court custom of display of and commentary on the imperial art collection came to an end.

Until recently, scholars did not have access to photographic reproductions of all the sections of the Qian Xuan scroll, which hindered an exploration of the scroll's provenance. The reproductions in figures 3 and 4 and the digitized version available on the Metropolitan Museum of Art's Web site fill that gap, allowing us to see what Yang Renkai included, what he excluded, and what he skewed in his discussion of the scroll's history. By failing to read objectively the evidence recorded on the Qian Xuan scroll, Yang presented an incomplete picture of the last phase of Chinese imperial art collecting. It is the very extensive verbal character of that evidence, with its scholarly and literary grounding, that is the chief way that provenance studies in Chinese painting and calligraphy differ from such studies in the West.

Today, the Qian Xuan scroll is no longer the object of only private viewings allowed by an emperor; it is accessible to commentators who can assess both it and the Taipei copy and can examine the written records of the Qianlong emperor and his successors. That type of examination brings new analyses and debates, for while the evidence of provenance and cultural history on a handscroll can be much richer than what a Western work of art typically provides, it can also be much more open to dispute.

Notes

I want to thank Gail Feigenbaum and Inge Reist for inviting me to present a case study of provenance questions in China. Wallace Weston provided a Western perspective from which I could reconsider comprehensively the last emperor's provenance problems. He proofread the manuscript and made critical improvements, for which I am deeply indebted. My thanks also are due to James Cahill, Alfreda Murck, and Celia Riely for reading the manuscript and offering valuable criticism, information, and suggestions.

Unless otherwise noted, all translations of quoted material from Chinese to English are my own.

1. See David Sensabaugh, "Suitable for Sons and Grandsons: The Qing Emperors and the Imperial Collection of Calligraphy and Painting," in *The Last Emperor's Collection: Masterpieces of Calligraphy and Painting from the Liaoning Provincial Museum=Mo di bao jian: Liaoning sheng bowuguan cang Qing gong san yi Ming Qing shu hua,* ed. Willow Weilan Hai Chang, exh. cat. (New York: China Institute Gallery, 2008), 17–31.
2. For information about Puyi's dramatic political career, see Puyi, *Wo de qian bansheng: Quanben* (The autobiography of Aisin-Gioro Puyi: A complete version) (Beijing: Qunzhong chubanshe, 2007). Also see the map "Puyi's Travel and Escape Routes," in Chang, *The Last Emperor's Collection,* xxiii.
3. See Yang Renkai, "The Story behind the Last Emperor's Dispersal of the Imperial Painting and Calligraphy Collection," in Chang, *The Last Emperor's Collection,* 1–11. Regarding the formation of a concept of "national treasure" in modern China, see Shou-Ch'ien Shih, "From Imperial Collection to National Treasure: Chinese Art and the Palace Museum in the 1st Half of the 20th Century," in *Moving Objects: Time, Space, and Context,* ed. Terry S. Milhaupt (Tokyo: National Research Institute for Cultural Properties, 2004), 73–83.
4. A selected bibliographic list of the pertinent publications is as follows: Qingshi shanhou weiyuanhui (The Committee for Taking Care of the Affairs of the Former Qing Royal Family), *Gugong yiyi shuji shuhua mulu sanzhong* (Three catalogs of the dispersed books, calligraphies, and paintings of the former palace; usually abbreviated as *Yimu* by scholars) (Beijing: Qingshi shanhou weiyuanhui, 1926), in *Gugong congkan* (The book series of the former palace), IV. Chen Rentao, *Gugong yiyi shuhua mu jiaozhu* (An annotated list of the lost calligraphies and paintings from the former palace collection) (Hong Kong: Tongying gongsi, 1956). Xu Bangda, *Congding Qing gugong jiucang shuhua mu* (Revised catalog of calligraphies and paintings in the former Qing Court collection) (Beijing: Renmin meishu chubanshe, 1997).
5. Yang Renkai, *Guobao chenfu lu: Gugong sanyi shuhua jianwen kaolüe* (Record of the vicissitudes of national treasures: Investigation of the dispersed and lost

calligraphies and paintings from the former palace that I have seen and heard about), first edition (Shanghai: Shanghai renmin meishu chubanshe, 1991).

6. Yang Renkai's book has had five editions, testifying to its importance: (1) The first edition (Shanghai: Shanghai renmin meishu chubanshe, 1991), part of which was translated by Yi Qing into Japanese and published by Nikasha in six sections in the free paper *Shuppan daijesuto* (Publishing digest) from 11 December 1993 to 1 April 1995. (I want to thank Kure Motoyuki for gathering the bibliographic information.) An English review of this edition by Thomas Lawton appears in *Artibus Asiae* 54, nos. 3–4 (1994): 378–80. (2) The second and revised edition (Shenyang: Liaohai chubanshe, 1999). (3) The third edition (Taipei: Xinzhongyuan chuban gongsi, 1999), with full-color illustrations. (4) The fourth and enlarged version (Shanghai: Shanghai guji chubanshe, 2007). (5) The fifth edition, abridged and annotated by Wang Di (Shanghai: Shanghai renmin meishu chubanshe, 2008).
7. *The Last Emperor's Collection: Masterpieces of Calligraphy and Painting from the Liaoning Provincial Museum* was the title of the show as well as of its catalog; see Chang, *The Last Emperor's Collection*.
8. Maxwell Hearn curated the exhibition; see Maxwell Hearn, *How to Read Chinese Paintings,* exh. cat. (New York: Metropolitan Museum of Art, 2008). The Qian Xuan scroll is reproduced on the catalog's back cover and was the centerpiece of a review of the exhibition in the *New York Times* by Holland Cotter, who praised the painting's serene mood. Holland Cotter, "The Art Is in the Detail," review of *Anatomy of a Masterpiece: How to Read Chinese Paintings,* Metropolitan Museum of Art, 1 March–10 August 2008, *New York Times,* 14 March 2008, http://www.nytimes.com/2008/03/14/arts/design/14asia.html. The Qian Xuan scroll can be accessed in its entirety online at http://www.metmuseum.org/Collections/search-the-collections/60007185.
9. See Igor Kopytoff, "The Cultural Biography of Things: Commoditization as Process," in *The Social Life of Things: Commodities in Cultural Perspective,* ed. Arjun Appadurai (Cambridge: Cambridge University Press, 1988), 64–90; Chris Gosden and Yvonne Marshall, "The Cultural Biography of Objects," *World Archaeology* 31 (1999): 169–78; and the essay by Rosemary Joyce, this volume, which considers the concept of "object biographies."
10. *Yimu,* which was compiled in 1924 and published in 1926, becomes the basic reference for all the later investigations.
11. There are 68 albums and 1,185 handscrolls. Yang points out that, because they were not easily portable, vertical hanging scrolls were not included in the collection. See Yang, *Guobao* (2007), 34. There were 21 hanging scrolls in Puyi's collection when it was transported from Beijing to Tianjin in 1924, but these were added to the collection later and came from sources other than the palace collection. See Yang, *Guobao* (2007), 47.
12. They were given as gifts by the last emperor to his siblings, who managed to take them out of the Forbidden City between 16 November 1922 and 28 January 1923. See Yang, *Guobao* (2007), 33–37.
13. Coined by Koryŏ (918–1392) collectors of paintings, the term was used by a Chinese poet, Lou Yue (1137–1213), in a poem titled "Ti Gaoli xingkanzi"

(Inscribing a [Tang] handscroll painting in the collection of a Koryŏ merchant), in his *Gongkui xiansheng wenji* (An anthology of Mr. Gongkui's writings) (Beijing: Beijing tushuguan chubanshe, 2005), 3:28b. This edition is a reprint of *Song Siming Loushi jiakeben* (The undated Song edition published by the Lou family from Siming) in the collection of the Beijing University Library. I want to thank Lu Xuanfei for gathering the bibliographic information.

14. Robert Hans van Gulik, *Chinese Pictorial Art as Viewed by the Connoisseur: Notes on the Means and Methods of Traditional Chinese Connoisseurship of Pictorial Art, Based upon a Study of the Art of Mounting Scrolls in China and Japan* (Rome: Istituto Italiano per il Medio ed Estremo Oriente, 1958), 38.
15. See Gulik's introduction of the various formats, in his *Chinese Pictorial Art,* 18–27, 33–41, and, especially, 67–69. For an in-depth discussion on the origin and application of this format in China and Japan, see Kohara Hironobu, "Narrative Illustration in the Handscroll Format," in *Words and Images: Chinese Poetry, Calligraphy, and Painting,* ed. Alfreda Murck and Wen Fong (New York: Metropolitan Museum of Art, 1991), 247–66.
16. They are even called "marks of vandalism"; see Martin Bailey, "In the Drawing Room: Louis-Antoine Prat on How He Has Amassed the Greatest Collection of French Drawings, Soon to Go on Show in Australia," *The Art Newspaper,* no. 216, September 2010, Features 35. I want to thank Wallace Weston for bringing this information to my attention. See also Gail Feigenbaum, " Manifest Provenance," in this volume.
17. See Hong Zaixin, "Huangjia mingfeng de queren yu zai queren: Qinggong zhi wei Manzhouguo gongting shoucang Quan Xuan Wang Xizhi guan e tu shimo kao" (Imperial identification claimed and reclaimed: A history of collecting Qian Xuan's *Wang Xizhi Watching Geese* from the 1740s to the 1940s), *Gugong bowuyuan yuankan* (Palace museum journal) 113, no. 3 (2004): 114–48. The appendix (141–48) contains detailed information on all the seals and colophons on the Qian Xuan scroll, including 27 seals of about ten collectors, such as Geng Zhaozhong and Geng Jiazuo, that predate the scroll's entry into the Qing imperial collection around 1746.
18. Yang, *Guobao* (1991), 91–92; Yang, *Guobao* (1999), 53–54; and Yang, *Guobao* (2007), 47.
19. Zhang Zhao et al., *Shiqu baoji chubian* (Catalog of calligraphies and paintings of the imperial collection, Part 1), in *Siku quanshu* (Complete library of the four treasuries), Yong Rong et al. (Beijing, 1773), vol. 43, Changchun shuwu (Live Forever Studio), 2b–5a. *Shiqu baoji chubian* is the first installment of volumes of a three-part catalog. It was begun in 1743 and finished in the next year but has some later insertions to the manuscript. For a recently reprinted edition, consult the Wenyuange edition of Yong Rong et al., *Siku quanshu* (Complete library of the four treasuries) (Hong Kong: Dizhi wenhua chuban youxian gongsi, 2007), 825:611–12. A 1918 reprint of *Shiqu baoji chubian* is listed in the bibliography in Sherman Lee and Wai-kam Ho, eds., *Chinese Art under the Mongols,* exh. cat. (Cleveland, Ohio: Cleveland Museum of Art, 1968), 386, no. 190. A reproduction of the first section, second section, and a portion of the third section (ending at the eighth colophon before 17 February 1918) appeared in Suzuki Kei,

Comprehensive Illustrated Catalogue of Chinese Paintings (Tokyo: University of Tokyo Press, 1982–83), 1:A1–012.

20. Wang Jie et al., *Shiqu baoji chongbian* (Catalog of calligraphies and paintings of the imperial collection, Part 2) (Beijing: 1791), in the National Palace Museum (NPM), *Midian zhulin shiqu baoji xubian* (Catalog of calligraphies and paintings of the imperial collection, Part 2) (Taipei: NPM, 1971).
21. These seals were cut in the 1780s, after the Qianlong emperor had turned eighty. See Chang, *The Last Emperor's Collection,* 341.
22. In fact, those provenance records, while unpublished until 2004, were available to Yang during his two visits to the Metropolitan Museum in the 1980s. Yang, *Guobao* (2007), 6. According to Alfreda Murck, former associate curator and administrator of Asian art at the Metropolitan Museum, "[Yang] certainly would have been given all the time he wanted to view and take notes as that was our practice. . . . He admired the painting, looked through the colophons and concluded that it was superior to the one in the National Palace Museum (NPM), Taipei (which confirmed my opinion). We (the Asian Art dept) likely provided him with b/w photos of the entire scroll, painting and colophons." Alfreda Murck, e-mail message to author, 28 July 2010.
23. Puyi, *Wo de qian bansheng,* 49, 104–5.
24. Between a colophon by Putong (1871–1952) dated February 1922 and a colophon by Zheng Xiaoxu dated 2 February 1926 on two different sheets that have been joined together, Puyi put his seal *Xuantong yulan* (inspected by Xuantong), on the newly remounted scroll to authenticate his subjects' inscriptions. This was Puyi's third seal on the Qian Xuan scroll. The other two had been added on the *huaxin* (the main body of the painting), see fig. 1, before he left the Forbidden City in 1924. For details of these two seals, see notes 40 and 41 below.
25. According to Chen Rentao, "The '*Watching Geese*' scroll was in Taiwan" (Chen, *Gugong yiyi,* 11b). But in an earlier account, Wang Shixiang, who visited the United States between 1947 and 1949 and saw the Qian Xuan scroll in C. T. Loo's place in New York, reported that "this scroll was dispersed in northeast China, and was sold to C. T. Loo by C. C. Wang." See Wang Shixiang, "Meiguo duhua ji" (Notes on reading paintings in the United States), *Wenwu cankao ziliao* (Reference materials about cultural relics), no. 11 (1950): 64–87. In the 1968 catalog (Lee and Ho, *Chinese Art under the Mongols,* cat. no. 185), only five of C. C. Wang's seals were mentioned, which indicates that C. C. Wang added two more seals on the scroll before he sold it to the Metropolitan Museum in 1973. In his e-mail to me dated 29 September 2010, James Cahill mentioned that "C. C. Wang had acted as an agent for Loo before he came to the U.S., buying paintings for Loo to receive and sell. Just what their financial arrangements were I can't say, nor can I say how Wang seems to have taken back some of the paintings he'd found after he moved to New York and became a kind of dealer himself. But this affects the story of how this painting and others moved between them."
26. In Zhang Zhao et al., *Shiqu,* 43:4b, we read that Qianlong inscribed the label without detail. The label reads: "Qian Xuan guan e tu zhenji, neifu yuwan" (A genuine work of Qian Xuan's *Watching Geese Scroll* for the imperial entertainment in the palace).

27. Modern scholars have made insightful observations and analyses of the theme and style of the Qian Xuan scroll: see James Cahill, *Chinese Painting* (Geneva: Skira, 1960), 101–2; Wen Fong and Marilyn Fu, *Sung and Yuan Paintings,* exh. cat. (New York: Metropolitan Museum of Art, 1973), 87; James Cahill, *Hills beyond a River: Chinese Painting of the Yüan Dynasty, 1279–1368* (New York: Weatherhill, 1976), 35; Richard Barnhart, *Along the Border of Heaven: Sung and Yüan Paintings from the C. C. Wang Family Collection,* exh. cat. (New York: Metropolitan Museum of Art, 1983), 108–10; Shou-chien Shih, "Eremitism in Landscape Paintings by Ch'ien Hsüan [Qian Xuan] (ca. 1235–before 1307)," (PhD diss., Princeton University, 1984), 260–66; Wen Fong, *Beyond Representation: Chinese Painting and Calligraphy, 8th–14th Century* (New York: Metropolitan Museum of Art, 1992), 319; Maxwell Hearn, "Archaism as Activist Art," in idem, *How to Read Chinese Paintings,* exh. cat. (New York: Metropolitan Museum of Art, 2008), 74–77; and James C. Y. Watt et al., *The World of Khubilai Khan: Chinese Art in the Yuan Dynasty,* exh. cat. (New York: Metropolitan Museum of Art, 2010), 186–87.
28. See Yang, *Guobao* (2007), 356–57; Xu, *Congding,* 60–61.
29. See John Hay, "Poetic Space: Ch'ien Hsüan [Qian Xuan] and the Association of Painting and Poetry," in *Words and Images: Chinese Poetry, Calligraphy, and Painting,* ed. Alfreda Murck and Wen Fong (New York: Metropolitan Museum of Art, 1991), 191.
30. See Hearn, *How to Read Chinese Paintings,* 74. Several English translations of the poem are available: see Fong and Fu, *Sung and Yuan Paintings,* 87, cited in Fong, *Beyond Representation,* 319; Lee and Ho, *Chinese Art under the Mongols,* cat. no. 185; and Hay, "Poetic Space," 191.
31. Cahill, *Chinese Painting,* 101.
32. Lee and Ho, for example, only briefly noted "the colophons by the Emperor Qianlong and his six [actually seven] subjects," Lee and Ho, *Chinese Art under the Mongols,* cat. no. 185.
33. Generally speaking, when a collector in Chinese collecting practice encounters the "twin" of a masterpiece by the same painter, he can easily remove the painter's inscription attached to the *huaxin* from one painting and mount the inscription on another painting of better quality. See Yang, *Guobao* (2007), 306.
34. The seals are (1) *Qianlong yulan zhibao* (treasure viewed by the Qianlong emperor), (2) *Sanxitang jingjian xi* (seal of authentication of the Three Rare Treasures Studio), (3) *Yi zisun* (good for sons and grandsons), (4) *Shiqu baoji* (treasured boxes of the Stone Channels), and (5) *Qianlong jianshang* (appreciated by Qianlong). Not only did Qianlong's subjects exclude the copy from Wang Jie et al., *Shiqu,* but his successors, such as the Jiaqing emperor and Xuantong, did not place seals on it—even though it had a colophon by Dong Qichang (1555–1636) datable to between 1607 and 1610. (Celia Riely pointed out this in her e-mail to me dated 29 September 2010, for which I am very thankful.) According to Wang Jiqian (C. C. Wang), however, not only is the Taipei piece "a Ming copy" but Dong's inscription is "a fake" as well. See *Wang Jiqian duhua biji* (Notes on paintings by Wang Jiqian), ed. Yang Kailin (Beijing: Zhonghua shuju, 2010), 174. The copy has been kept in the imperial family collection ever since. See the NPM, *Gugong shuhua lu* (Catalog of calligraphies and paintings in the NPM), rev. ed.

(Taipei: NPM, 1965), 4:73, and the NPM, *Gugong shuhua tulu* (Illustrated catalog of calligraphies and paintings in the NPM) (Taipei: NPM, 1989), 16:381–84. I want to thank Wang Yaoting for facilitating my viewing of the copy in the NPM in 2004.

35. The Qian Xuan scroll, for example, came from the collections of the Geng brothers. See Hong, "Huangjia," 141–42.
36. See Patricia Ebrey, *Accumulating Culture: The Collections of Emperor Huizong* (Seattle, Wash.: University of Washington Press, 2008).
37. For a comparative observation on Zhao's calligraphy masterpiece *Youjun sishi juan* (Four anecdotes from the life of Wang Xizhi) in relation to Qian Xuan's calligraphic writing of the poem for the Qian Xuan scroll, see Hearn, *How to Read Chinese Paintings,* 85–87.
38. See my discussion on Luo Zhenyu, one of Puyi's controversial loyalists, in "A Newly Made Marketable 'Leftover': Luo Zhenyu's Scholarship and Art Business in Kyoto (1911–1919)," in *Lost Generation: Luo Zhenyu, Qing Loyalists and the Formation of Modern Chinese Culture,* ed. Chia-ling Yang and Roderick Whitfield (London: Saffron, 2012), 142–71.
39. See Liu Zhengcheng et al., *Zhongguo shufa quanji,* vol. 78, *Jinxiandai bian: Kang Youwei Liang Qichao Luo Zhenyu Zheng Xiaoxu juan* (The complete works of Chinese calligraphy, vol. 78, Modern period: Kang Youwei, Liang Qichao, Luo Zhenyu, Zheng Xiaoxu) (Beijing: Rongbaozhai, 1993), which includes two of the most acknowledged calligraphers among all Puyi's contributors.
40. Puyi's seal reads *Wuyizhai jingjian xi* (seal of authentication of the Diligent Studio). As Sensabaugh highlights in the title of his essay "Suitable for Sons and Grandsons," the Qianlong emperor's seal *Yi zisun* (suitable for sons and grandsons) is symbolic, however; Sensabaugh does not establish a special connection between the two monarchs.
41. Below *Jiaqing yulan zhibao* (treasure viewed by the Jiaqing emperor) is Puyi's *Xuantong jianshang* (appreciated by Xuantong).
42. For a more general discussion on the literature of concept and problems of provenance in China, see Joseph Alsop, *The Rare Art Traditions: The History of Art Collecting and Its Linked Phenomena Wherever These Have Appeared* (New York: Harper & Row, 1982), 18–19, 212–51.

PART TWO

The Time and Place of Provenance

ROSEMARY A. JOYCE

FROM PLACE TO PLACE

Provenience, Provenance, and Archaeology

Seen in print or heard in passing, the terms *provenience* and *provenance* may seem nothing more than variations of the same word. Yet listen briefly to archaeologists and art historians use these two terms, and differences in their understandings of the life histories of things become evident. The differences are consequential and reveal the dissimilar values these disciplines impute to the same material objects.[1] At the same time, the terms are not entirely unrelated, and object itineraries, a modification of the concept of "object biographies,"[2] may bridge the distinctions scholars wish or need to make in tracing the progress of things from place to place.

Archaeologists usually understand *provenience* to be the original findspot of an object. In contrast, the *provenance* of the same object is normally defined by art historians as its chain of ownership. While in theory the chain of ownership should begin with the making of the object, in practice the provenance of antiquities often starts with the removal of the object from its context of archaeological recovery. This distinction illuminates the reason these two concepts promote such different understandings: provenience is a fixed point, while provenance can be considered an itinerary that an object follows as it moves from hand to hand. Where the two concepts intersect is the place that the archaeological provenience singles out as the only important location in this itinerary, the find site.

The mere fact that there is such a point of intersection suggests that these concepts are inherently related; they are links in a single chain of places that an object has occupied. Moreover, these places are not randomly connected; they can and indeed, for understanding, must be arranged in temporal order, forming a history of the circulation of the archaeological object.

The recovery of the archaeological object is a moment of significant rupture in that history of circulation. It begins with the object's journey through modern institutions that organize, present, and attribute value to it: universities, museums, and academic disciplines. The construction of provenance by assembling a record of these movements is both chronological and at the same time geographical, a mapping of where the object has been located over its life. Because provenience and provenance are both emplaced histories, we are in a position to extend our interpretation of these related concepts to embrace a more complete history of the object, while also understanding the deeper implications of using one term or the other.

Archaeological Provenience

Archaeologists usually define *provenience* as the place where a secure, interpretable archaeological context was established for an object. The definition officially endorsed by the Society of American Archivists is "the site of an archaeological excavation."[3] Archaeologists are more precise; for them, provenience refers to a three-dimensional location in space: "Provenience is another word which has a slightly different meaning when used archaeologically. The dictionary defines provenience . . . as 'origin' or 'derivation.' . . . More technically, in archaeology the term refers to the actual position of the object in three dimensions. Thus, an object's provenience can be stated as being 30m north, 22m east, and 3.5m down from an arbitrary fixed point on the site (called the datum point)."[4]

Although the term *provenience* is understood today as being clearly distinct from *provenance,* definitions of the two words remain confusing, even among archaeologists.

In notes on entries for archaeology-related *Wikipedia* pages—arguably a good sample of contemporary thought among informed, if not professional, Internet users—objections were raised to using the term *provenience,* which was considered a synonym for *provenance* that was perhaps "more obscure."[5] Where does this understanding of provenance and provenience come from, and does it tell us anything about the professional discriminations now made in the use of these words?

Provenience and Provenance

The meaning of *provenance* in museological and art-historical practice is different from the archaeological *provenience:* it is a chain of ownership, ideally beginning with the creation of the object. This is not well understood by many North American and British archaeologists, who assume that the two terms are simply variants of a single word, often assigning the use of *provenance* to European scholars and understanding it as having essentially the same meaning as the Americanist *provenience.*[6]

Even though it is demonstrably not accurate either as a historical explanation or as a description of contemporary practices, this simple explanation of the *provenience/provenance* distinction as a matter of dialect is of long standing.

In 1926, the eminent British archaeologist V. Gordon Childe commented on what he took to be excessive Americanisms in a book he was reviewing. Among the terms to which he objected was the use of *provenience* instead of what he took as its equivalent, *provenance*.[7] Assignment of the two terms to United States and British scholars, respectively, continues to be a staple in more recent archaeological writing as well. For example, in a general book published in 1994 and directed at an international archaeological audience, Sarah Wisseman and Wendell Williams clarify their terminology by saying "the term 'provenience' ('provenance' to European scholars)...."[8]

The Society of American Archivists appears at first glance to share this common archaeological assumption that the two terms are merely dialectical variants, but the archivists identify the groups by whom they are used quite differently—not in terms of nationality but in terms of profession: "Provenience and provenance are fundamentally synonyms for source or origin. However, provenance is used in archives and museology, whereas provenience is used in archaeology."[9] Yet the definition offered for *provenance* goes far beyond the brief description of *provenience* as archaeological site cited above: *provenance* is defined as "arrangement; context; creator; custodial history; entity of origin; *fonds* [the entire body of records of an organization, family, or individual that have been created and accumulated as the result of an organic process reflecting the functions of the creator]; office of origin; original order."[10] The author of this archivists' guide notes that "provenance is a fundamental principle of archives, referring to the individual, family, or organization that created or received the items in a collection. The principle of provenance or the *respect des fonds* dictates that records of different origins (provenance) be kept separate to preserve their context."[11] For an archivist, the "significance of archival materials is heavily dependent on the context of their creation, and... the arrangement and description of these materials should be directly related to their original purpose and function."[12]

Archaeological provenience does not privilege the origin of materials, nor is their significance dependent on the context of their creation, which this definition suggests is critical to provenance. Archaeological provenience instead foregrounds context in its broadest sense: "everything that the object is embedded in, both natural or cultural, the whole web of relationships that touch any object. In archaeology, context is often defined more precisely as the matrix, provenience, and associations of any object."[13] It is this bundle of associations that makes provenience so important for archaeologists and distinguishes it from provenance.

Morag Kersel and Christina Luke, in a pointed commentary on the reasons archaeologists are concerned about the lack of precise records of archaeological findspots, define *provenience* as "an artefact's context and provenance as the artefact's recent history."[14] Here, they echo other scholars writing about issues of the international traffic in antiquities. For example, Clemency Coggins writes that "provenience signifies original location—an archaeological site, a church—while provenance refers to the history of ownership of an object—art dealer, private collection, museum."[15]

For such contemporary scholars, *provenance* is understood not as the entire chain of ownership beginning with the making of the archaeological object but only as that part of the chain that follows the moment of archaeological recovery at the find site, the provenience. Because of its implication in debates about cultural property, this division has come to stand for a fundamental difference in understanding between contemporary archaeology and art history. Kersel and Luke's position, that a secure original record of provenience provides *irreplaceable* information, is to some extent contested in contemporary art-museum practice. As Ildiko DeAngelis notes, "The art community also maintains that important information about a culture that created an object may be gleaned from the object's style and appearance even if its provenience is unknown," supporting this point by citing James Cuno's 1997–98 *Annual Report of the Harvard University Art Museums.*[16]

The distinction between *provenience* and *provenance* has thus come to demarcate a sharp division in a contemporary debate. In this debate, *provenience,* understood as perhaps adapted from an Americanism, is strongly associated with archaeology and is seen as jargon or specialized language through which archaeologists differentiate themselves from those who use *provenance* as their preferred designation.

Yet this conclusion ignores the very long coexistence of these two terms within archaeology and art history. Writers with less investment in contemporary disciplines whose boundaries are demarcated by such choices of language have explored this earlier history and more complex contemporary patterns of usage and presented their findings on the Internet. For these broader public communities, the point of understanding provenance and provenience is less to illuminate disciplinary disputes and more to gain a better idea of the lives of things themselves.

Provenience and Provenance in Place on the Web

In August 2003, the author of the blog Eudaemonist recounted an exploration of the meanings of *provenance* and *provenience.*[17] Beginning with an exchange with a friend about a legal case involving the Metropolitan Museum of Art, the blogger admitted initially assuming "that provenience was a highly specialized museo-/archeo-logical term, similar but not identical to the more familiar provenance." This writer merges the specialist groups who actually use these two terms in distinctive ways into a single academic community understood to be employing the less familiar *provenience,* implicitly, as an affectation.

What makes this blog entry interesting for the present purpose is that the author proceeded to explore the history of usage of the two terms. This blogger's Google search showed that *provenance* is overwhelmingly the more common term in digitized works: 704,000 results versus 26,000 for *provenience.* Following up with a JSTOR search, the author of Eudaemonist found greater parity in the academic literature: *provenience* yielded 1,252 results and *provenance* 1,481, while 112 articles in that database used both *provenance* and *provenience.* (My own reproduction of the JSTOR search in 2008 found that, since 2003, the number of articles with both terms had increased to 508.) All of this supports what one might conclude based on the discussion of academic writing presented above: there are two roughly equal academic dialect communities employing distinct terms.

Somewhat surprisingly, however, the author of Eudaemonist demonstrated that the earliest use of *provenience* identifiable in the JSTOR article database already was trying to differentiate an archaeological find site from an assignment of origin based on style. Percy Gardner, the author of this nineteenth-century article, was British, not American, thus disposing of the explanation Childe used some forty years later to account for what he viewed as an objectionable neologism.

The author of Eudaemonist noted that, in 1883, only a year before publishing an article using the term *provenience* (the term's first occurrence in a JSTOR journal), Gardner had used the term *provenance* in another article in the same journal. Even though he did not use the word *provenience* in the earlier article, it is clear that Gardner was already making the modern differentiation that identifies the findspot as distinctive by labeling it the *provenience.* Gardner explicitly notes that he does not know where the object was found, instead discussing the attributed origin based on stylistic features as the provenance of the piece:

> I am unable to state positively where the statuette was found. The Princess of Wales supposes it to come from Tanagra: but on grounds of style this provenance would seem scarcely probable. The fact that it was gilt points strongly to Asia Minor as its source; gilding being a marked characteristic of the statuettes of Asia Minor, especially those of Smyrna. And the style of art is most distinctly that of Asia and not that of Greece proper. We might search in vain among the figures from Tanagra for anything like it; but

> turning to the plates of M. Froehner's *Terres Cuites d'Asie Mineure* we at once find several statuettes, and even several figures of Eros, which bear a strong family resemblance to the present figure.[18]

A year later, Gardner, commenting on the origin of Etruscan reliefs in cemeteries, uses the term *provenience* in its modern sense, of find site: "As to their provenience, it seems to be established that in some cases at all events they come from cemeteries and the close neighborhood of tombs; one published by M. Fränkel for instance was found close to an actual tombstone."[19]

In other words, in the nineteenth century, Gardner was already using the pair *provenience/provenance* to make the kind of distinction that has in the last half-century come to signify differences in archaeological and art-historical values. Gardner seeks his comparisons for *provenance* in the pages of the authoritative publication that allow comparison of the "family resemblance" of style. For *provenience,* the cited authority is the documented location where the piece was found. The same distinctions were deployed by other authors within the next decades, in archaeology and in manuscript studies.[20]

Thus, it would seem that what is often seen as a contemporary issue—a debate about the value of secure knowledge of the findspot—has actually long been a part of the motivation of scholars to use *provenience* instead of or in addition to *provenance. Provenience* is, as so many archaeologists insist, fundamentally different from *provenance.*

In 2006, the online forum at About.com dedicated to archaeology, moderated by K. Kris Hirst, fostered a substantive discussion of the perceived difference between *provenience* and *provenance* among the generally educated users of the site. This conversation began with an article in which *provenience* was parenthetically equated with *provenance,* both defined as "the original location of an artifact, where it was recovered, its context."[21] These three things do not, of course, have exactly the same meaning. The place where an object was recovered in an archaeological site is set here as the same as its "original location," implicitly raising the question of how we think about the life of things *before* they were deposited where the archaeologist finds them. More interesting, perhaps, is the conflation of the find site with the "context" of the object. This suggests that the place where the archaeologist found an object is the place in which it makes (the most?) sense. These are in fact the underlying assumptions in most archaeologists' use of the term, and they precisely frame what is at stake for archaeologists in the loss of *provenience,* understood as the one securely interpretable context for the object.

The poll called for in the original post produced the now predictable results—an almost even split, in this case with a slight bias toward the use of *provenience* by what presumably was a largely archaeological readership. But the debate did not end there. Within a week, response to the original story led Hirst to propose to "call the whole thing off."[22] She noted that the picture had become more confusing, with art historians using the terms differently from archaeologists. Interestingly, she nonetheless felt she could now clearly define the two terms and offered an illuminating hypothetical example:

> Provenience: The precise location where an artifact or archaeological sample was recovered archaeologically.
>
> Provenance: The detailed history of where an artifact has been since its creation.
>
> Take as an example a Roman coin. The provenance of that coin could include its creation in a mint in Italy, its loss in a shipwreck off Alexandria, its recovery by shell divers, its purchase first by an antiques dealer, then by a tourist who left it to her son who eventually sold it to a museum. The artifact's archaeological provenience would be the location in the shipwreck where it was found.[23]

This is a major step forward in relating the two terms. Even though at first glance it appears simply to recapitulate contemporary distinctions drawn between *provenance* and *provenience,* it extends provenance to include the time before the moment when archaeological provenience is established, to correspond to a history that begins with the creation of the object.

Since the archaeological find site itself is part of the chain of places where the object "has been since its creation," these two definitions clearly suggest that the archaeological readers who informed this discussion see provenience as a specific place in the chain of provenance. Nor did the ensuing discussion stop with this useful connection between two terms often viewed (ahistorically) as opposed. In a comment on Hirst's original posting about provenience and provenance, the geology guide on About.com wrote:

> Geological provenance seems to differ from archaeological provenience. To the geologist, provenance is where something comes from, where it was before it arrived here. For instance, the pebbles in this conglomerate have a provenance in an ancient mountain range to the east. The provenance of these pebbles tells us something about ancient geography. What you define as provenience is something else: it's where those pebbles ended up. A Roman coin in the rubble would have an ancient Roman provenance, but its provenience is in the rubble, whether that's a Roman ruin or the remains of a coin shop.[24]

That is to say, materials research can extend provenance even before the manufacture of objects, to their origin as raw materials.

A geologist critical of a study of catlinite calumets in the United States published in 1989 used *provenience* and *provenance* to make the same distinctions, exploring issues with deriving "meaningful provenance-provenience (i.e., initial geological source to final archaeological occurrence) relations" in the absence of precise materials analyses.[25] In terms of Hirst's example of the Roman coin, the provenance she imagined would need to start even earlier, with the acquisition of raw materials.

For archaeological materials scientists, this distinction between object provenience and materials provenance entirely replaces the dichotomy more familiar in contemporary debates about collecting of objects excavated without professional documentation:

> To avoid confusion, the distinctions between the terms provenience and provenance must be clarified. Provenience is an archaeological term that refers to the precise location where an artifact was unearthed. The provenience of an artifact involves its vertical and horizontal position in relation to a set of coordinates. Provenance, on the other hand, is a geological term that refers to the source from which geological material is derived, such as a specific quarry, outcrop, mine, or other geologic feature. In common usage, these terms are often used interchangeably; however, their meanings are different with respect to the topic at hand. Any recovered artifact made from geological material has both a provenience and provenance. Many artifacts are not recovered where they were fabricated, so their proveniences and provenances are different. Consequently, provenance studies do not answer questions about where a certain artifact was fashioned, only the geologic source of the material from which it was manufactured.[26]

Moving Places: Object Itineraries

Objects move from place to place before they reach their archaeological findspot, and they continue in motion from the moment they are archaeologically recovered. *Provenience* and *provenance,* variably used by scholars in different disciplines, both reference *places* in a series of chronologically arranged spatial locations. Only discipline-specific considerations provide reasons to privilege one part of an object's itinerary: thus, the geologist is concerned with the raw-material provenance and archaeological provenience but not particularly with the steps that intervened between these; the archaeologist decries the loss of provenience that comes when objects are not professionally excavated;

and the art historian understands that, using stylistic and other clues, a provenance can be reconstructed from the place of manufacture through to the present. But the object itself is more than any one of these descriptions.

These differences in emphasis undoubtedly become heated in contemporary situations, where the different values placed on parts of an object's life history—and differences in understanding of how its itinerary can securely be known—are critically tied to debates about cultural property. Art historian Karen Mack, in a comment posted in response to Hirst's second article on provenience and provenance, wrote:

> I resent the statement that art historians don't really care about provenience, although I must admit most art historians are unfamiliar with the term. The provenience of religious sculpture and paintings in Japan is crucial for reconstructing the history of temples and shrines destroyed during the persecution of Buddhism in the 17th century. Also, when the provenience of such works is lost it is often impossible to identify the local deities depicted in these works. *Often art historians trace the provenance in an effort to recover the provenience* [emphasis added].[27]

What Mack was objecting to would appear to any archaeologist like a relatively neutral statement of fact. Hirst wrote:

> When archaeologists lament about the loss of provenience from a looted art object, what we really mean is that part of the provenance has been lost—we are interested in how the coin got from the Roman mint into the museum; *while art historians don't really care, since they can generally figure out what mint a coin came from.* "It's a Roman coin, what else do we need to know?" says an art historian; "The shipping trade in Roman era Mediterranean Sea" says an archaeologist. I should have known: it all comes down to a question of context. It's interesting, don't you think? *Because provenance for an art historian is important to establish ownership, but provenance is interesting to an archaeologist to establish meaning* [emphasis added].[28]

From an archaeologist's point of view, the provenience cannot be "recovered," and thus part of the history cannot be reconstructed if the find site was not professionally documented.

But what is lost when the archaeological provenience is undocumented is also the ability to truly document the full provenance. For example, collecting practices in the past created significant histories of ownership for objects—as heirlooms, relics, or the like—before they reached their archaeological location.[29] This part of the provenance of the object also cannot be reconstructed, whether by materials analyses that tell us the geological provenance of raw materials, or stylistic studies that tell us where the object likely was made.

As Hirst's final sentence quoted above implies, provenance properly understood is thus of interest for both archaeologists and art historians, even though it cannot replace provenience for the archaeologist. When DeAngelis suggests that provenance actually references "the history of the life of the work," she points us toward one way to bridge what has become in practice a polar opposition between provenance and provenience.[30]

Provenience, Provenance, and Object Itineraries

We might want to listen carefully to the thoughtful author of Eudaemonist, who closes the blog entry on provenance and provenience with a critical commentary on what appears to be an unresolvable debate: "Very few items spring miraculously out of the ether: they have a provenience, even if it is unknown.... Scholars will argue about the dates of objects, about the craftsman who made it, about its role in history, which suggests that the primary characteristic of such facts is their mutability."[31] *Mutability* here is meant to suggest that what we as scholars think about objects changes, not necessarily that the characteristics of objects themselves change.

Yet even such things as "the dates of objects" *do* change. Provenance, more than provenience, captures that sense of the biography of an object as composed of many potentially meaningful chronological moments. When one date is singled out of the biography of an object made by ancient artists working for a patron, it is as likely to be the dates of the patron's life as the date of the creation of the object. Archaeologically documented objects not infrequently are associated with much later dates of use and burial than any original date of creation that could be inferred from stylistic details, which themselves point to the workshop, not the patron's residence. Exceptional objects may be reworked into new, striking forms, as when Olmec altars were reworked into monumental heads, or painted beakers from Chaco Canyon were scraped and repainted.[32] Calling this experience of objects held and reused long after they were created "heirlooming" or "recycling" doesn't really resolve the challenge of talking about their significance in time, in history. A richer concept of life history would allow us to trace the multiple historical circumstances in which an object was significant, including those associated with the recovery of objects as scientific specimens and their circulation as items of cultural property, personal luxury, or public heritage. *Mutability* also clearly applies not just to *knowledge* about the roles of objects in history but to those very roles themselves.

Provenience and *provenance* each index only part of the dynamic itinerary of an object, and they do so in such variable ways that, in some senses, they fail to discriminate usefully how objects pass in and out of meaningfulness. As references to the movement of objects from place to place, *provenance* and *provenience* can be seen as ways of framing parts of the object's itinerary as it moved from hand to hand. That itinerary itself provides a framework to begin to consider the biography of the object more broadly.

The biographical approach "seeks to understand the way objects become invested with meaning through the social interactions they are caught up in. These meanings change and are renegotiated through the life of an object."[33] For studies of historical provenance, this means attending to the social circumstances through which ownership by certain people increases the prestige and visibility of an object. For studies of archaeological provenience, this means acknowledging that the same kinds of objects found in different settings within sites or in different geographic locations have different kinds of value in the same way that objects with different historical provenances do. For example, recovery in burials rather than domestic debris, near the workshop, in the residence of a presumed patron, or far abroad from the geological source as a product of gifting or other socially mediated exchange alters the significance of the object just as ownership does in art-historical provenance. Neither segment of an object biography is better, nor are they so very different from each other. Each alone is incomplete, and the biography of the object is necessarily more than either or even both of these combined.

Notes

1. For example, see the discussion by Claire Lyons in her "Objects and Identities: Claiming and Reclaiming the Past," in *Claiming the Stones, Naming the Bones: Cultural Property and the Negotiation of National and Ethnic Identity,* ed. Elazar Barkan and Ronald Bush (Los Angeles: Getty Research Institute, 2002), 116–37.
2. Chris Gosden and Yvonne Marshall, "The Cultural Biography of Objects," *World Archaeology* 31 (1999): 169–78; and Igor Kopytoff, "The Cultural Biography of Things: Commoditization as Process," in *The Social Life of Things: Commodities in Cultural Perspective,* ed. Arjun Appadurai (Cambridge: Cambridge University Press, 1986), 64–91.
3. Richard Pearce-Moses, *A Glossary of Archival and Records Terminology* (Chicago: Society of American Archivists, 2005), http://www.archivists.org/glossary/index.asp.

4. H. Arthur Bankoff, "Context," online source consulted 13 August 2007 at http://depthome.brooklyn.cuny.edu/anthro/SCP50/archaeology/context.html (no longer available).
5. "Provenience," in "User Talk: Adamsan/Talkie Talkie Talkie Happy Talk (2004)," *Wikipedia,* http://en.wikipedia.org/wiki/User_talk:Adamsan/Talkie_talkie_talkie_happy_talk_(2004).
6. For example, Christopher Chippindale and David W. J. Gill, "Material Consequences of Contemporary Classical Collecting," *American Journal of Archaeology* 104 (2000): 467.
7. V. Gordon Childe, "Review of *Italic Hut-Urns and Hut-Urn Cemeteries: A Study of the Early Iron Age in Latium* by W. R. Bryan," *Man* 26 (1926): 171.
8. Sarah U. Wisseman and Wendell S. Williams, eds., *Ancient Technologies and Archaeological Materials* (Langhorne, Pa.: Gordon & Breach Science, 1994), 18.
9. Pearce-Moses, *Glossary of Archival and Records Terminology.*
10. Pearce-Moses, *Glossary of Archival and Records Terminology.*
11. Pearce-Moses, *Glossary of Archival and Records Terminology.*
12. Steven L. Henson, "The First Shall Be First: APPM and Its Impacts on American Archival Description," *Archivaria* 35 (1993): 67; cited in Pearce-Moses, *Glossary of Archival and Records Terminology.*
13. Bankoff, "Context."
14. Morag Kersel and Christina Luke, "Comment: The Battle for the Past," *Culture without Context* 13 (2003), http://www.mcdonald.cam.ac.uk/projects/iarc/culturewithoutcontext/issue%2013/kersel-krowitz.htm.
15. Clemency C. Coggins, "Property and Heritage: Whose Property? Whose Heritage? A View from Latin America" (paper presented at the Second Annual Ename International Colloquium, "Who Owns the Past? Heritage Rights and Responsibilities in a Multicultural World," Ghent, 22–25 March 2006); see also Chippindale and Gill, "Material Consequences"; and David W. J. Gill and Christopher Chippindale, "Material and Intellectual Consequences of Esteem for Cycladic Figures," *American Journal of Archaeology* 97 (1993): 601–59.
16. Ildiko Pogany DeAngelis, "How Much Provenance Is Enough? Post-Schultz Guidelines for Art Museum Acquisition of Archaeological Materials and Ancient Art," in *Art and Cultural Heritage: Law, Policy, and Practice,* ed. Barbara T. Hoffman (Cambridge: Cambridge University Press, 2006), 398–408.
17. See http://www.eudaemonist.com/aged/0803.
18. Percy Gardner, "A Statuette of Eros," *Journal of Hellenic Studies* 4 (1883): 266.
19. Percy Gardner, "A Sepulchral Relief from Tarentum," *Journal of Hellenic Studies* 5 (1884): 112.
20. For examples from archaeology, see William N. Bates, "Archaeological Discussions," *American Journal of Archaeology* 19 (1915): 179–214; and J. Arthur Munro, H. A. Tubbs, and Warwick Wroth, "Excavations in Cyprus, 1890: Third Season's Work, Salamis," *Journal of Hellenic Studies* 12 (1891): 59–198; for manuscript studies, see Karl Young, "Some Texts of Liturgical Plays," *Proceedings of the Modern Language Association* 24 (1909): 294–331.
21. K. Kris Hirst, "Provenience or Provenance? A Poll," About.com, http://archaeology.about.com/b/a/257567.htm.

22. K. Kris Hirst, "Provenience, Provenance, Let's Call the Whole Thing Off," About .com, http://archaeology.about.com/b/a/257574.htm.
23. Hirst, "Provenience, Provenance."
24. Andrew Alden, "Comment on 'Provenience or Provenance? A Poll,'" About.com, http://archaeology.about.com/b/a/257567.htm.
25. James Novotny Gunderson, "'Catlinite' and the Spread of the Calumet Ceremony," *American Antiquity* 58 (1993): 561.
26. Ellery Frahm, "Analysis in Archaeology, Part 2: Provenance Studies," *Electron Microprobe Analysis in Archaeology,* http://web.archive.org/web/20090322055725/http://web.mac.com/elleryfrahm/iWeb/Microprobe/Electron%20Microprobe%20Analysis%20in%20Archaeology/5E256B37-4965-46CC-A1AA-BC41A18DF8ED.html.
27. Karen Mack, "Comment on 'Provenience, Provenance, Let's Call the Whole Thing Off,'" About.com, http://archaeology.about.com/b/a/257574.htm.
28. Hirst, "Provenience, Provenance."
29. See Byron Hamann, "The Social Life of Pre-Sunrise Things," *Current Anthropology* 43 (2002): 351–82; Rosemary A. Joyce, "Concrete Memories: Fragments of the Past in the Classic Maya Present (500–1000 AD)," in *Archaeologies of Memory,* ed. Ruth van Dyke and Susan Alcock (Oxford: Blackwell, 2003), 104–25; and Katina Lillios, "Objects of Memory: The Ethnography and Archaeology of Heirlooms," *Journal of Archaeological Method and Theory* 6 (1999): 235–62.
30. DeAngelis, "How Much Provenance Is Enough?," 398n6.
31. "Of Doubtful Origin," Eudaemonist, http://www.eudaemonist.com/aged/0803.
32. James Porter, "Olmec Colossal Heads as Recarved Thrones: 'Mutilation,' Revolution, and Recarving," *Res* 17–18 (1989): 23–29; and Patricia Crown and Wirt H. Wills, "Modifying Pottery and Kivas at Chaco: Pentimento, Restoration, or Renewal?" *American Antiquity* 68 (2003): 511–32.
33. Gosden and Marshall, "Cultural Biography of Objects," 170.

DOMINIQUE POULOT

PROVENANCE AND VALUE
The Reception of Ancien Régime Works of Art under the French Revolution

A remarkable series of debates took place in revolutionary France; as much political as cultural, they concerned the ways in which the provenance of a work of art should be treated and the consequences that this entailed, particularly within the new museums. These new ways of understanding and presenting a work's provenance were connected with the peculiar relationship that the Revolution enjoyed with temporality: its ambition to begin time anew and cut itself off entirely from the past has fascinated interpreters of the revolutionary decade, from the contemporary witness Edmund Burke to Alexis de Tocqueville and the historians of the twenty-first century. As François Furet puts it: "Bizarre as it may seem in the light of the inevitable continuity of any nation's historical evidence, the idea that society could be made over starting with a clean slate drew considerable power from the people's revolt against inequality and the elite's faith in the philosophy of the Enlightenment."[1] In Furet's account, the emergence and subsequent radicalization of the term *ancien régime* perfectly illustrates this aspiration to break with a past that was now identified with ignorance, ignominy, and memory—in short, with all the most dangerous adversaries of change. By the time of Maximilien Robespierre and the Reign of Terror, "the phrase had come to denote any manifestation of resistance or even mere inertia in the face of the collective effort to establish a new order for the common good. It also implied a range of habits of mind, customs, and mores that impeded progress toward the republican goal of creating a new man. The Ancien Régime was the antagonist, which lurked not only in the shadows of conspiracy but also in the dark recesses of memory.... [It] was not simply a curse, it was the enemy."[2] The moderate François Antoine Boissy d'Anglas summed up the overall view of the revolutionary generation with respect to everything that had preceded it: "In another forty, fifty or sixty years at the most, people will remember the Ancien Régime only in order to despise and hate it"[3] (fig. 1). This new expectation that the future "be sensed as progressive or catastrophic" brought with it a new concept, as Reinhart Koselleck has shown, that of the "Revolution" in history and, more broadly, a new critical self-consciousness about the science of history itself.[4] Awareness of the origins and provenance of objects and forms of behavior was increasing, underpinned

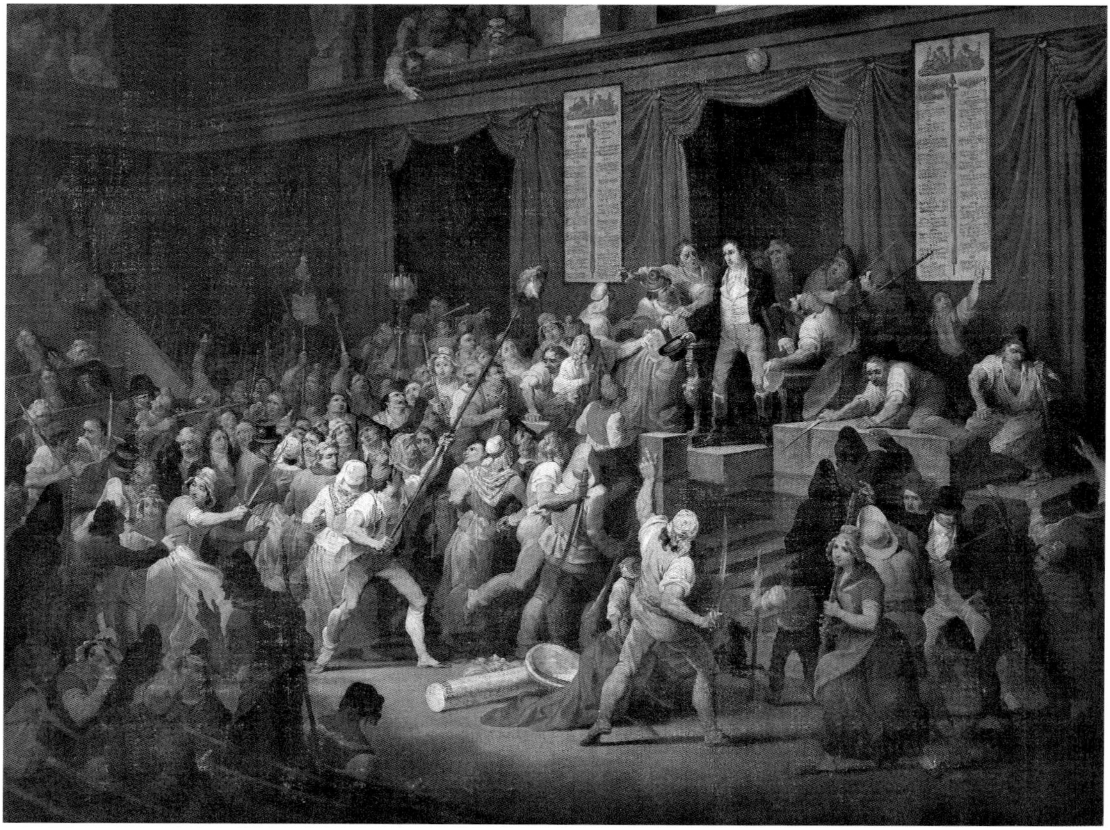

Fig. 1.
Joseph Auguste Tellier (French, act. 1800s).
From the Tribune of the Convention, Boissy d'Anglas Salutes the Head of Deputy Féraud, 20 May 1795, 1830, oil on canvas, 85 × 110 cm (33½ × 43⅜ in.). Versailles, Châteaux de Versailles et de Trianon, MV5516.

by the unprecedented attention then being accorded to the notion of context. This new relationship with "context" gave rise to the human sciences and more specifically to the history of literature and art.[5] But the representation of "provenance" within the range of mechanisms invented by the Revolution to deal with its artistic and cultural heritage has not been much studied, despite the fact that it exemplifies the ambiguities and paradoxes of this overall reorganization of the relationship between past and future.

An Unprecedented Revolution

François Grille, the prolix author of *La France au dix-neuvième siècle* (France in the nineteenth century)—a description of the French *départements* and their wealth—was also the editor of *Mémoires sur la Révolution française* (Memoirs on the French Revolution), for which he wrote the introduction in 1825. With the advantage of hindsight, he admirably summarized the implications of the revolutionary break with the past: "France had one foot in the grave; the knell had been tolled; it faced ruin and death. All of a sudden, it turned back to its cradle in search of the common origin of all its children. . . . What a triumph for immutable nature over fragile society!"[6] Indeed, the refusal to trust any reference to the past and therefore to conceive of a provenance for the revolutionary inspiration other than nature itself (or a version of antiquity so primitive and primordial as to be all but indistinguishable from nature) was concomitant with the claim that this was an unprecedented break with the past.

Yet the question of the provenance of the nation had long mobilized intellectual energy in what have recently been called the "incredible genealogies"[7] of modern Europe. In the case of France, the debate over whether the nation owed its origins to Gauls or Germans exercised intellectuals during the pre-revolutionary years.[8] For Élie Carcassonne, the separation of history from politics took place around 1760 to 1770; thereafter, no legitimacy could be sought in the factual past, and reform could therefore be justified only through the quest for principles.[9] The concept of "nation" played a major role in this quest both in terms of the continuity of France and in terms of the dissatisfaction with the present that fueled civic protests and demands. But by 1789, reference to history had become aligned with the defense of privilege, and the search for historical precedent was definitively condemned. The Revolution thus declared itself to be without provenance though it continued to perceive itself as belonging to the continuity of civilization and thus to the progress of morals and intellect.

On 28 frimaire, year II (18 December 1793), in a report to the Convention on the new Commission temporaire des arts (Temporary commission for the arts), Jean-Baptiste-Charles Mathieu-Mirampal (who was briefly president of the Comité d'instruction publique) characterized the Revolution as "the fall of everything that had no basis in nature."[10] But at the same time, he spoke of the need to conserve "monuments and antiquities still of interest; those that time, having spared and consecrated them, seems to bestow on us afresh because it does not destroy them; those that history consults, the arts study, and philosophy observes; such as our eyes love to gaze upon with the sort of interest inspired by the very age of things and by everything that imparts a kind of life to the past."[11] In the process of regeneration, the argument runs, the new era should benefit from the experience and natural talents of humanity. Works inherited from the past were thus required to bear witness in the present to the abilities naturally exhibited by humanity. This double imperative paved the way for a philosophical inquiry into the place that the arts should occupy between history and morality, memory and nature, model and bogeyman. At the heart of this reflection, the question of provenance took on particular importance since it brought to bear the knowledge of the expert and inevitably led to assessments of value.

Under the ancien régime, thinking about the provenance of objects was a geographical and juridical procedure. One of the characteristics of consumption under the ancien régime, as William Reddy notably has shown in his analysis of dictionaries of merchandise,[12] was the emphasis on the capacity of the buyer to make an expert assessment of the product supplied. The expectation was that goods on the market would encounter expert consumers likely to be capable of discerning the marks of a legitimate production-source and recognizing the guarantees afforded by products whose nature and origin were regulated. Reflecting this situation and answering the need for ad hoc tools, works were published on the marks of craft production: the first dictionary devoted exclusively to marks in artworks was published in Paris in 1750.[13] As the terms of this dictionary imply—*monogram, mark, inscription* (the word *signature* became conventional in art only in the nineteenth century)—the presence of such indications of provenance was connected with guild traditions.

In the picture galleries, the notion of a national school appeared at the end of the century and afforded a form of classification at once hierarchical, encyclopedic, and patriotic.[14] In France, however, the system was less developed than in other places, and hanging by provenance took second place; the priority was to distribute the different kinds of beauty in line with academic doctrine or a balanced representation of the painters' qualities.[15] However, a concern for provenance accompanied the unprecedented expansion of the Parisian market and reinforced the rapid rise during the second half of the eighteenth century of expertise involving attribution.[16] A part of the literature of art was now concerned with the new scholarship of provenance, which made it possible to create catalogues raisonnés; this was a genre that developed over the course of the century.[17] Finally, the mention of an illustrious provenance sometimes constituted a decisive argument in favor of purchase, as we can see from sales-catalog introductions and publicity material.

With the advent of the Revolution, awareness of provenance was primarily related to such massive phenomena as the nationalization of church property, the confiscation of émigré property, and the plundering of conquered countries. When the first museums opened, notes on the provenance of works confiscated and exhibited by the authorities constituted a manifestation of collective and popular approval, and this aspect temporarily overrode the certificate of quality that provenance might also afford. If the public was so ill informed as to mistake an ancient bust for a representation of the noble who possessed it, taking the label triumphantly specifying provenance to be part of an explanation of the work's subject, too bad; better accommodate such error than fail to signal the triumph of the Revolution.[18] Removing works from the place for which

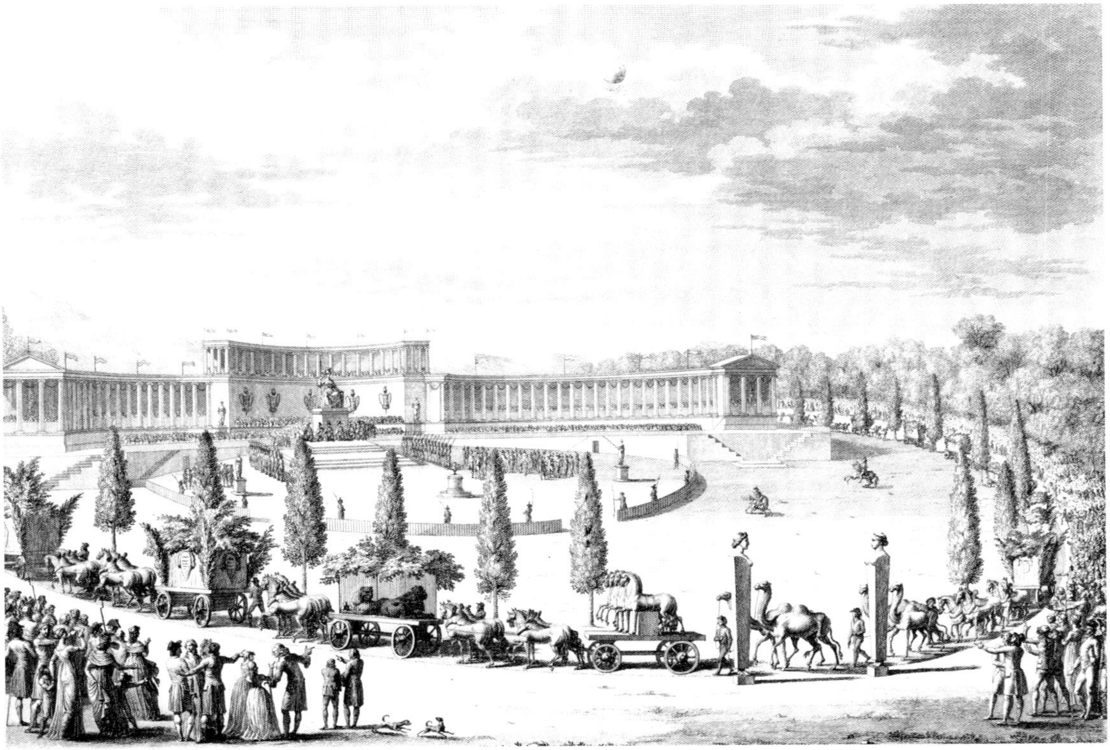

Fig. 2.
Pierre Gabriel Berthault (French, ca. 1748–ca. 1819).
Triumphal Entry into France of the Monuments of the Sciences and Arts, 1798, engraving, 24 × 30 cm (9½ × 11¾ in.).
Los Angeles, Getty Research Institute.

they had been created became part and parcel of the practice of the modern museum and more especially of its revolutionary version. The representation of provenance might nevertheless prove opportune in the revolutionary museum if it enhanced value. Provenance was deliberately emphasized in the Fête des Arts (fig. 2) and in all the exhibitions at the Louvre intended to celebrate the victories of French armies on foreign soil, for example the exhibition of German art.[19] The appeal to provenance became, by contrast, a strong argument in the mouths of counterrevolutionaries, particularly as regards their opposition to the seizure of works in Italy for exhibition in the Louvre and other French museums; this opposition was inaugurated by Antoine Quatremère de Quincy in his famous *Lettres sur le projet d'enlever les monumens de l'Italie* (Letters on the plan to abduct the monuments of Italy, 1796).[20] Thus, evocation of a work's provenance became an integral part of the political struggle as it was mobilized by those who opposed or supported the revolutionary museums. The counterrevolutionaries imagined the original state of the works in terms of a golden age of the artwork's destination (*destination* here being used in the sense ascribed to it by Quatremère).[21] The revolutionaries argued that the work's aesthetic and moral power—and thus the pleasure that it might give—could be enhanced by its removal to a museum. In other words, recognition and appreciation of an artwork in the revolutionary present seemed to run counter to respect for its provenance.

Public Recognition of Works of Art versus a Concern with Provenance

One feature of French eighteenth-century philosophical writing about the works of the past was the idea that certain of them should be allowed gradually to disappear or (a more radical view) be destroyed, while others were perpetuated by various mechanisms of commemoration. This project is particularly evident in utopian literature, which was governed entirely by reason and morality and intent on annihilating all harmful institutions. In utopia, says Bronislaw Baczko, historical discourse becomes "a discourse that one might describe as 'monumental' in the sense that it can be perfectly translated into a series of monuments, a series of images distributing to the people edifying examples and lessons in morality."[22] In Daniel Jost de Villeneuve de Listonai's utopian Selenopolis, the palace square receives the equestrian statue of the reigning king. At the death of the monarch, "his effigy is removed and placed in a special rotunda. But this is done only on condition that the deceased contributed to the happiness of the people, otherwise he simply falls into oblivion.... In the other squares are assembled the statues of great men who have deserved the gratitude of the country"[23] (fig. 3). The form of such towns imitates that of a

Fig. 3.
Jean Duplessis-Bertaux (French, 1747–1819) and R. Daudet (French, 1737–1824), after Louis-Jean Desprez (French, 1743–1804).
Transport of the Antiquities of Herculaneum from the Museo [Ercolanese] di Portici to the Palazzo degli Studi in Naples. From Jean Claude Richard de Saint Non, *Voyage pittoresque; ou, Description des royaumes de Naples et de Sicile*, vol. 2 (Paris: Imprimerie de Clousier, 1782), no. 95.

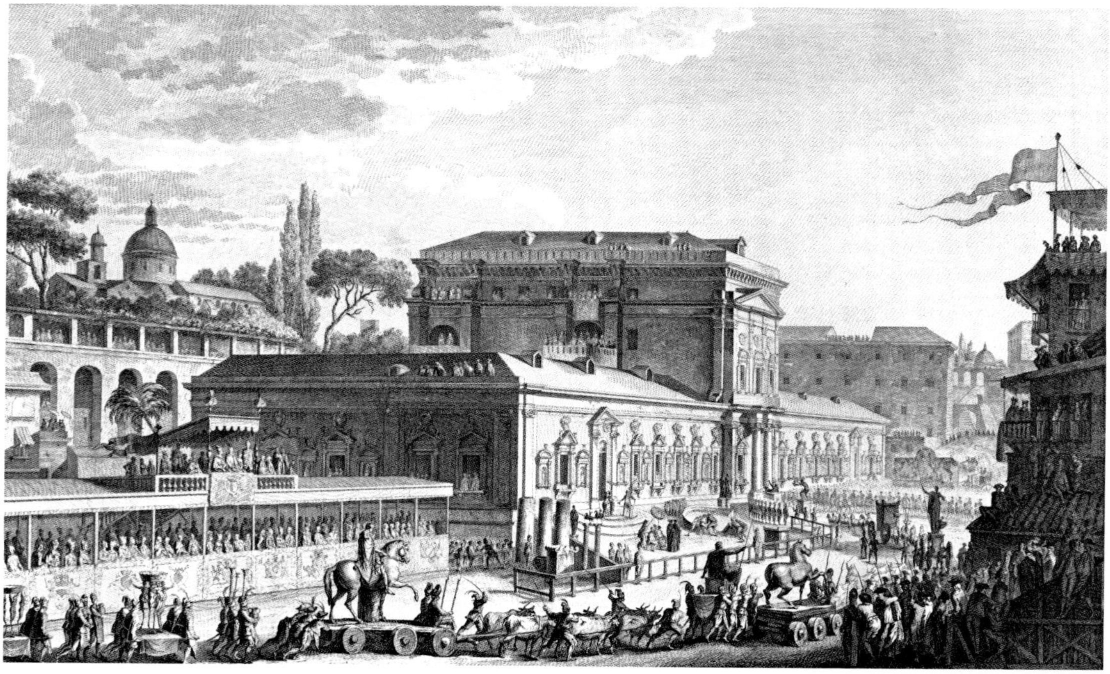

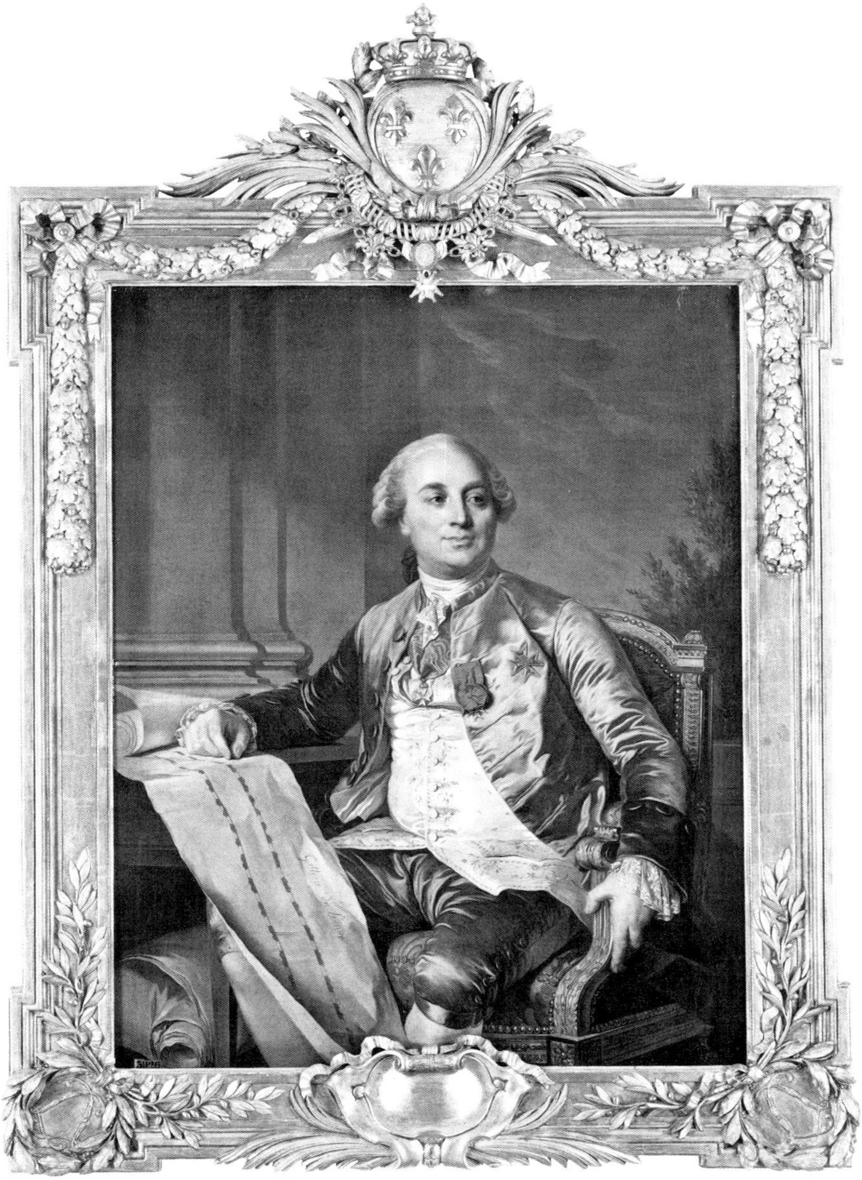

Fig. 4.
Joseph-Siffred Duplessis (French, 1725–1802).
Charles-Claude de La Billarderie, Count d'Angiviller, Director of the King's Buildings in 1774, Presenting a Plan for the Development of the Grand Gallery of the Louvre, ca. 1779, oil on canvas, 144 × 106 cm (56¾ × 41¾ in.). Versailles, Châteaux de Versailles et de Trianon.

Panthéon—or indeed a museum in which the provenance of monuments is systematically forgotten in favor of a new kind of recognition taking the form of their translation to a special place of memory.

Under Louis XVI, the comte d'Angiviller (1730–1809) (fig. 4), a Rousseauiste appointed to the Direction des Bâtiments (Superintendence of buildings)[24] in December 1774, decreed that "history paintings and statues" would be commissioned every year "whose subject would be great French men." The series of sculptures produced illustrates a morally and historically significant attitude and continued from 1776 to 1787: "Great captains are clearly in a minority compared to the representatives of literature and science ('the sages of the Nation'). As a sign of the times, a contemporary 'philosophe' was admitted to this empyrean: Montesquieu."[25] The purpose of this program was to provide works for the museum planned in the Louvre, which was to be dedicated "to the glory of the Kings of France and to that of the Illustrious Men of the Nation"[26] (fig. 5). Rhetoric of this kind, which gave rise to other plans for public squares and galleries,[27] proves that glory—in its new acceptation—occupied a central position in the way in which the past was regarded. Finally, this concern with the transmission of the past brought attention to bear on the material supports of that past—and thus on their conservation—in a perspective combining scholarship and morality.[28]

The revolutionary enterprise inherited these considerations. But for the Revolution, the only agency legitimating the past's existence in the present was the recognition conferred by its own authorities. Thus the decree of 20 June 1790: "It concerns the glory of the nation that no monument should survive capable of evoking ideas of slavery.... It befits the dignity of a free people to celebrate only such actions as it has itself assessed and deemed great and useful."[29] It therefore became a permanent undertaking to ensure the victory of enlightened memory over prejudice and routine; we might compare this with the way that, in Hayden White's view, the historians of the Enlightenment wrote history against the past.[30] The exemplary illustration of this is the Panthéon, in which the act of "decreeing eternity"[31]—the coming together of a politics of memory with the judgment of posterity—is played out. The paradox here was that memory should not recall the former state of affairs—that being the most dangerous perspective imaginable—but must be entirely oriented toward the future in order to reinforce the progress of reason and guarantee the stability of the most recent stage attained in that progress.

To restore French glory in all its authenticity and transcend the aberrations of despotism and fanaticism required a combination of restoration and censorship that was determined by the provenance of the monument in question. In practice, certain mausoleums could be allowed to survive in their capacity as historical monuments, while others were newly erected to replace the excessively modest tombs formerly bestowed on genius; the new monument was sometimes a considerable distance from the original place of burial. When Lazare Carnot, the minister of war, made a speech early in year IX in front of the tomb of Henri de Turenne,[32] which was being moved to the church of Saint-Louis des Invalides (fig. 6)—having previously been removed from Saint-Denis and exhibited for a while at the Musée des monuments français—he addressed

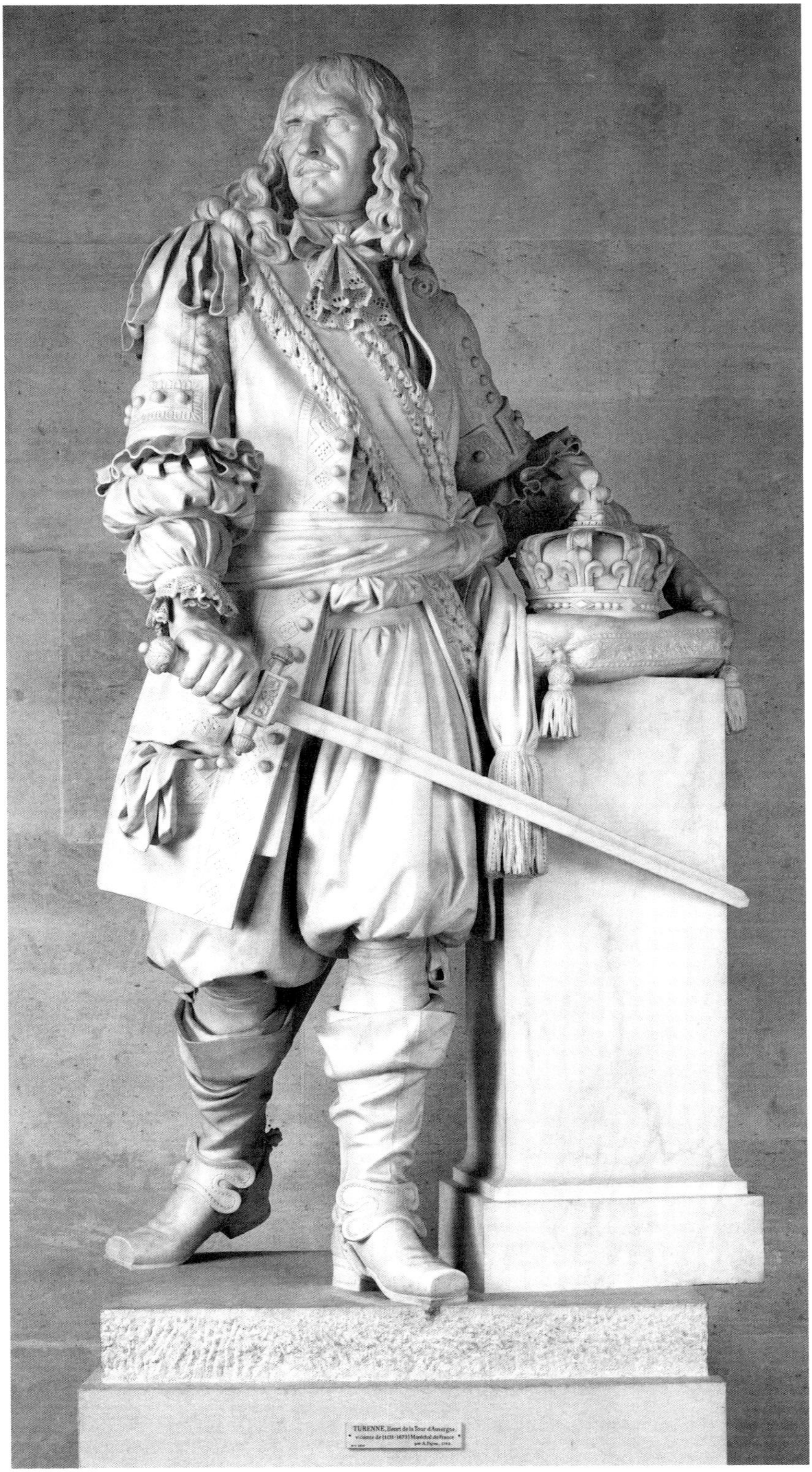

Fig. 5.
Augustin Pajou (French, 1730–1809).
Henri de La Tour d'Auvergne, Viscount of Turenne, Marshal of France (1611–1675),
1782–83, marble, 209 × 107 × 74 cm ($82\frac{3}{8}$ × $42\frac{1}{8}$ × $29\frac{1}{8}$ in.). Versailles, Château de Versailles.

Fig. 6.
Gaspard Marsy (French, 1624–81) and Jean Tuby the elder (French, 1635–1700).
Tomb of Henri de La Tour d'Auvergne, Viscount of Turenne, Marshal of France, 1675–80, bronze and marble, larger than life size.
Paris, Hôtel des Invalides.

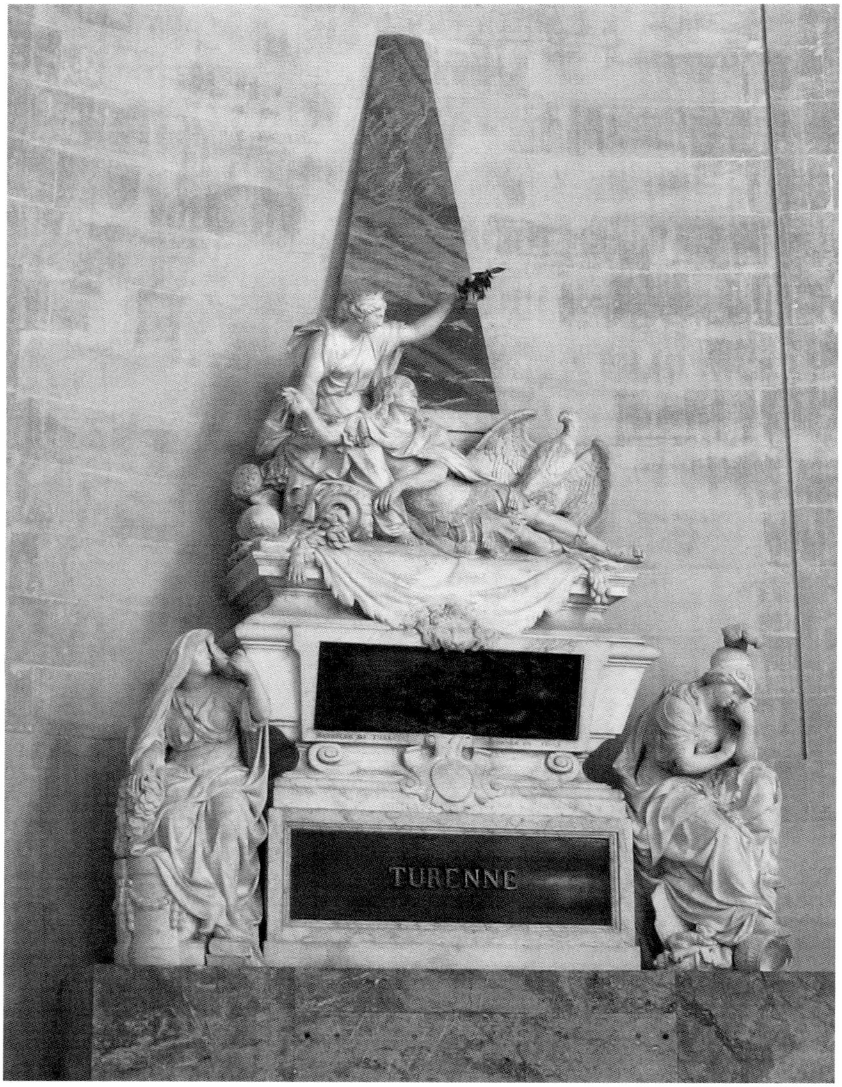

this issue: "The remains of Turenne were until our own day conserved amid the tombs of kings. The republicans have rescued them from this ostentatious oblivion."[33] The evocation of this provenance served to condemn a form of false recognition; glory bestowed by the ancien régime could, in the new perspective, be negligent and confused at best and might be simply ignominious. This fallacious glory could now be contrasted with true (revolutionary) glory, of which the museum was one of the privileged sites.

In museums, pedagogic intention trumped any other, and the effort put into lucidity and educational efficacy was wholly unprecedented. The requirement that the historical heritage be rendered intelligible in the Musée des monuments

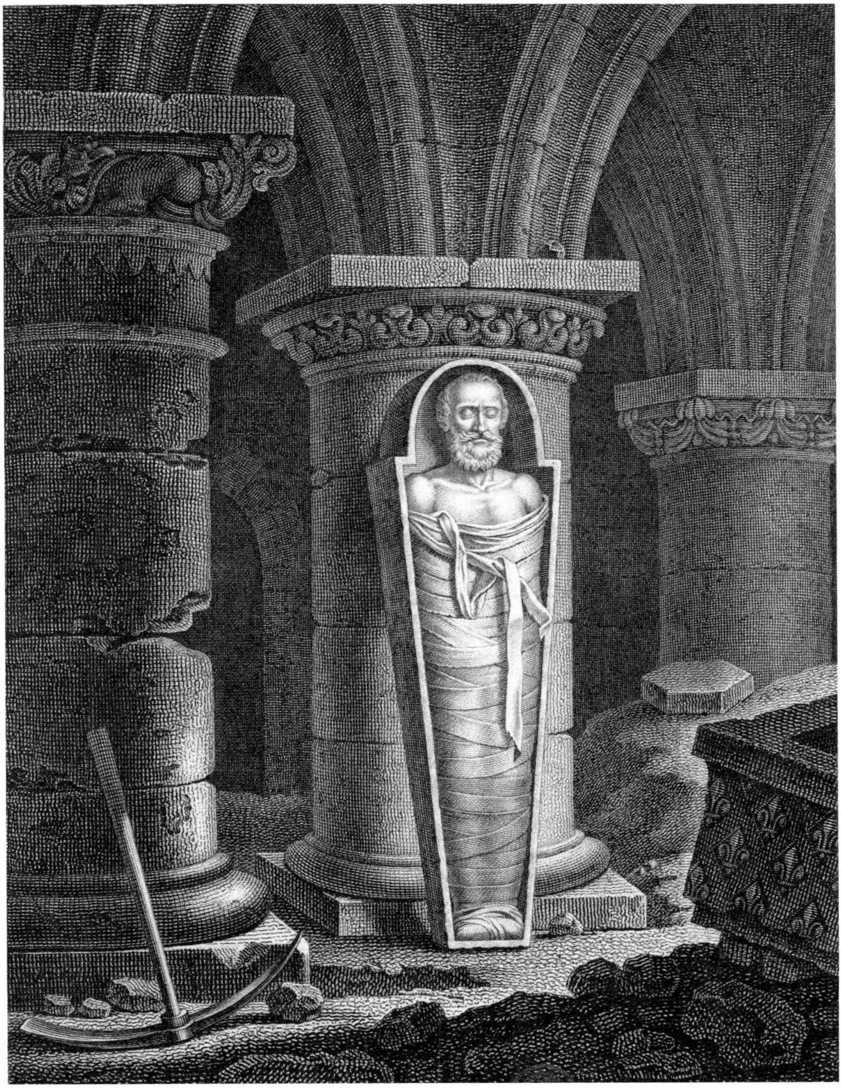

Fig. 7.
Alexis Chataignier (French, 1772–1817) and Edme Bovinet (French, 1767–1832), after Eustache-Hyacinthe Langlois du Pont de l'Arche (French, 1777–1837) and François Gabriel Théodore Busset de Jolimont (French, 1787–1854).
Henry IV Exhumed, 1817, engraving with aquatint, page: 40.3 × 29 cm (15⅞ × 11⅜ in.), engraving: 33.2 × 25.1 cm (13⅛ × 9⅞ in.).
Versailles, Château de Versailles.

français (founded in 1795) led to a clear and eloquent arrangement of the tombs taken from Saint-Denis and the Parisian churches, one that was in marked contrast with their previous disorder.[34] Winckelmannian in approach, this was a museum of the progress of art, yet it also sought to be a "French Westminster." This was paradoxical: the royal figures, with very few exceptions,[35] were thought to embody barbarity and ignorance prevailing at the point of the sword. One such exception was Henry IV (fig. 7). The opprobrium visited on most royals emphasized the contrasting glory of the present; it was intended to reinforce an account of history that unfolded in a series of antitheses according to a logic that was as much ideological and political as it was aesthetic.[36] Provenance arrived

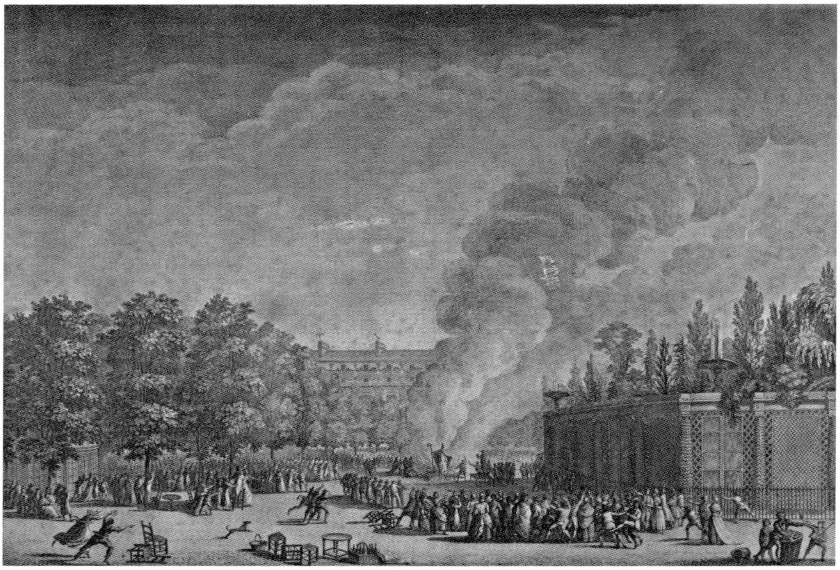

Fig. 8.
Pierre Gabriel Berthault (French, 1737–31), after Jean Louis Prieur Le Jeune (French, act. 1759–95).
Pope Burnt in Effigy at the Palais Royal, 6 April 1791,
ca. 1791, engraving, 31.3 × 48.5 cm (12⅜ × 19⅛ in.).
Private collection.

at the Musée des monuments français under duress, since the objects and human remains exhibited there had been torn from their original context. And it was humbled there, since the objects were re-exhibited in an unprecedented context; they became the material basis for a particular image of history.[37] But the citation in the museum's catalog of the sometimes incongruous vicissitudes that works of art underwent subsequent to the sale of church property and the crisis of vandalism also constituted a celebration of the salvage of certain monuments by the curator (fig. 8).[38]

Works of Art Freed of Their Provenance and Restored to the Art of Liberty[39]

Reflection on the provenance of artworks harbored in the new museums could not be confined to condemning the past, for all that the past was identified with the faults and errors that might, on occasion, have distorted the artist's original intention; it also meant preserving—in the form of the works bequeathed by the past—the materials of the future. From that perspective, a monument regenerated by the museum would have to be extracted from the past to serve present and future against that past; it would have to show that the values of the present day existed no less in history but had been oppressed. The works of times gone by thus bore witness both to the deviations of art caused by social influences (errors of taste and artistic failures attributable to ignorance or maleficent regimes) and to the permanence of artistic talent. Artworks showed themselves to be indices of good or bad government and thus veritable moral images of justice and injustice. The museum hoped, via the historical provenances that it could bring to bear on each work, to make of each visitor a citizen-legislator. In this respect, the revolutionary museum might almost be defined as a collection of provenances through which one could effortlessly read a philosophical history of the political conditions required for the perfection of art.

Any work of art from the ancien régime thus reflected its execrable times; its hated provenance afforded a guarantee that despotism would never permit true art to emerge let alone manifest itself freely. That a work of this kind could nevertheless serve as a model for republican artists therefore required legitimation. One solution was to distinguish between context and form, between a monument to the detested despotism and the authentic talent of the artist who had been forced to serve the regime against his will. In other words, whereas the intention behind this regeneration of the arts was to celebrate their virtuous finality and severe taste in some future world, the assessment of works bequeathed by the past called for a fundamental dissociation between the effort and technique of the artist and the meaning required by the patron who had commissioned the work. This process was directly linked to a way of thinking about history that distinguished between the continuity of human nature and the vicissitudes of more or less perverted societies.

In the early days of September 1793, Pierre Cossard and François-Valentin Mulot, envoys from the Commission des monuments, signaled that a medallion of Louis XIV in the Troyes town hall should be conserved. They had had to "remove it at all speed from the eyes of those republicans who, because of their hatred of despotism, would soon have found the sight of it unbearable." But "these ornaments, the fruit of the art of Girardon, must be preserved out of respect for art, in gratitude to their maker, and in the interest of the students whose training they will serve."[40] The protection of the work against vandalism speaks of a patriotic cult of talent. And their recommendation also suggests the need to ensure the continuity of "professional" memory and the indispensability of the service rendered by artistic models. This in turn reflects a world of art answering to specific and relatively constant criteria rather than to the "revolutions" of history that were otherwise considered decisive. Different strategies are simultaneously operative inside this conceptual framework: for some of these, the work can be fully acknowledged in the present and its status therefore reestablished; for others, a distinction must be made between its eternal qualities and those that are time-specific, with provenance ranked among the latter.

In the simplest interpretation, art and politics were simply out of phase. In a widely known speech given on 18 floreal, year II (7 May 1794) (*Rapport sur les rapports des idées religieuses et morales avec les principes républicains, et sur les fêtes nationales*), Robespierre famously spoke of "men of letters [who] in general covered themselves in shame during this Revolution." He suggested the existence of a clear contrast between the arts and philosophy: "The peoples of Europe have made astonishing progress in what we call the arts and sciences yet they seem ignorant of the first notions of public morality. . . . Whence comes this mixture of genius and stupidity?"[41] Antoine Claire Thibaudeau, speaking in the name of the Comité d'instruction publique on 21 floreal, year II (10 May 1794), similarly evoked the "centuries of base adulation" that artists would have to "efface by in future devoting their talents to honoring virtue and making tyranny abhorrent." And he concluded that "the arts have long been retarded relative to the Revolution."[42]

Another solution to the dilemma was to suppose the exact opposite: that artistic genius had been able to anticipate the future triumph of liberty. Instead of endeavoring to "force" works otherwise utterly tainted with the past to bear witness to at least some acceptable precepts, as Casimir Varon, one of the curators of the Louvre put it, one should acknowledge that art had been several steps ahead and that political regeneration was only now catching up.[43] This idea is also found in the report by Jean-Baptiste-Charles Mathieu-Mirampal cited above: "It is for the Convention nationale to do today for the arts, sciences, and the progress of philosophy what the arts, sciences, and philosophy did to bring about the reign of liberty; they too are creditors of the Revolution and the Revolution must do all that it can for them."[44] Boissy d'Anglas, in his report to the Convention and the Comité d'instruction publique (*Quelques idées sur les arts . . .*) printed on 25 pluviôse, year II (13 February 1794), recommends that "despotism, whose pride encouraged and protected the arts that taught people to destroy it, should in this respect be surpassed by liberty."[45] He further expressed his conviction that for the French nation, the homeland of the arts and model of all peoples, this was something of a mission. Such theories bear witness to an awareness of the long history of arts at the service of the new political ideal. But by this very fact, they weakened the sense of an unprecedented break with the past and made revolutionaries the students of the old masters.

The disadvantage of the "Robespierre" philosophy of provenance was its implication that the art of the ancien régime was inferior to that of the future. In Pierre-Jean-Baptiste Chaussard's terms, this meant acknowledging the success of its techniques—recognizing the pleasure that it could offer and the virtuosity of its practitioners—while rejecting its goals.[46] True art was inaugurated with the republic and artists were required to redeem their previous complacency. This was, ipso facto, to devalue the museum; it meant that in exhibiting the art of the past, it could exhibit only examples of technical expertise rather than models for future artists; worse still, it might be limited to presenting manifestations of error and specimens whose function was deterrent. The disadvantage of the "Varon" philosophy was that it implied an autonomous history of art, detached from political contingency; this indirectly implied that the republican art of the future was not, after all, unprecedented and entirely superior. In short, the dilemma appears to have been as follows: either recognize the provenance of ancien régime art as a historical fact and thereby assume it to be evil in its very conception—with all the consequences that this implied—or integrate this provenance with the present in which authenticity had been restored and thus create an enigma: authentic art that predated liberty.

The latter hypothesis freed the art of the past from the need to undergo an iconoclastic or restorative "cleanup" before it could edify the republic; moreover, it postulated something permanent about truth and beauty. Under the ancien régime, it was argued, these elements had been disdained or misunderstood but they now stood revealed. In short, this theory required one to believe that works could be freed of their provenance. Thus, in parallel with the process by which the corrupt images of the ancien régime were sorted, banned, or smashed, the Revolution also claimed to bring to light true works of art till then relegated to the obscure storehouses of despotism. In this perspective, the purpose of republican collections, museums, and libraries was to exhibit neglected works that bore witness to the contempt in which truth had hitherto been held. Works till then unnoticed or forgotten were considered in a more favorable light since their very obscurity suggested a great and unsuspected talent deprived of acknowledgment, if not indeed suffocated or forced to hide its light under a bushel. Revolutionary management of the past was thus a work of rehabilitation, and its task was to undo the harm inflicted in equal measure by the malice of humanity and the passage of years.

Abbé Henri Grégoire explained in his *Rapport sur la bibliographie,* "Peerage lists, genealogical treatises, all those works in which despotism set down its rage and extravagance, were almost invariably honored with morocco leather, while the immortal books could only escape the judgment of censorship and the persecution of the Inquisition of the time by taking refuge in obscure corners under a modest parchment cover."[47] From this perspective, disputes about the restoration of works of art clearly showed the republic as under an obligation to elect as privileged figures in its heritage these symbolic "victims" of oppression and misfortune.

The New Discourse of Provenance in the Museum

The museum therefore sought to impose a new discourse of provenance that put behind it all previous exhibition arrangements as invariably unsatisfying and inappropriate, if not indeed nefarious. In the museum, the picture was to be valued for itself, stripped of the circumstances in which it had previously been exhibited and of any legends pertaining to these—stripped, in short, of its entire heritage, which was regarded as useless or even damaging. Yet it was precisely this assemblage of representations, legends, and memories that Quatremère and his friends identified as the truth of the work. This complete blanking of the successive provenances that might have altered or distorted the work was done in the name of the artist's original intention within the framework of a philosophy of the liberty of art deriving from a vulgarized version of Johann Joachim Winckelmann's thought. It is not therefore a complete negation of provenance but rather an attempt to filter out from the historical provenances one that might be considered primordial and be singled out in the name of respect for the artist's intention. This principle is clearly illustrated in the policy of restoration, which theorizes a superior form of provenance: a primitive state deriving from the artist's independence and its recovery from the historical provenances subsequently layered over the work by its successive ownership and sales.

In the earlier mercantile economy, the movement of paintings and the modification of their dimensions had been closely linked; paintings were altered in order to adapt them to a changing context or satisfy the caprices of taste.[48] The cessation of such revisions—indeed, the ban on their practice—was linked to a change in the way paintings were represented. At the end of the eighteenth century, the treatment of pictures as if they were mere articles of furniture was very widely condemned. This condemnation became commonplace with the ideal of a museum open to the public and intended to educate the public. One consequence of this was that, during the early years of the Louvre, regular declarations were made of respect for the dimensions of the work and indeed of the need for it to be returned to its original size. In 1794, following a suggestion on the part of the restorer Jean-Michel Picault, certain works in the national collection were returned to their original form.[49]

Regard for the original dimensions of the picture became explicit during the "Marin affair," which, while it crystallized tensions between certain of the Louvre's staff members, also bore witness to these new values. In his attacks on the museum, Representative Anthelme Marin[50] particularly emphasized consideration for the materiality of the work, offering highly significant arguments about the need for the museum to distance itself from the kind of private opulence for which artistic value was an irrelevance: "There have been increasing numbers of complaints about the fact that—following the example of the financier who, having had the shelves of a bookcase made in richly decorated mahogany, had the volumes cut down to fit the shelves—paintings by Guercino have had sections six inches and sometimes even a foot wide cut off in order to match them in size with some other picture."[51] The stereotype of the ignorant rich man who is unaware of his treasures or simply despises them here coincides with the jibes of the philosophes (for example, Voltaire in *Candide*)[52] but above all with the carefully cultivated stereotype of idiotic and grasping royal mistresses, who were said to have secured for their own pleasure certain masterpieces from the national collections; all of these themes featured in the literature of year II at the opening of the Louvre.

The administration then admitted to having modified the dimensions of three works, two Guercino pictures and a painting by Bartolomeo Schedoni. In the first case, the experts explained the removal of some inches in terms of the need to create a matching pair and therefore reduce one painting to the size of the other. In the second, they pointed out that the edges were black and that their disappearance therefore had no effect on the painting. In the third, they stated that they had simply removed extensions that had been added in the past and that they had not therefore diminished the painting but merely restored it to its original dimensions, a point that Marin contested.[53] It is clear that the Louvre team was well aware of the scandal caused by their actions.

The committee appointed by the Assemblée législative consequently published a report declaring that the original dimensions of objects belonging to the museum should be strictly respected: "It will therefore be necessary to restore to their original dimensions all those pictures in which it is indubitably recognized that parts have been added, parts that, not being by the hand of the master, were added merely with the intention of extending them to the size required to fill a larger location."[54] The history of the provenance of the work had at this point become indispensable; without it, respect for original form was impossible. But this provenance espoused a specific interest; it defined the authenticity of the piece as its original form, stripped of subsequent historic vicissitudes, of the contexts in which the work had been hung and interpreted. Sweeping away previous owners and audiences, the museum appealed to a new notion of provenance, which accurately matched its intention to exalt the autonomy of the picture and the liberty of the artist.

The revolutionary episode affords a remarkable field in which to observe awareness of the provenance of works of art. Over the course of a decade, a variety of attitudes prevailed. Provenance could be denied or forgotten and works reused as if they were simple materials; it could be invoked for its historical interest as one of many examples of the intolerable subordination of artists, in which case it served as a proof of infamy or bore witness to historical criminality; or it could be respected for the greater glory that the works—now exhibited in the new museums—could be expected to draw from it. What emerges from these contradictory solutions is the conviction that to respect the provenance of works in the same terms as the ancien régime would be to confuse principles with aberrations and positive values with ignominy.

The theme of the restoration of truth in art was accompanied by the rehabilitation of the victims of despotism and a corresponding fall in the status of artists favored by royalty. The detestable patronage under which their works had been produced was emphasized, but it never led to lasting ignominy for the works themselves. Thinking about provenance under these conditions principally meant constructing a specific form of knowledge linked to the process of musealization and in particular detaching works from their context in order to establish their status as models or paradigms. This led to a new investment in the notion of provenance; the objective was to pass over in silence the particular vicissitudes undergone by a work in favor of an origin that one might describe as delusive, general, and abstract: that of the production of art by the eternal genius of humanity.

The fact remained that although the revolutionary museum was able to stage the provenance of its works for its own benefit, in order to vaunt their fame or celebrate their rescue, it nevertheless had to negotiate the comparison with earlier hangings; that might involve a variety of criteria, from memories of the emotion earlier felt in situ by sentimental visitors or the detection by experts of alterations to the material state or condition of a work. Museal discourse on provenance functions in this way with every picture, but the revolutionary museum prioritized the notion of an original artistic performance that it considered superior to the conditions of commission and the constraints of the historical situation. The ideal of transmission that it embodied required absolute respect for the material conservation of the work and for the dimensions recorded when it left the studio; the counterpart of this was the erasure of both context and the nonmaterial memories with which the work was invested.

Notes

This essay was translated from the French by Chris Miller. All foreign-language quotations within the essay were also translated by him, unless otherwise indicated.

1. François Furet, "Ancien Régime," in *A Critical Dictionary of the French Revolution*, ed. François Furet and Mona Ozouf, trans. Arthur Goldhammer (Cambridge, Mass.: Harvard University Press, 1989), 604–15, here p. 608.
2. François Furet, "Ancien Régime," 609.

3. Quoted in Diego Venturino, "La naissance de l'ancien regime," in *The French Revolution and the Creation of Modern Political Culture,* ed. Colin Lucas, vol. 2, *The Political Culture of the French Revolution* (Oxford: Pergamon, 1988), 11–40. The form of words used by Boissy d'Anglas (1756–1826) is particularly significant given that he was an active member in all the revolutionary assemblies and was notable for his liberal positions on religion and freedom of the press. His fame is owed to the events of 1 prairial year III (20 May 1795); presiding that day over the Convention, he faced down a mob brandishing the decapitated head of another *conventionnel,* confining himself to raising his hat to his dead colleague and otherwise remaining impassively in his place. In this way, though he continued to consider the Revolution a complete break from the past, he became a hero in the liberal pantheon, as evidenced by the commission made in September 1830 by Guizot, prime minister under Louis Philippe, of a picture of these events intended to be hung in the Chambre des députés. See Christine Le Bozec, *Boissy d'Anglas, un grand notable liberal* (Privas, France: FOL de l'Ardèche, 1995).
4. Reinhart Koselleck, *Futures Past: On the Semantics of Historical Time* (New York: Columbia University Press, 1963), 60; see also the third chapter, "Historical Criteria of the Modern Concept of Revolution," 43–57.
5. See Peter Burke, "Context in Context," *Common Knowledge* 8, no. 1 (2002): 152–77.
6. François-Joseph Grille, *Introduction aux mémoires sur la Révolution française; ou, Tableau comparatif des mandats et pouvoirs donnés par les provinces aux députés aux États-Généraux de 1789* (Paris: Pichard, 1825), 9–10.
7. Robert Bizzocchi, *Genealogie incredibili: Scritti di storia nell'Europa moderna* (Bologna: Mulino, 2009).
8. Claude Nicolet, *La fabrique d'une nation: La France entre Rome et les Germains* (Paris: Perrin, 2003).
9. Élie Carcassonne, *Montesquieu et le problème de la constitution française au XVIIIe siècle* (Paris: Presses Universitaires de France, 1927).
10. *Rapport fait à la Convention au nom du comité d'instruction publique, par Mathieu, député. Le 28 frimaire, l'an IIe de la république française* (Paris: Impr. nationale, 1793). On the basis of this report, the Commission des monuments, instituted on 4 August 1972, was abolished and replaced by the Commission temporaire des arts on 28 frimaire, year II (18 December 1793). The members of the Comité d'instruction publique (Mathieu, Villars, Fourcroy, Massieu, Grégoire) constituted the essential elements of the Commission temporaire, recruiting scholars, artists, and men of letters to serve on it with them; these were divided into sections or classes to facilitate the work of the Commission. See James Guillaume, *Procès-verbaux du Comité d'instruction publique de la convention nationale,* vol. 3, *1er frimaire an II–30 ventôse an II* [21 November 1793–20 March 1794] (Paris: Impr. Nationale, 1897), 180. See also the new edition: Josiane Boulad-Ayoub and Michel Grenon, eds., *Édition nouvelle et augmentée des procès-verbaux du Comité d'instruction publique de l'Assemblée législative et de la Convention publiés et annotés par James Guillaume,* 9 vols., preface by Michel Vovelle (Paris: L'harmattan, 1997).
11. Quoted in Guillaume, *Procès-verbaux du Comité d'instruction,* 3:180.

12. William Reddy, *The Rise of Market Culture: The Textile Trade and French Society, 1750–1800* (Cambridge: Cambridge University Press, 1984).
13. Johann Friedrich Christ, *Dictionnaire des monogrammes, chiffres, lettres initiales, logogryphes, rébus, sous lesquels les plus célèbres peintres, graveurs, et dessinateurs ont dessiné leurs noms,* trans. Gottfried Sellius (Paris: S. Jorry, 1750; 1st ed, Leipzig, 1747). On the notion of expertise in relation to the arts, see Charlotte Guichard, "Les formes de l'expertise artistique en Europe (XVI–XVIIIe siècle)," *Revue de synthèse* 132, no. 1 (2011): 1–11.
14. Robert W. Scheller, "La notion de patrimoine et la formation du musée au XVIIIe siècle," in *Les musées en Europe à la veille de l'ouverture du Louvre: Actes du colloque organisé par le service culturel du Musée du Louvre du 3 au 5 juin 1993,* ed. Édouard Pommier (Paris: Klincksieck, 1995), 113–24.
15. Andrew McClellan, "The Politics and Aesthetics of Display: The Museum in Paris, 1750–1800," *Art History* 7, no. 4 (1984): 438–64; and Andrew McClellan, *Inventing the Louvre: Art, Politics, and the Origins of the Modern Museum in Eighteenth-Century Paris* (Cambridge: Cambridge University Press, 1994).
16. Krzysztof Pomian, *Collectionneurs, amateurs et curieux: Paris-Venise, XVIe–XVIIIe siècles* (Paris: Gallimard, 1987). See also Sophie Raux, "From Mariette to Joullain: Provenance and Value in Eighteenth-Century French Auction Catalogs," this volume.
17. Pascal Griener, *La république de l'oeil: L'expérience de l'art au siècle des Lumières* (Paris: Odile Jacob, 2010), 213–16.
18. Dominique Poulot, *Musée, nation, patrimoine, 1789–1815* (Paris: Gallimard, 1997).
19. The "Program of the Festivals of Liberty" included the "triumphal entry of the objects of sciences and the arts collected in Italy." The administrators of the Musée central des arts, the Musée spécial de l'école française, and the Musée des monuments français took part in this "entry," processing behind a banner bearing the slogan "Fine Arts. The arts seek the land where the laurels grow." On the following banner was written: "Monuments of ancient sculpture. Greece gave them; Rome has lost them. Their fate has twice changed but will change no more." The four horses of Saint Mark's Basilica in Venice were displayed on the first two carts with the following inscription: "Horses transported from Corinth to Rome and from Rome to Constantinople, from Constantinople to Venice and from Venice to France. At last they find themselves in a land of freedom"; *Le moniteur,* 9 thermidor, year VI (27 July 1798), 322–24. On the German exhibitions, see Marie-Anne Dupuy, Isabelle le Masne de Chermont, and Elaine Williamson, eds., *Vivant Denon: Directeur des musées sous le Consulat et l'Empire; Correspondance, 1802–1815* (Paris: Réunion des Musées Nationaux, 1999); and Bénédicte Savoy, *Patrimoine annexé. Les biens culturels saisis par la France en Allemagne autour de 1800,* 2 vols. (Paris: Maison des Sciences de L'Homme, 2003).
20. See Antoine Quatremère de Quincy, *Letters to Miranda and Canova on the Abduction of Antiquities from Rome and Athens,* trans. Chris Miller and David Gilks, intro. Dominique Poulot (Los Angeles: Getty Research Institute, 2012).
21. In Quatremère, the notion of "destination" is linked with that of necessity: "A work may be called necessary if it has a fixed and determined purpose, a use

so positive that it imposes an obligation on its author to impart a particular character to it, forces the spectator to judge it in a way consistent with the reasons for which it was produced and the public to take from it determinate and uniform impressions." Antoine Quatremère de Quincy, *Considérations morales sur la destination des ouvrages de l'art; ou, De l'influence de leur emploi* (Paris: Impr. de Crapelet, 1815), 2 (available online via Google Books). See my introduction, "The Cosmopolitanism of Masterpieces," in Antoine Quatremère de Quincy, *Letters to Miranda and Canova on the Abduction of Antiquities from Rome and Athens* (Los Angeles: Getty Research Institute, 2012), 1–91.

22. Bronislaw Baczko, *Lumières de l'utopie* (Paris: Payot, 1978), 322–23.
23. Daniel de Villeneuve (Listonai, pseud.), *Le voyageur philosophe dans un pays inconnu aux habitants de la terre* (Amsterdam, 1761), 73–93, according to Baczko, *Lumières,* 294–303. Though not precisely utopian, from the purview of a politics of memory and recognition, this image (fig. 3) of an imaginary transfer of antiquities from one museum to another—from an old museum to a new one that is more enlightened in its policies of conservation and display—serves the same function as the triumphal display in procession through the city of monuments or relics. See Jean Duplessis-Bertaux, "Transport des antiquités d'Herculanum du museum de Portici au Palais des Études à Naples," in Jean Claude Richard de Saint Non, *Voyage pittoresque; ou, Description des royaumes de Naples et de Sicile* (Paris: Impr. de Clousier, 1781–86), 1782, 2:54–55, pl. 95. The commentary accompanying the image speaks of "a sort of ceremony or festivity... a march or a kind of triumph rendered infinitely interesting, since this spectacle would present a justified homage, paid by a nation during an enlightened century, to the fine arts handed down to us, the brilliance of which has given new lustre to Italy and modern Europe." On such processing of works of art, see Dario Gamboni, "Walking Icons," in *The Modern Procession,* ed. Francis Alÿs (New York: Public Art Fund, 2004), 35–43.
24. Jacques Silvestre de Sacy, *Le comte d'Angiviller, dernier directeur des bâtiments du roi* (Paris: Plon, 1953).
25. François Souchal, "Situation de la sculpture en France en 1778," *Dix-Huitième siècle* 11 (1979): 117–21.
26. This was the dedication of a plan to reform and rebuild the Louvre-Tuileries area (the project included a "French museum") created in 1783 by Abbé Lubersac de Livron: see Mark K. Deming, "Louis XVI en l'Île. Contribution à l'étude des places royales parisiennes à la fin de l'ancien régime," *Revue de l'art* 83, no. 1 (1989): 86–92, 92nn45–46.
27. See the exhibition *Le Louvre au temps des Lumières (1750–1792),* Musée du Louvre, 11 November 2010–7 February 2011.
28. Jacques Guillerme, *L'atelier du temps: Essai sur l'altération des peintures* (Paris: Hermann, 1964), 117–89. See also Philippe Sénéchal, "The Fantasy of the Imperishable in the Modern Era: Towards an Eternal Painting," *Diogenes* 46 (1998): 69–81.
29. The Assemblée nationale constituante was preparing the Fête de la Fédération and intending to purge the capital of all unsuitable monuments before the arrival in the city of representatives from "all parts of France." One consequence was

the removal of the "four chained figures at the foot of the statue of Louis XIV" ("Décret pour l'enlèvement des quatre figures de la place des Victoires, pris le 23 juin"); see Jean Baptiste Duvergier, ed., *Collection complète des lois, décrets, ordonnances, réglements, et avis du Conseil d'Etat*, vol. 1 (Paris: A. Guyot et Scribe, 1824), 256.

30. Hayden White, *Metahistory: The Historical Imagination in Nineteenth-Century Europe* (Baltimore: Johns Hopkins University Press, 1973), 63.
31. Bronislaw Baczko, "Le calendrier républicain: Décréter l'éternité," in *Les lieux de mémoire*, ed. Pierre Nora, vol. 1, *La république* (Paris: Gallimard, 1984), 37–83.
32. See Thomas F. Hedin, "Tomb of the Vicomte de Turenne," in idem, *The Sculpture of Gaspard and Balthazar Marsy: Art and Patronage in the Early Reign of Louis XIV, with a Catalogue Raisonné* (Columbia: University of Missouri Press, 1983), 82–85, and no. 43, pp. 197–202. On the overall context, see M. J. Harvey, "Death and Dynasty in the Bouillon Tomb Commissions," *Art Bulletin* 74, no. 2 (1992): 271–96; Bénédicte Gady, *L'ascension de Charles Le Brun: Liens sociaux et production artistique*, vol. 29 of *Passages/Passagen* (Paris: Maison des Sciences de L'Homme, 2010); and, more generally, Claire Mazel, *La mort et l'éclat: Monuments funéraires parisiens du grand siècle* (Rennes, France: Presses Universitaires de Rennes, 2009). On the fate of monuments during the French Revolution, see Louis Courajod, *Alexandre Lenoir, son journal et le Musée des monuments français*, 3 vols. (Paris: H. Champion, 1878–87), 1: documents 695, 712, 719, 1055, 1132; Pierre Arizzoli-Clémentel, "Le mausolée de Turenne aux Invalides: Quelques documents inédits," *Revue de la Société des amis du Musée de l'armée* 76 (1972): 4–12; and Suzanne Glover Lindsay, "Mummies and Tombs: Turenne, Napoleon, and Death Ritual," *Art Bulletin* 82, no. 3 (2000): 478–502.
33. Carnot's speech in "Fête de la fondation de la République, 1er vendémiaire an IX," *Le moniteur*, 3 vendémiaire, year IX (25 September 1800), quoted in Bronislaw Baczko, "Turenne au temple de Mars," in idem, *Politiques de la Révolution française* (Paris: Gallimard, 2008), 742n28. Turenne was the first to enter the church of Saint-Louis des Invalides, on 22 September 1800, due to a consular *arrêté* from 18 fructidor, year VIII (5 September 1800): subsequent to this event, Les Invalides, founded in 1670 by Louis XIV, became a center for the memory of military heroes.
34. The disorder perhaps related to the issue of royal transcendence; see Jean-Marie Le Gall, "La nécropole dynastique des Bourbons à Saint-Denis; ou, L'impossible simple corps du roi," *Revue historique*, no. 637 (2006): 61–80.
35. Among others, of course Henri IV, and Louis XII; cf. Laurent Avezou, "Louis XII: Père du peuple; Grandeur et décadence d'un mythe politique, du XVIe au XIXe," *Revue historique*, no. 625 (2003), 95–125; and Laurent Avezou, "Du retour aux sources à la nostalgie du bon vieux temps: Sully dans les arts de Louis XVI à Louis-Philippe," *Bibliothèque de l'Ecole des Chartes* 163 (2005): 51–78.
36. All these projects can be found in the *Commission de l'Inventaire général des richesses d'art de la France: Archives du Musée des monuments français* (Paris: Ministère de l'Instruction Publique et des Beaux-arts, in association with E. Plon Nourrit, 1883), 1:196–98, 383–85, nos. 182, 400. See Dominique Poulot, *Surveiller et s'instruire: La Révolution française et l'intelligence de l'héritage historique* (Oxford: Voltaire Foundation, 1996).

37. The Musée de Cluny is particularly revealing in this respect: see Stephen Bann, *The Clothing of Clio: A Study of the Representation of History in Nineteenth-Century Britain and France* (Cambridge: Cambridge University Press, 1984); see also Dominique Poulot, *Une histoire des musées de France* (Paris: Découverte, 2005).
38. On engraving in general in this context, see Claudette Hould, Alain Chevalier, and Emmanuelle Macaigne, *La Révolution par la gravure: Les tableaux historiques de la Révolution française, une entreprise éditoriale d'information et sa diffusion en Europe (1791–1817)* (Paris: Réunion des Musées Nationaux, 2002).
39. On this formula, which is not contemporary, see Édouard Pommier, *L'art de la liberté: Doctrines et débats de la Révolution française* (Paris: Gallimard, 1991).
40. L. Tuetey, "Procès-verbaux de la Commission des monuments (1790–1794)," in Société de l'histoire de l'art français, *Nouvelles archives de l'art français,* third series, vol. 17 (1901), and vol. 18 (1902) (Paris: N. Charavay, 1902–3); here, 18:170–71.
41. His own answer was as follows: "Because, to become able in the arts, all one need do is follow one's passions, whereas to defend one's rights and respect those of others, one must win those rights. There is another reason: the kings who decide earthly fate do not fear great geometers, great painters, or great poets; they fear philosophers and those who defend humanity." *Rapport fait au nom du Comité de salut public, par Maximilien Robespierre, sur les rapports des idées religieuses et morales avec les principes républicains, et sur les fêtes nationales. Séance du 18 floréal, l'an second de la République française une et indivisible* (Paris: Imprimé par Ordre de la Convention Nationale (18 floréal, year II [7 May 1794]), 4.
42. See James Guillaume, ed., *Procès-verbaux du Comité d'instruction publique de la convention nationale,* vol. 4 (Paris: Impr. Nationale, 1901) (1 germinal, year II [21 March 1794]–11 fructidor, year II [28 August 1794]), 176–88. Thibaudeau's *Rapport* is found in *Instruction publique et beaux-arts* (Paris: Bibliothèque Historique de la Ville de Paris), document 12296, vol. 5. Note that the situation subsequently changed: as Lynn Hunt has noted, on 29 November 1794, "several months after the fall of Robespierre and David, Thibaudeau suggested that the artists themselves name a jury" for the competition of works of art (this report was adopted but was never implemented). Lynn Hunt, "Hercules and the Radical Image in the French Revolution," *Representations,* no. 2 (1983): 95–117, here 112.
43. Casimir Varon, *Rapport fait au nom des commissaires envoyés dans le département de Seine et Oise, à la Commission temporaire des arts, par Varon, membre de cette commission et du conservatoire du muséum national, le 10 messidor an deuxième de la république française* (Paris: Impr. Nationale, 1794). See also Alexandre Tuetey and Jean Guiffrey, eds., *La commission du muséum et la création du Musée du Louvre (1792–1793)* (Paris: H. Champion, 1910).
44. *Rapport fait à la Convention,* 6.
45. François-Antoine de Boissy d'Anglas, *Essai sur les fêtes nationales, suivi de quelques idées sur les arts et sur la nécessité de les encourager adressé à la Convention nationale* (Paris: Impr. Polyglotte, 12 messidor, year II [30 June 1794]).
46. In the view of the Theophilanthropist Pierre-Jean-Baptiste Chaussard (1766–1823), "We have till now considered the arts as the ornament of the social edifice

but they are part of its basis.... We confused their *method,* which consists in giving pleasure, with their *object,* which is to be useful." See his *Essai philosophique sur la dignité des arts* (Paris: Impr. des Sciences et des Arts, ventôse, year VI [March 1798]).

47. Henri Grégoire, *Rapport sur la bibliographie présenté à la Convention nationale le 22 germinal an II* [11 April 1794] (Paris: Mckean, 1873).
48. For a general picture of restoration issues, see the collection of essays by Gilberte Emile-Mâle, *Pour une histoire de la restauration des peintures en France* (Paris: Somogy, 2008).
49. "Following Picault's proposal, the Conservatory decrees that Champagne's Christ [*sic*], which was elongated by around fifteen inches, shall be restored to the size in which its author painted it and Citizen Picault is authorized to have the chassis made," 25 vendémiaire, year III [16 October 1794]. Quoted in Yveline Cantarel-Besson, *La naissance du Musée du Louvre* (Paris: Réunion des Musées Nationaux, 1981), 1:104.
50. Anthelme Marin (1758–1825) was elected member of the Convention for the *département* of Mont-Blanc on 1 February 1793 and deputy to the Conseil des cinq-cents (Council of the five hundred) on 14 October 1795. He kept his post as deputy until 20 May 1798.
51. A. Marin, *Motion d'ordre par Marin, député du Mont-Blanc, sur le Muséum central des arts: Corps législatif, Conseil des cinq-cents; Séance du premier nivôse an VI* [21 December 1797] (Paris: Impr. Nationale, 1797).
52. For example, François-Marie Arouet (commonly known as Voltaire), "A Visit to Signor Pococuranté, a Venetian Nobleman," in idem, *Candide* (1759), trans. Theo Cuffe (London: Penguin, 2005), 74.
53. *Procès-verbal de l'assemblée des savants et artistes réunis au museum le 11 nivôse an 6 de la république, en vertu de l'arrêté du Directoire exécutif du 7 du même mois,* in Yveline Cantarel-Besson, *Musée du Louvre, janvier 1797–juin 1798: Procès-verbaux du Conseil d'administration du "Musée central des arts"* (Paris: Réunion des Musées Nationaux, 1992), 209.
54. *Rapport de la Commission nommée dans l'Assemblée du 11 nivôse de l'an 6* (1798), reprinted in Yveline Cantarel-Besson, *Musée du Louvre, janvier 1797–juin 1798: Procès-verbaux du Conseil d'administration du "Musée central des arts"* (Paris: Réunion des Musées Nationaux, 1992), 218. For other aspects of the *Rapport,* see Sarah Lowengard, *The Creation of Color in Eighteenth-Century Europe* (New York: Columbia University Press, 2008) (also available online at http://www.gutenberg-e.org/lowengard/print.html); and Noémie Etienne, "Restaurer la peinture à Paris (1750–1815)," (PhD diss., Université de Genève, 2011), 208.

PART THREE

Provenance and Commerce

SOPHIE RAUX

FROM MARIETTE TO JOULLAIN
Provenance and Value in Eighteenth-Century French Auction Catalogs

> The demand for authenticity . . . is reflected in an obsession with certainty—specifically, certainty as to the origin, date, author, and signature of a work. The mere fact that a particular object has belonged to a famous or powerful individual may confer value on it.
> —Jean Baudrillard[1]

During the eighteenth century, France experienced a significant increase in collecting and an expansion of the art market. While many studies have been devoted to this phenomenon, little attention has been paid to the advent of the concept of provenance as an element contributing to the identity of a work and also as a criterion to assess its value and its radiance. William McAllister Johnson paved the way to these issues more than twenty years ago with two remarkable studies. The first stressed the importance of the earliest provenance index for paintings, published by the art dealer François-Charles Joullain in the 1780s.[2] The second analyzed the process through which the location of cabinet paintings was mediatized and transmitted in France from the 1730s to the 1760s, thanks to engravings that ostentatiously associated the name of an owner to the reproduction of a painting.[3] Since then, despite insightful recent publications, these topics have not been closely investigated.[4] Yet they offer stimulating perspectives in the context of the growing interest, during the French Enlightenment period, in the knowledge of objects, the history of their origins, their description, and the criteria according to which they were classified and cataloged.

Likewise, the spread of the notion of provenance must be connected to the development of both collecting and connoisseurship, which led to new means of documenting and promoting works of art. This essay analyzes one of the most evolutionary and innovative forms of publication: the auction catalog. Indeed, in catalogs written by the greatest art dealers, such as Pierre-Jean Mariette, Edmé-François Gersaint, Pierre Rémy, and Jean-Baptiste-Pierre Lebrun, one can observe a growing awareness of the importance of the concept of provenance, an awareness eventually leading to François-Charles Joullain's famous *Répertoire de tableaux, dessins et estampes, Ouvrage utile aux Amateurs,* published in 1783 and commonly known as Joullain's *Répertoire*.[5] This essay also investigates the motivations that led auction-catalog writers to emphasize the history and the provenance of a work: What was the extent of the writers' historical consciousness as they documented the works of art that way? What sort of emulation did they intend to arouse in the art lovers and buyers who would read the catalogs? What commercial outcome were they expecting?

The Memory of Provenances

The concept of provenance in France during the Enlightenment is tightly bound to the development of collecting and to the attendant reflection on cataloging. The word *collection* derives from the Latin *colligere,* which means to choose and to gather. It implies a major difference from the principle of accumulation, insofar as the author of a collection exerts a choice.[6] The collector makes his own work, in turn, thanks to the relevance of his choices, the quality of his taste, and his sense of discrimination. The collection thus becomes a factor of social elevation, likely to raise the prestige of its owner, whatever his birth, his rank, or his titles. Gersaint—a clever art dealer interested in arousing new vocations for collecting—clearly emphasizes this argument in 1744 in the introduction of the Louis Quentin de Lorangère sales catalog: an *amateur* "is to be on an equal footing with those indulging in such a noble passion, who are above himself according to rank or condition."[7]

A collection is generally short-lived and is likely to be scattered after the death of its owner. Keeping track of collections and the memory of the individuals who built each one led to the development of a thriving literary genre: the catalog. As Joullain put it, in 1786: "without the publication of a catalog keeping the description of these objects, we wouldn't know such a cabinet had existed nor that its constitution had been the work of such a distinguished *amateur*."[8] The word *catalog* comes from the Greek *katalogos* (to list completely) and implies the display of a set of objects according to a founding order. This principle of order distinguishes the collection catalog and the sales catalog from the inventory; the latter is a mere enumeration arranged at best according to a topographic order.[9] Collection catalogs and sales catalogs were designed as mediation tools; in the process of creating those catalogs, a description and commentary methodology was devised. As in other branches of knowledge, notably in the natural sciences, there was a desire to organize, classify, and rationalize knowledge according to objective criteria. But, unlike the *naturalia,* works of art cannot be analyzed into distinct, universally recognizable elements. Indeed, they are rated according to taste and sensorial analysis, factors whose subjectivity is all too likely to lead to uncertainty and variableness.

The irreducibility of a work of art cannot fit within the limits of description, of *ekphrasis* and language. Because of this obstacle, the authors of collections and sales catalogs created two different sets of standards to describe a work of art: on the one hand, a formal analysis or stylistic commentary, which reflected the author's subjective judgment; on the other hand, an account of the mere material identity of the work, which was an objective description. The criteria of material description were gradually worked out; provenance developed into a major criterion, one that reflected different intentions, as we will see.

Mariette: The Forerunner

A book devoted to a set of royal and private collections, the so-called *Recueil Crozat,* gave a critical impetus to the question of provenance.[10] This anonymous book came from the circle of Pierre Crozat (1665–1740), who was one of the most prominent patrons and art collectors of his time. This publication was not the first in France to show an interest in the provenance of the works. Indeed, at the end of the seventeenth century and beginning of the eighteenth century, André Félibien and Louis-François Dubois de Saint-Gelais, for instance, mentioned the history of a number of works, but they did not do so consistently and were much less thorough, showing no conscious desire to rigorously document the works' "biography."[11] However, the *Recueil Crozat* was a turning point in that direction, thanks to the systematic care and attention paid to the history of a work as being an essential element of its material existence. This intention is clearly displayed on the title page of the book, whose first volume was published in 1729: *Recueil d'estampes d'après les plus beaux tableaux et d'après les plus beaux desseins qui sont en France... divisé suivant les différentes écoles; avec un abbregé de la vie des peintres, & une description historique de chaque tableau* [emphasis added] (fig. 1).

The book is generally attributed to Pierre Crozat's closest artistic adviser, Pierre-Jean Mariette.[12] The rationale behind the book's structure is explained in the preface: it first aims to establish the artists' biographies in order to extend our knowledge on their life and work; "secondly, as the history of the fate known by the works of a great master during his lifetime and after his death being a natural continuation of his life, we are giving here the history of the paintings and of the drawings that we have had engraved; we even say the name of those who owned them successively, going back as far as possible to the very first owner."[13] It was indeed the first time that such an exhaustive account of a work's history is given, and it was done so as a duty to the memory of both the artist and his works. However, an additional aspect emerges from the book's new heuristic approach, one described in an announcement that appeared in

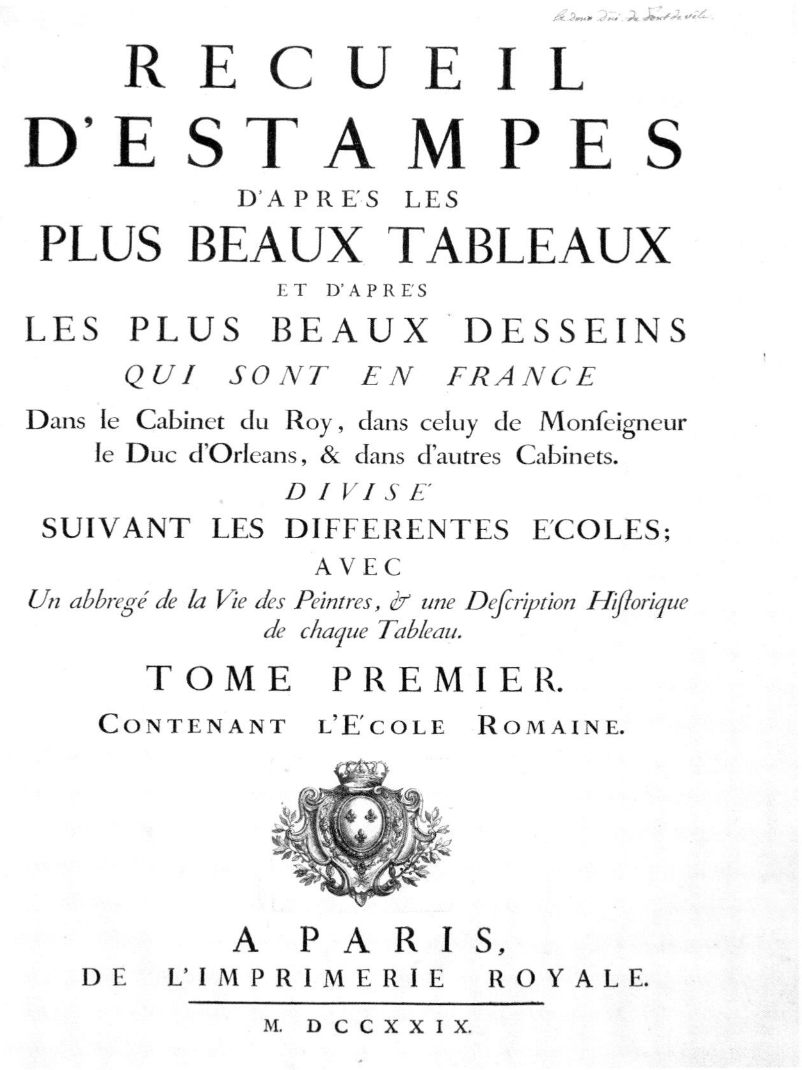

RECUEIL
D'ESTAMPES
D'APRE'S LES
PLUS BEAUX TABLEAUX
ET D'APRE'S
LES PLUS BEAUX DESSEINS
QUI SONT EN FRANCE
Dans le Cabinet du Roy, dans celuy de Monſeigneur le Duc d'Orleans, & dans d'autres Cabinets.
DIVISE'
SUIVANT LES DIFFERENTES E'COLES;
AVEC
Un abbregé de la Vie des Peintres, & une Deſcription Hiſtorique de chaque Tableau.
TOME PREMIER.
CONTENANT L'E'COLE ROMAINE.

A PARIS,
DE L'IMPRIMERIE ROYALE.
M. DCCXXIX.

Fig. 1.
Title page of the first volume of *Recueil d'estampes d'après les plus beaux tableaux et d'après les plus beaux desseins* [known as the *Recueil Crozat*] (Paris: Imprimerie Royale, 1729).
Los Angeles, Getty Research Institute, 1366-334.

the *Mercure de France* in May 1728, a few months prior to the book's publication: "we have added to these lives a brief description of the paintings and drawings... followed by the name of those who owned them successively, to establish and certify their originality more authentically."[14] Thus, the idea that recounting the provenance of the work could serve as a means of asserting its originality was already set, in this publication, as early as the 1720s; that idea flourished during the second half of the century, alongside the development of theories and practices of connoisseurship and the spectacular booming of the art market. But it also epitomizes an evolution by which originality is gradually replaced by authenticity as a privileged notion: the latter became a major criterion for market practices in the nineteenth century and played a critical role in the construction of art history as a discipline endowed with a specific methodology. The urge to establish and certify the paintings' "originality more authentically" by mentioning the history of their ownership entails the emergence of a new kind of discourse on the uniqueness of the artwork. Indeed, during the Renaissance and the Baroque eras, when one spoke of the originality of a given work, the word called forth ideas such as the invention (*inventio*) of the artist, or the visual features associated with his name, and not those of unicity, singularity, or autography. But from then on, one can evidence the biography of the work and trace its previous provenances (what Joullain would call its *filiation*), hence endowing it with a proper, unique, and singular identity. It must be stressed, though, that at this stage the term was not yet a synonym for authenticity as we mean it today. Indeed, what is at stake here is to guarantee the uniqueness of the artefact as such, not its autographic dimension. The latter concern would become increasingly crucial over the course of the eighteenth century, thereby reflecting the growing importance given to both judgments about attribution and the status of autography, and would eventually culminate at the beginning of the nineteenth century, in keeping with the gradual consolidation of the myth of the singular genius.[15]

Francis Haskell underlines the fact that Mariette's text in the *Recueil* "does indeed mark a new departure in the appraisal of paintings, both in what it says and what it omits; for it takes a decisive step away from the interest in what is painted to an interest in who painted it and how it is painted"[16]—and, I might add, to the way it falls within a history. The systematic attention being paid to the biography of works bears witness to a new awareness that artistic values were objectified in the process of time, an awareness that would develop throughout the eighteenth century. Later, in 1741, Mariette published the sales catalog of Crozat's drawing collection. This collection is universally considered as the most important in France in the first half of the eighteenth century. In the catalog, Mariette dedicates a long passage to the collection's history. He also mentions and praises the numerous cabinets that supplied Crozat and the famous auction sales he attended, in France as well as abroad. Mariette concluded that "these are not, as we can see, some drawings bought one by one, but first-rate cabinets bought altogether and gathered by M. Crozat, thus making his own cabinet the largest one ever created, if I may say so, for drawings."[17] This comment expresses the notion that the aura of Crozat's collection partly originates in the reputation of older cabinets from which it had been built up. Later, in the lots description, the prestige of provenance is emphasized: the names of Everhard Jabach, François de La Noue, Roger de Piles, and Giorgio Vasari, among others, are invoked as a way of guaranteeing the probity of a work's origin.

A renowned connoisseur and dealer, Mariette is famous today for initiating a new type of auction catalog, one that was used as a model by generations of dealers. He pioneered the classification of works of art by schools and introduced new criteria for identification and description in which provenance held a significant role. His interest in the "biography" of an object may have proceeded at first (in the *Recueil Crozat*) from a historical concern, but it rapidly reached the world of art dealing, where the most innovative dealers soon understood the impact that a prestigious provenance could have on a work of art's value. Understandably, this preoccupation grew as the supply of paintings found on the Parisian art market soared, from the middle of the eighteenth century on.

From Gersaint to Lebrun

In 1744, Gersaint complained in the Quentin de Lorangère auction catalog that cabinet paintings were dispersed after their owner's death "without the possibility of knowing into whose hands most of them fell: we have experienced such a situation during the famous sales that took place successively: I mean those of M. de La Faye, Madame la Comtesse de Verrue, M. le Maréchal d'Estrées, M. Le Cardinal de Polignac, and M. Le Prince de Carignan: we could have thought that such a prodigious amount of paintings could not have found an equal number of *amateurs:* yet, hardly could we mention today the cabinets where even a tenth part of these paintings is kept."[18] This was only 1744, and Gersaint, who would die six years later, could certainly not imagine that between the 1730s and the 1780s the supply of paintings would be multiplied more than sixty times and that the question of the provenance of works of art would become crucial (table 1).[19] This increase highlights the growing need to provide the

Table 1. Paintings sold at auctions in Paris between 1730 and 1789, by decade.

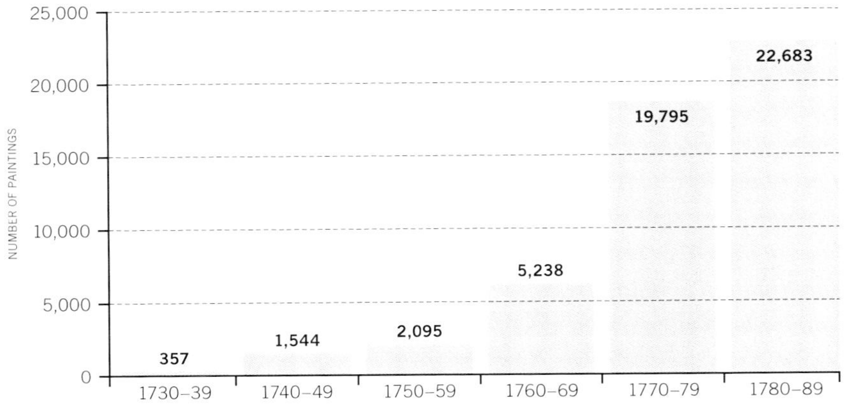

public with reliable landmarks guaranteeing the authenticity and the origin of the works in order to reassure distrustful buyers facing a profusion of works on the market whose origin and authenticity were questionable.

In 1748, in the Angran de Fonspertuis catalog, Gersaint connected for the first time the prestige of a work with that of its provenance. Concerning *Peasant Wedding* (1650, Saint Petersburg, State Hermitage Museum), by the Flemish painter David Teniers the Younger (no. 424), he made this radical statement: "In praise of this painting and to acknowledge its superiority, it is sufficient to say that among all the paintings belonging to the comtesse de Verrue, whose taste was so refined, this was the one that she considered as the most beautiful and most interesting to be found."[20] The comtesse de Verrue was famous for having built the most remarkable collection of Dutch and Flemish paintings to be seen in Paris during the first third of the eighteenth century. After her death, the auction sale of one part of her collection, in 1737, was considered a major event in the art market, not only because of the quality of the works but also because prices on the market had suddenly soared. About ten years later, the prestige of de Verrue's provenance had lost nothing of its aura. On the contrary, its mention alone would suffice to guarantee, for Gersaint and his public, the excellence of the painting: *Peasant Wedding* by Teniers remained attached to the person of the comtesse de Verrue. The painting's singularity, its uniqueness, was strengthened by that attachment. To possess *Peasant Wedding,* more than any other object of desire, became the ultimate achievement in ownership. In fact, the painting reached by far the highest price of the sale: 6,000 livres; the average price of the 132 lots was 315 livres.

Another remarkable exception should also be underlined concerning this sale: the unusual price fetched by two works by Rembrandt (nos. 434 and 435) sold together for 2,750 livres: *The Beautiful Gardener* (ca. 1640, New York, Metropolitan Museum of Art, as by Govert Flinck) and *A Girl at a Window* (fig. 2). The latter was already associated with a legendary past. It had belonged to Roger de Piles, and its popularity mainly originated in an anecdote related by de Piles in his book *Abregé de la vie des peintres:* Rembrandt was said to have displayed the painting at his window. For days, passersby had been fooled and believed an actual girl was standing there, until they eventually noticed that she never moved and realized that it had to be a painting.[21] As apocryphal as this anecdote may seem, Gersaint was eager to reference it, quoting de Piles's note in full. Then he provided a complete history of the work, more detailed than in previous auction catalogs, by relating the succession of its five owners: Roger de Piles; Monsieur Duvivier; Charles-Henry, comte d'Hoym; Charles-Jean-Baptiste Fleuriau, comte de Morville; and Louis-Auguste Angran de Fonspertuis. From then on, the painting achieved a mythic dimension; the

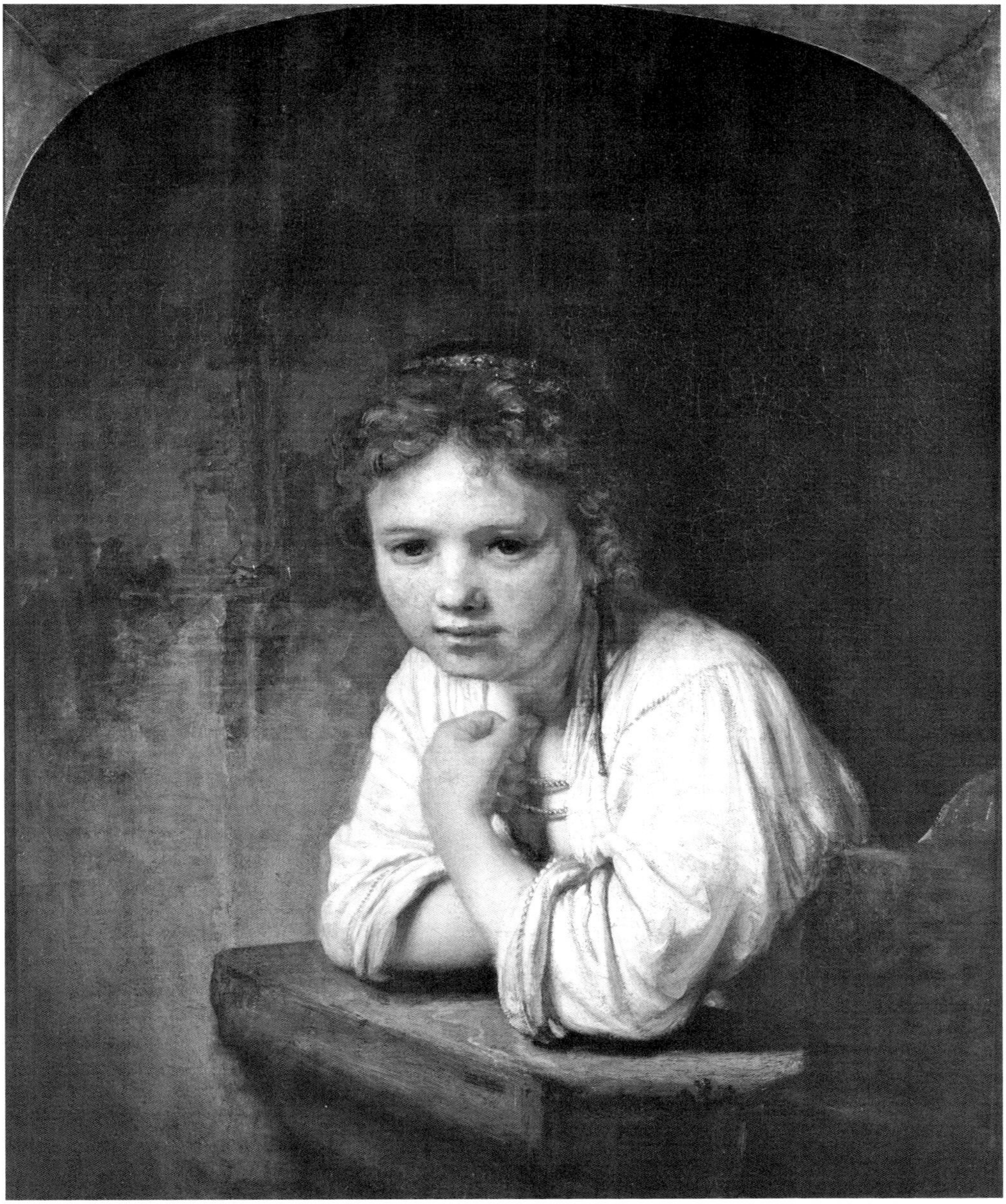

Fig. 2.
Rembrandt Harmensz. van Rijn (Dutch, 1606–69).
A Girl at a Window, 1645,
oil on canvas, 77.5 × 62.5 cm
(32¼ × 25⅞ in.).
London, Dulwich Picture Gallery.

assurance of its authenticity and its social distinction made it absolutely unique and raised its value. These few examples are enough to show that before 1750, highlighting a prestigious provenance was already an essential tool used to increase the value of a work, sometimes even more powerful than praising its intrinsic qualities.

After Gersaint's death, Pierre Rémy gave new impetus to the criterion of provenance, thanks to a more documented approach. In 1755, in the Louis

Pasquier sales catalog, Rémy was the first to mention the sources, as far as they were known, that enabled him to ascertain the provenance of some lots.[22] Previous auction catalogs became reference tools. This is the case, for instance, in Rémy's description of lot no. 4, two paintings by Philips Wouwerman, *A Departure for the Hunt* and *After the Hunt* (both paintings ca. 1650, Dresden, Gemäldegalerie): "they come directly from the Cabinet of the Chevalier d'Orléans, Great Prieur of France, who had purchased them from the Vicomte de Fonspertuis' sale. See Gersaint's catalog; p. 202, item 436." As the text unfolds, cross-references to the sales catalogs of Gersaint, Angran de Fonspertuis, and Prince de Carignan multiply. Rémy sometimes went further, as in the Selles catalog (1761), where, in the margin, he underlined a reference to the previous sales catalog in order to make it stand out from the rest of the information.[23] Eventually, provenance information would be seen first.

In the 1770s, some major collections were dispersed and therefore the number of works of art on the market suddenly increased; the most famous sales, the Paul Randon de Boisset, Augustin Blondel de Gagny, and Prince de Conti sales, were considered landmark events. With a wide variety of works on the market, the details of a painting's history became more and more refined. From the beginning of the 1780s onward, it was not unusual to find three filiations or more in sales catalogs, notably in entries written by Rémy and Lebrun.

Joullain's *Répertoire*

The need for a tool to aggregate and present information about ownership led the dealer François-Charles Joullain to publish, in 1783, the first repertory on provenance, *Répertoire de tableaux, dessins et estampes, Ouvrage utile aux Amateurs* (fig. 3).[24] Three years later, Joullain updated the *Répertoire* in a more general book, *Réflexions sur la Peinture*.[25] In the foreword to the *Répertoire*, Joullain justified his book's relevance by emphasizing the importance of recent sales, which had sped up the circulation of artworks on the market and had given rise to new questions concerning the volatility of provenances and the variability of prices: "since those of M. Mariette, M. Neyman, M. de Gagny, Mgr. Le P. de Conti, M. De Boisset &c. the quantity of catalogs to which they gave birth, the difference of prices from one year to another, the changes of owners, all these grounds made me think of this Répertoire in which I indicate the filiation of an object, the different cabinets to which it went successively, the prices it sold for, and the cabinet where it is currently located."[26] In addition to the newness, originality, and completely atypical nature of this publication, perfectly described by McAllister Johnson,[27] it also included an element of major importance: for the first time, the prices fetched by works

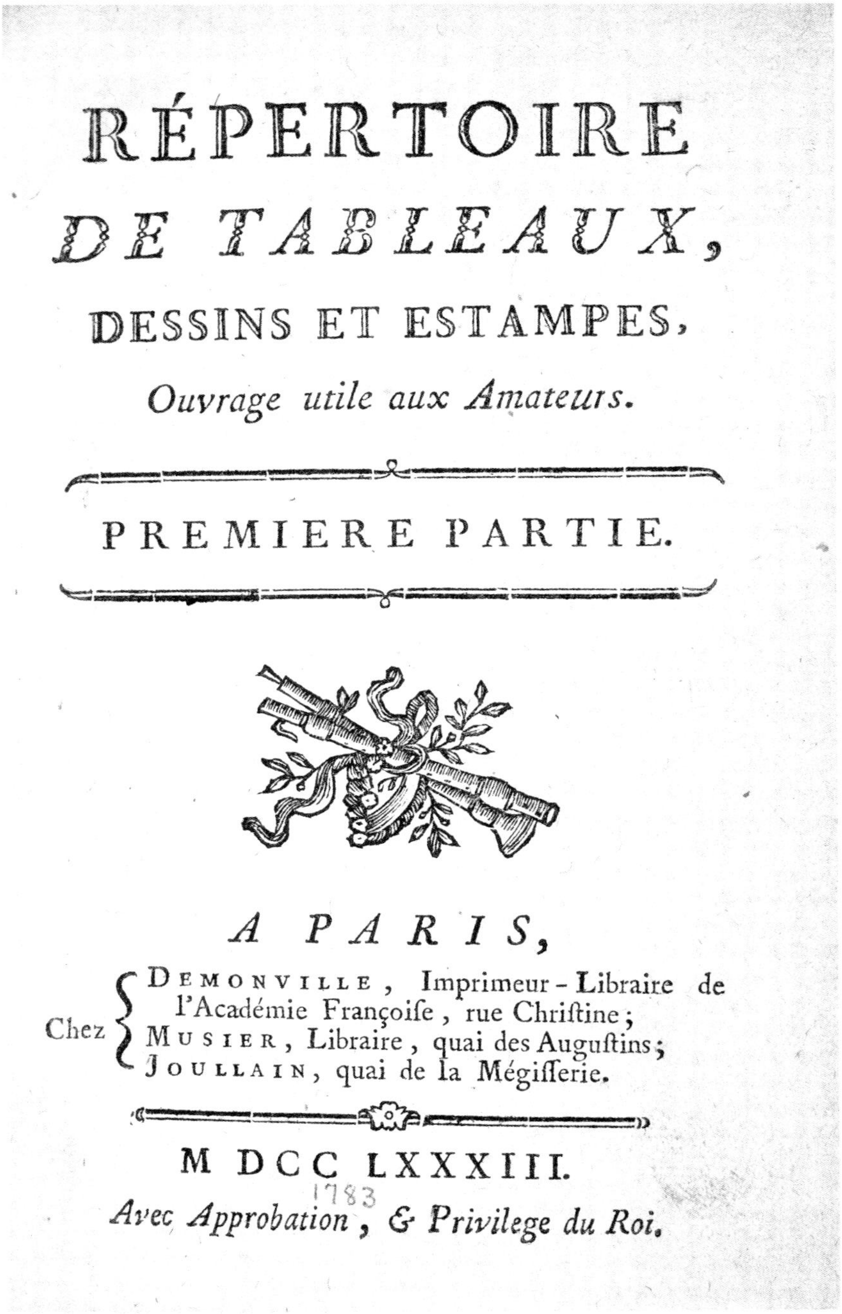
RÉPERTOIRE
DE TABLEAUX,
DESSINS ET ESTAMPES,
Ouvrage utile aux Amateurs.

PREMIERE PARTIE.

A PARIS,
Chez { DEMONVILLE, Imprimeur-Libraire de l'Académie Françoiſe, rue Chriſtine; MUSIER, Libraire, quai des Auguſtins; JOULLAIN, quai de la Mégiſſerie.

M DCC LXXXIII.
1783
Avec Approbation, & Privilege du Roi.

Fig. 3.
Title page of [François-Charles Joullain,] *Répertoire de tableaux, dessins et estampes, Ouvrage utile aux Amateurs* (Paris: Demonville, 1783).
Los Angeles, Getty Research Institute, 26274833-B.

during successive sales were mentioned in a way that highlighted the relation between provenance and value as well as the variability of prices from one sale to another.

The *Répertoire* is a 113-page book devoted to indicating the former provenances and the current location of 368 paintings considered the most

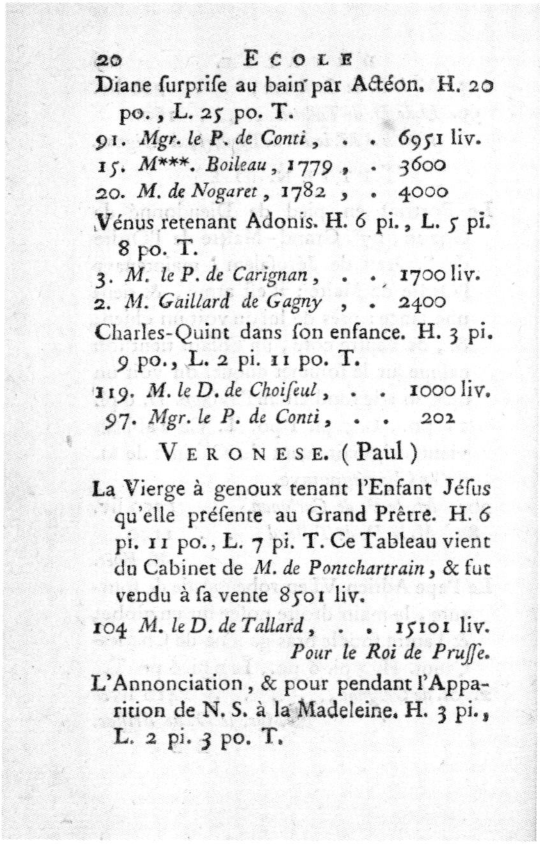
20 ECOLE

Diane ſurpriſe au bain par Actéon. H. 20 po., L. 25 po. T.

91. *Mgr. le P. de Conti*, . . 6951 liv.
15. *M***. Boileau*, 1779, . 3600
20. *M. de Nogaret*, 1782, . 4000

Vénus retenant Adonis. H. 6 pi., L. 5 pi. 8 po. T.

3. *M. le P. de Carignan*, . . 1700 liv.
2. *M. Gaillard de Gagny*, . 2400

Charles-Quint dans ſon enfance. H. 3 pi. 9 po., L. 2 pi. 11 po. T.

119. *M. le D. de Choiſeul*, . . 1000 liv.
97. *Mgr. le P. de Conti*, . . 202

VERONESE. (Paul)

La Vierge à genoux tenant l'Enfant Jéſus qu'elle préſente au Grand Prêtre. H. 6 pi. 11 po., L. 7 pi. T. Ce Tableau vient du Cabinet de *M. de Pontchartrain*, & fut vendu à ſa vente 8501 liv.

104 *M. le D. de Tallard*, . . 15101 liv.
Pour le Roi de Pruſſe.

L'Annonciation, & pour pendant l'Apparition de N. S. à la Madeleine. H. 3 pi., L. 2 pi. 3 po. T.

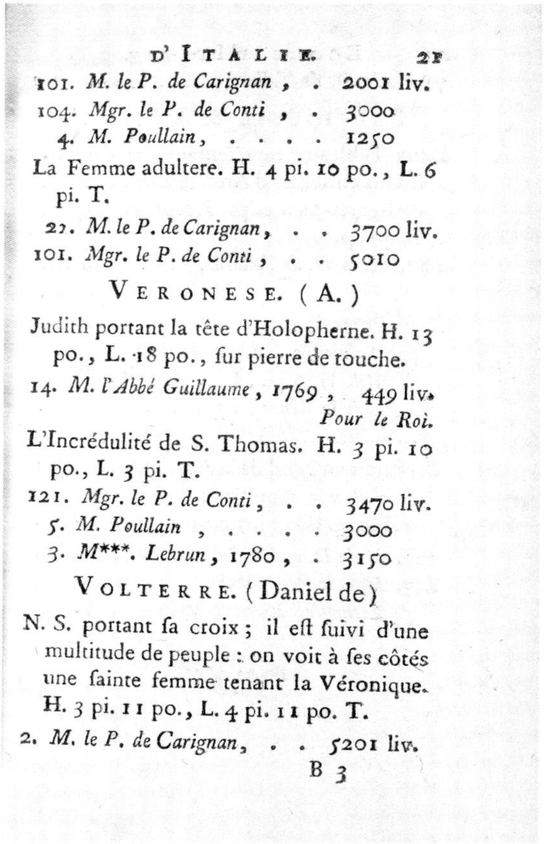
D'ITALIE. 21

101. *M. le P. de Carignan*, . 2001 liv.
104. *Mgr. le P. de Conti*, . 3000
4. *M. Poullain*, ... 1250

La Femme adultere. H. 4 pi. 10 po., L. 6 pi. T.

27. *M. le P. de Carignan*, . . 3700 liv.
101. *Mgr. le P. de Conti*, . . 5010

VERONESE. (A.)

Judith portant la tête d'Holopherne. H. 13 po., L. 18 po., ſur pierre de touche.

14. *M. l'Abbé Guillaume*, 1769, 449 liv.
Pour le Roi.

L'Incrédulité de S. Thomas. H. 3 pi. 10 po., L. 3 pi. T.

121. *Mgr. le P. de Conti*, . . 3470 liv.
5. *M. Poullain*, ... 3000
3. *M***. Lebrun*, 1780, . 3150

VOLTERRE. (Daniel de)

N. S. portant ſa croix; il eſt ſuivi d'une multitude de peuple: on voit à ſes côtés une ſainte femme tenant la Véronique. H. 3 pi. 11 po., L. 4 pi. 11 po. T.

2. *M. le P. de Carignan*, . . 5201 liv.

B 3

Figs. 4a, 4b.
[François-Charles Joullain,] ***Répertoire de tableaux, dessins et estampes, Ouvrage utile aux Amateurs*** **(Paris: Demonville, 1783), 20–21.**
Los Angeles, Getty Research Institute, 26274833-B.

interesting in Paris (figs. 4a, 4b). It retrieved up to six provenances for a single painting. Joullain's *Répertoire* was the first autonomous publication to provide such a mine of information and to function as a tool to fulfill a dual purpose: to establish the pedigree of the works of art and to provide the public with the information necessary to establish the quotation of both works and artists. Before Joullain's *Répertoire,* no comparable publication related to art sales existed. However, two earlier attempts deserve a closer look, even though their goals and methodology are rather different.

The first was launched in 1752, when the Dutch painter and dealer Gerard Hoet II began publishing an index of Dutch sales from 1648 onward that provided the price each painting fetched at auction.[28] Although Hoet's index offers a valuable basis for studying thousands of prices of paintings sold at Dutch auctions over a century, it does not document their provenances. Indeed, Hoet showed no real interest in connecting the different sales and collections related to a specific painting. The mention of a painting in a given sale thus remained isolated, and any recurrence of the same work in other sales and collections was disregarded.

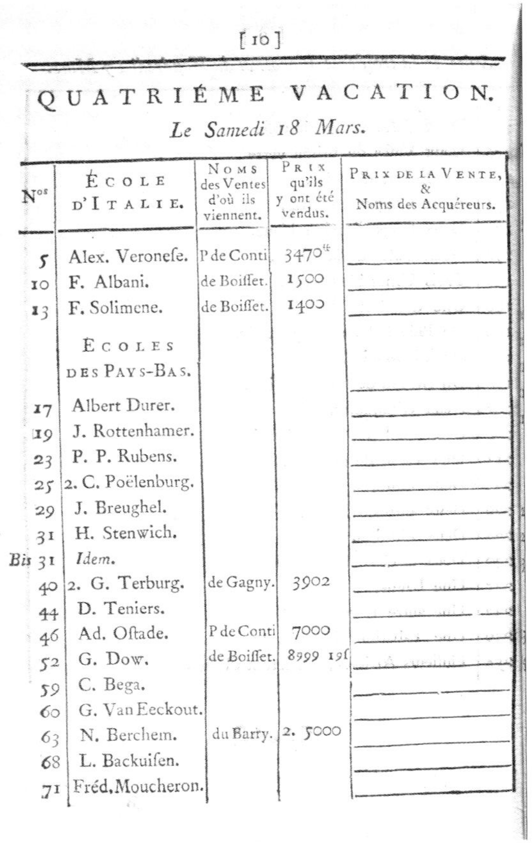

[10]

QUATRIÉME VACATION.

Le Samedi 18 Mars.

Nos	École d'Italie.	Noms des Ventes d'où ils viennent.	Prix qu'ils y ont été vendus.	Prix de la Vente, & Noms des Acquéreurs.
5	Alex. Veroneſe.	P de Conti	3470 ₶	
10	F. Albani.	de Boiſſet.	1500	
13	F. Solimene.	de Boiſſet.	1400	
	Ecoles des Pays-Bas.			
17	Albert Durer.			
19	J. Rottenhamer.			
23	P. P. Rubens.			
25	2. C. Poëlenburg.			
29	J. Breughel.			
31	H. Stenwich.			
Bis 31	*Idem.*			
40	2. G. Terburg.	de Gagny.	3902	
44	D. Teniers.			
46	Ad. Oſtade.	P de Conti	7000	
52	G. Dow.	de Boiſſet.	8999 19ſ	
59	C. Bega.			
60	G. Van Eeckout.			
63	N. Berchem.	du Barry.	2. 5000	
68	L. Backuiſen.			
71	Fréd. Moucheron.			

Fig. 5.
***Feuilles de distribution for the fourth auction* (18 March 1780).**
From Jean-Baptiste-Pierre Le Brun, *Catalogue raisonné des tableaux... qui composoient le cabinet de feu M. Poullain, receveur général des Domaines du Roi: Suivi d'un abrégé historique de la vie des peintres dont les ouvrages formoient cette collection* (Paris: Chez Langlier... Le Brun... Julliot fils, 1780).
Los Angeles, Getty Research Institute, 85-P7777.

The second was introduced by Jean-Baptiste-Pierre Lebrun in the catalog of the Antoine Poullain sale of 1780.[29] Indeed, it was the first time a dealer would mention the very last provenance and last purchase price of works put at auction. Nevertheless, such price information is relegated to the end of the catalog, in the *Feuilles de distribution,* an appendix displaying a synoptic table (fig. 5). It is not included in the full written descriptions of the lots in the catalog, where the premium is given to documenting their provenance: in the *Feuilles de distribution,* Lebrun would select only the most recent and most famous Parisian sales—none were prior to 1776 and all had caused a stir. Though emphasized in the catalog, the Verrue, Carignan, Lassay, and Jullienne provenances, just to name a few, do not appear in the appended *Feuilles de distribution.* By not accounting for variations in prices over time, Lebrun turned the latest price that a work fetched into a reference price.

Reactions to Joullain's *Répertoire* came quickly: as early as May 1783, in the *Petites Affiches de Paris,* Abbot Jean-Louis Aubert criticized it strongly, describing it as a "tariff" that provided a range of prices for everyone's knowledge.[30] Joullain denied this and claimed that his intention was to underscore the variability of prices for the most famous paintings of the time. He concluded: "Everyone knows that all the productions of the sciences and of the arts are not in the least subject to an intrinsic value, and that their more or less price depends on the competition between art-lovers and on the distinction of the object."[31] Thus, with unfailing lucidity and pragmatism, Joullain identifies the level of desire that a work of art arouses and its "distinction" (to use his own word) as primary factors of the work's pecuniary value. Needless to say, for Joullain, the prestige of the provenance fully partakes in this distinction.

Whatever Joullain's true intentions, the *Répertoire*—thanks to its historical and documentary dimensions—represents a clear move toward more transparency in the market[32] and a stepping-stone in the methodological development of a still-nascent history of art. The influence of Joullain's *Répertoire* was soon felt: the following year, in his catalog of the comte de Vaudreuil's sale in November 1784, Lebrun began associating (in written description of the lots) a work's successive provenances and the prices it had previously fetched.

Provenance as a Guarantee of Originality

Investigating how the provenance of a work affects its commercial value is not as easy as it seems. I have already mentioned the striking effect of prestigious provenances on the price of paintings, starting with Gersaint's sales in the 1740s. However, although generally advantageous for the value of a work, this effect was not systematic. To refine the analysis of ties between provenance and value, a statistical approach based on econometrics is required.[33] One of the central issues discussed in artistic circles during the eighteenth century concerned the criteria for judging a work of art's quality and value. Important dealers, who emerged as true connoisseurs throughout the century, had much to say on the topic. The aesthetic quality of a painting and the reliability of its attribution and of its authenticity were the recurrent standards used by dealers, depending on priorities that evolved through the century. As Krzysztof Pomian has shown, the primacy of the aesthetic assessment, as practiced by Gersaint, gradually declined while, starting with Rémy, attribution became an increasingly important criterion.[34] However, the methodological principles of attribution were still frail, as were those used to prove originality. The latter relied on the analysis of the *manière,* which only the most informed connoisseurs were able to perform. Their stylistic judgment, as acute as it may have been, was not flawless; neither was their honesty. In the absence of certainties, and out of fear of being fooled (intentionally or not), buyers were looking for the most reliable guarantees available at the time.

Oddly enough, the artist's signature, which today is considered essential for authenticating a painting, went completely unmentioned in the material descriptions of paintings in eighteenth-century catalogs, as if signatures did not exist at all. Yet many older paintings were signed; indeed, engravers imitated signatures faithfully in their reproductive prints, clearly regarding them as an integral part of a work. For instance, a painting by Teniers illustrates this phenomenon, which deserves a proper study: *The Feast of the Prodigual Son* (1644, Paris, Musée du Louvre) is signed in the lower right-hand corner, on the rock: "DAVID TENIERS FEC.//AN 1644." It was part of the Blondel de Gagny sale (no. 80) in 1776. In the catalog, Rémy wrote a sixteen-line commentary with a precise description, but he did not mention the signature. In the print (fig. 6a), though, Jacques-Philippe Le Bas took care to reproduce faithfully and obviously Tenier's signature and date (fig. 6b). Why such a relevant sign of authenticity

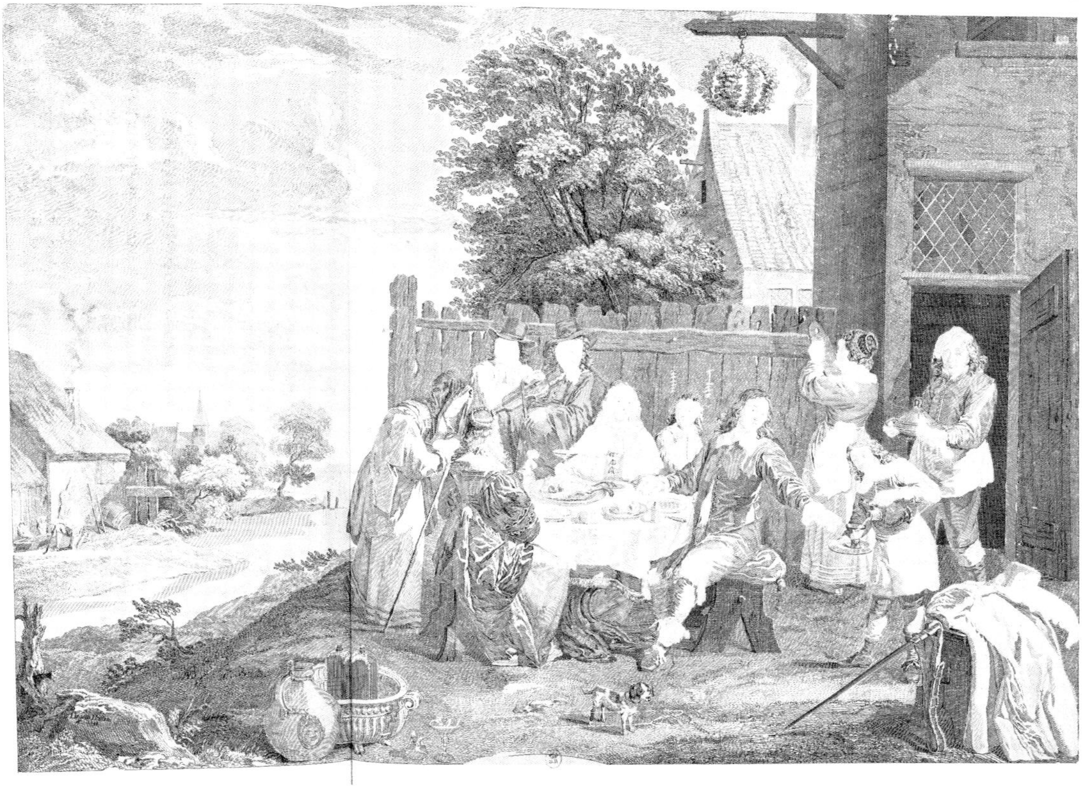

Fig. 6a.
Jacques-Philippe Le Bas (French, 1707–83), after David Teniers the Younger (Flemish, 1610–90).
The Feast of the Prodigal Son, 1749–51, etching, first state, 51.4 × 63.4 cm (20¼ × 25 in.).
Paris, Bibliothèque nationale de France, Département des estampes et de la photographie.

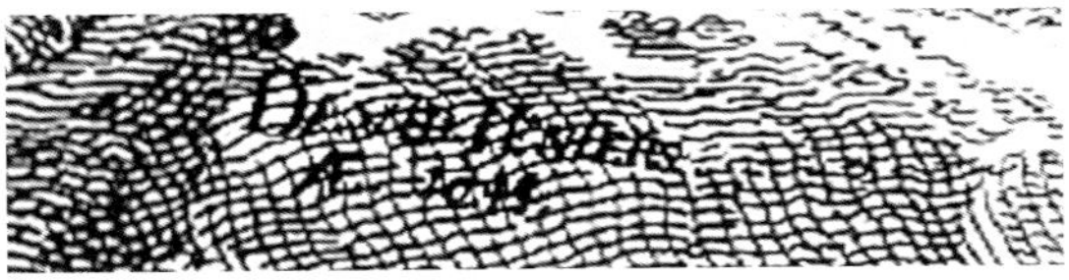

Fig. 6b.
Detail of figure 6a showing Le Bas's reproduction of Teniers's signature.

was not mentioned is unclear and remains to be investigated. Nevertheless, provenance—that is, an explication of the filiation of several more-or-less famous owners—was the tool used to guarantee a work's pedigree.

Mentioning previous owners, especially if they were famous for the distinction of their choices, indicated that the painting had already gone through several selection and ratification processes, thereby building a consensus on the painting's value and enhancing its prestige. In a surprising shift, the provenance, which is a testified and verifiable fact, became the guarantee of originality, a notion subjected to the uncertainties of judgment and expertise. Thus, Rémy wrote in the preface of the Prince de Conti's catalog: "The originality of these paintings is beyond doubt. We know their filiation; we were able to mention, as far as we could, the different cabinets in which they had been kept."[35]

Linking originality to provenance was not unanimously approved of; the approach was especially disputed among those art theorists who defended the analysis of the *manière* as the specific expertise of the "true connoisseur." In 1762, Antoine-Joseph Dézallier d'Argenville criticized the approach harshly by using a demonstration on drawings that he believed could be applied to paintings: "The history of a drawing and its filiation, which tell us the names of the different *amateurs* who owned it, the great collections it belonged to, are only suitable for dealers, whose sole interest is to sell with a benefit. Such a sterile knowledge dazzles only the ignoramus. Little is proved about the originality of a drawing by this supposed authenticity.... Attention should be paid to the object itself, to its intrinsic value."[36] However, the dealers, led by Rémy and Lebrun, continued to emphasize provenance. From the late 1770s onward, paintings from the collections of Blondel de Gagny, Randon de Boisset, and Prince de Conti were regarded as ultimate indications of prestige. They were highlighted in sales catalogs, not only in lot entries but also in the preface, in order to underscore a sale's high quality and to satisfy the obsession with hierarchy and distinction, which grew ever stronger in a context of a steadily expanding supply.

Conclusion

In eighteenth-century France, the notion of provenance became a central criterion in the elaboration of a discourse on works of art and their valuation. This interest fell within general trends of thought devoted to the origin of objects and to the way to preserve their memory and locate them in the flow of time. In *Les mots et les choses,* Michel Foucault demonstrates that the activity of the mind in the classical age consisted in distinguishing—that is, in establishing identities—according to a new relation to order. Collecting became a privileged field that produced knowledge and led to a new era in the way history was studied. Foucault writes: "The ever more complete preservation of what was written, the establishment of archives, then of filing systems for them, the reorganization of libraries, the drawing up of catalogues, indexes, and inventories, all these things represent, at the end of the Classical age, not so much a new sensitivity to time, to its past, to the density of history, as a way of introducing into the language already imprinted on things, and into the traces he has left, an order of the same type as that which was being established between living creatures."[37] The growing interest during the eighteenth century in the history of works of art, their biography, perfectly illustrates the phenomenon that Foucault describes. Whether the connoisseurs who set out to keep track of the provenance of works were motivated by commercial or historical purposes, they clearly embodied a new relationship to the history of works of art. Their approach marks a definite turning point in the methodology used in the history of art, and we are still indebted to them, whether we are art historians, art dealers, or collectors.

Notes

I gratefully aknowledge the Institut de Recherches Historiques du Septentrion (IRHiS-CNRS) at the Université Lille and the Samuel H. Kress Foundation for providing funding for the presentation of an earlier version of this essay at the annual conference of the College Art Association, held in Dallas in February 2008. I wish to express my gratitude to the chairs of the session, Gail Feigenbaum and Inge Reist, for inviting me to such a stimulating forum. I would like to thank Peter Fuhring, Neil De Marchi, and Hans J. Van Miegroet for their comments and suggestions. Unless otherwise indicated, all translations are mine with the invaluable help of Michael Smith and Isabelle Decobecq.

1. Jean Baudrillard, *The System of Objects,* trans. James Benedict (London: Verso, 2005), 81; originally published as *Le système des objets* (Paris: Gallimard, 1968).
2. William McAllister Johnson, "Paintings, Provenance and Price: Speculations on 18th-Century Connoisseurship Apparatus in France," *Gazette des Beaux-Arts* 107 (1986): 191–99.
3. William McAllister Johnson, "From Verrue to Vence: Systematic Engraving of Private Collections in France to 1760," *Gazette des Beaux-Arts* 117 (1991): 77–92.
4. The most extensive approach is in Charlotte Guichard, *Les amateurs d'art à Paris au XVIIIe siècle* (Seyssel, France: Champ Vallon, 2008), 100–116. See also Patrick Michel, *Le commerce du tableau à Paris dans la seconde moitié du XVIIIe siècle* (Villeneuve d'Ascq, France: Presses Universitaires du Septentrion, 2007), 237–38, and Neil De Marchi and Hans J. Van Miegroet, "The Rise of Dealer-Auctioneers in Paris: Information and Transparency in a Market for Netherlandish Paintings," in *Art Market and Connoisseurship: A Closer Look at Paintings by Rembrandt, Rubens, and their Contemporaries,* ed. Koenraad Jonckheere and Anna Tummers (Amsterdam: Amsterdam University Press, 2008), 149–74.

5. [François-Charles Joullain], *Répertoire de tableaux, dessins et estampes, Ouvrage utile aux Amateurs* (Paris: Demonville & Musier, 1783).
6. Baudrillard, *System of Objects* (note 1), 111.
7. Edmé-François Gersaint, *Catalogue raisonné des diverses curiosités du cabinet de feu M. Quentin de Lorangère* (Paris: Jacques Barois, 1744), 2.
8. François-Charles Joullain, *Réflexions sur la Peinture et la Gravure, accompagnées d'une courte Dissertation sur le Commerce de la Curiosité, et les Ventes en général* (Paris: Demonville & Musier, 1786), 108.
9. Victor I. Stoichita, *L'instauration du tableau* (Geneva: Droz, 1999), 150–52.
10. *Recueil d'estampes d'après les plus beaux tableaux et d'après les plus beaux desseins qui sont en France, dans le cabinet du Roy, dans celuy de Monseigneur le duc d'Orleans, & dans d'autres cabinets, divisé suivant les différentes écoles, avec un abbregé de la vie des peintres, & une description historique de chaque tableau* (Paris: Imprimerie Royale, 1729).
11. André Félibien, *Entretiens sur les vies et les ouvrages des plus excellens Peintres anciens et modernes* (Paris: P. Le Petit, 1666–85), 5 vols.; Louis-François Dubois de Saint-Gelais, *Description des Tableaux du Palais-Royal avec la Vie des Peintres à la tête de leurs ouvrages* (Paris: D'Houry, 1727).
12. Francis Haskell, *The Painful Birth of the Art Book* (London: Thames & Hudson, 1987).
13. *Recueil d'estampes*, 7.
14. *Mercure de France*, May 1728, 1006.
15. On the notions of originality and authenticity, see Rosalind E. Krauss, "Retaining the Originals? The State of the Question," in *Retaining the Original: Multiple Originals, Copies and Reproductions*, ed. Kathleen Preciado (Washington, D.C.: National Gallery of Art, 1989), 7–11; Richard E. Spear, "Notes on Renaissance and Baroque Originals and Originality," in Preciado, *Retaining the Original*, 97–99; Jeffrey M. Muller, "Measures of Authenticity: The Detection of Copies in the Early Literature on Connoisseurship," in Preciado, *Retaining the Original*, 141–49; Ernst Van de Wetering, "The Question of Authenticity: An Anachronism? (A Summary)," in *Rembrandt and His Pupils*, ed. Görel Cavalli-Björkman (Stockholm: Nationalmuseum, 1993), 9–13; Maria H. Loh, "Originals, Reproductions, and a 'Particular Taste' for Pastiche in the Seventeenth-Century Republic of Painting," in *Mapping Markets for Paintings in Europe, 1450–1750*, ed. Neil De Marchi and Hans J. Van Miegroet (Turnhout: Brepols, 2006), 237–60; Charlotte Guichard, "Du 'nouveau connoisseurship' à l'histoire de l'art. Original et autographie en peinture," *Annales. Histoire, Sciences sociales* 6 (2010), 1387–1402.
16. Haskell, *The Painful Birth*, 42.
17. Pierre-Jean Mariette, *Description sommaire des dessins... du cabinet de feu M. Crozat* (Paris: Mariette, 1741), x.
18. Gersaint, *Catalogue raisonné des diverses curiosités*, 107.
19. The number of paintings put at auction rose from around 350 paintings in the 1730s to more than 22,680 in the 1780s according to data provided in Frits Lugt, *Répertoire des catalogues de ventes publiques intéressant l'art ou la curiosité* (The Hague: Nijhoff, 1938), 1. However, this book is far from being comprehensive and

needs to be updated, and considering that many paintings were sold at auctions without a catalog printed (notably in the first half of the eighteenth century), we can get only a sense of a proportional increase.

20. Edmé-François Gersaint, *Catalogue raisonné... de la succession de M. Angran, vicomte de Fonspertuis* (Paris: Barrois, 1747), 185–88, lot no. 424.
21. Roger de Piles, *Abregé de la vie des peintres* (Paris: Jacques Estienne, 1715), 423.
22. [Pierre Rémy], *Catalogue des tableaux... de feu M. Pasquier* (Paris: Barrois, 1755).
23. Pierre Rémy, *Catalogue des effets curieux du cabinet de feu M. De Selles* (Paris: Didot l'Aîné, 1761).
24. [Joullain], *Répertoire.*
25. Joullain, *Réflexions.*
26. [Joullain], *Répertoire,* v.
27. McAllister Johnson, "Paintings, Provenance and Price."
28. Gerard Hoet, *Catalogus of naamlyst van Schilderyen met Derzelver Pryzen Zedert een langen reks van Jaaren zoo in Holland als op andere Plaatzen in het openbaar verkogt* (The Hague: Van Baalen, 1752), vol. 2. A third volume was published by Pieter Terwesten in 1770.
29. Jean-Baptiste-Pierre Lebrun, *Catalogue raisonné des tableaux... qui composoient le cabinet de feu M. Poullain, receveur général des Domaines du Roi: Suivi d'un abrégé historique de la vie des peintres dont les ouvrages formoient cette collection* (Paris: Chez Langlier... Le Brun... Julliot fils, 1780).
30. Joullain, *Réflexions,* 189.
31. Joullain, *Réflexions,* 189–90.
32. See De Marchi and Van Miegroet, "The Rise of Dealer-Auctioneers."
33. The first tests I have initiated with Luc Champarnaud, an economist from Lille University, have shown that in the eighteenth century the effect of provenance can be clearly isolated as one of the most significant variables among all those contributing to the value of works of art.
34. Krzysztof Pomian, "Marchands, connaisseurs, curieux à Paris au XVIIIe siècle," *Revue de l'Art* 43 (1979): 23–36.
35. Pierre Rémy, *Catalogue d'une riche collection de Tableaux... de Mgr le Prince de Conti* (Paris: Muzier, 1777), v.
36. Antoine-Joseph Dézallier d'Argenville, *Abrégé de la Vie des plus fameux Peintres* (Paris: De Bure, 1762), xl, lxv.
37. Michel Foucault, *The Order of Things: An Archaeology of the Human Science* (London: Routledge, 2001), 143; originally published as *Les mots et les choses: Une archéologie des sciences humaines* (Paris: Gallimard, 1966).

ELIZABETH A. PERGAM

PROVENANCE AS PEDIGREE

The Marketing of British Portraits in Gilded Age America

While studies of Gilded Age collecting often focus on larger-than-life collectors such as Henry Clay Frick, Henry Edwards Huntington, and John Pierpont Morgan, the crucial role that dealers played in the formation of art collections in turn-of-the-century America is often overlooked.[1] The parentheses or square brackets that surround dealers' names in catalogs' provenance sections belie the role of dealers as a driving force behind the radical geographic redistribution of art from Europe to the United States. To a large extent, however, it was the dealers' marketing strategies that led to their own minimization in the provenance record. Even as dealers such as Joseph Duveen (1869–1939) were removing paintings from ancestral homes by the cartload, they were, when the time came to sell the works, referencing the paintings' connections to those previous owners. As the details of provenance, exhibition history, and bibliographic references attest, the presentation brochures assembled by Duveen Brothers and other dealers emphasized the cachet associated with aristocratic families.[2] That these newly formed collections included a preponderance of portraits—a genre of lower status in academic hierarchies—demonstrates the effectiveness of the dealer's emphasis on provenance as a guarantor of authenticity. By looking first at the rising taste for portraits in the late nineteenth and early twentieth centuries and then examining two commercial exhibitions that focused exclusively on portraits, we will see how dealers took advantage of the close conceptual connection between a portrait's provenance and its genealogical bona fides.

In using the vocabulary of breeding, dealers reinforced the idea that the quality of a painting could be judged by the prestige of the family who had owned it. Both Duveen Brothers and M. Knoedler & Co. explicitly called a painting's provenance and its exhibition history the work's "pedigree." These pedigrees required careful research. An internal Knoedler memorandum regarding Giovanni Bellini's *St. Francis* includes an instruction to provide the correct catalog number of that painting as it appeared in the Manchester *Art Treasures Exhibition* of 1857.[3] Although an erroneous catalog number might seem to be a minor mistake, this episode reveals the premium placed upon accuracy and documentation in the presentation of a painting's history.[4] Provenance spans the concerns of both the art market and art-historical

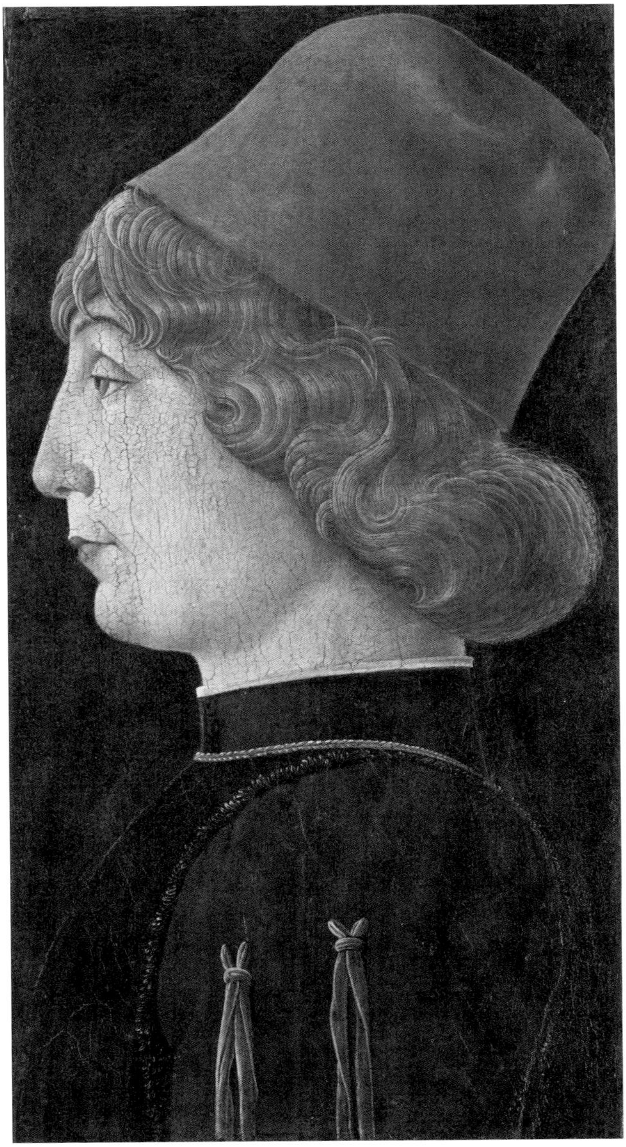

Fig. 1.
Cosmè Tura (Italian, ca. 1433–95).
Portrait of a Young Man, mid-1470s, tempera on wood, 28.3 × 19.7 cm (11⅛ × 7¾ in.).
New York, The Metropolitan Museum of Art, 14.40.649.

scholarship; thus an examination of how dealers exploited a painting's history during the height of the transatlantic art trade can illuminate the intersection of scholarship and the art market at the turn of the twentieth century.

The association of a painting with an aristocratic name or, better yet, a princely one was particularly important when selling a portrait. Bernard Berenson's opinion that a bust-length profile portrait (fig. 1) was painted by Cosmè Tura and represented the fifteenth-century nobleman Borso d'Este allowed him to claim that it was a "masterpiece by the greatest artist of the Ferrarese School, representing the greatest ruler the Ferrarese State ever had."[5]

Armed with this ducal identification, Duveen offered the painting to the department-store magnate Benjamin Altman in 1913. Altman duly purchased the painting; when he died later that year, it was part of his bequest to the Metropolitan Museum of Art. Today, Berenson's identification of the artist has proven to be correct, but his identification of the sitter has not been sustained.[6] This episode points to the difficulty in determining the sitter's identity after a portrait has been separated from its original owner. Portraiture, therefore, represents a special category in any study of provenance, because the identity of both sitter and artist is inextricably linked to the history of a painting's ownership. Within that category, no other school of painting has as much bearing on our understanding of the elision of provenance and pedigree than that of British portraits of the eighteenth and nineteenth centuries.

The notion that the turn-of-the-century American predilection for portraits of British aristocrats was based on a desire to acquire "instant ancestors" has recently been called "the great chestnut."[7] This interpretation acquires an important nuance in Malcolm Warner's account of British art in American collections; he describes the economic and cultural conditions that allowed Americans to regard Britain with fellow feeling and no longer as their principal enemy.[8] Warner argues that as icons of "an idyllic, leisured, pre-industrial society," British portraits appealed to the nostalgia of barons of industry.[9] It is certainly true that portraits represented a specific lifestyle associated with the Old World. More importantly, however, portraits were an easily accessible form of fine art both materially and figuratively. While the Settled Land Act of 1882 in Britain and the Payne-Aldrich Tariff Act of 1909 in America eliminated legal and economic barriers to the transatlantic art trade, the discourse surrounding portraiture provided a conceptual underpinning for the accessibility of the genre.[10] From the mid-nineteenth century on, discussions about portraits addressed the inherent tension between classifying a portrait as an important work of art by virtue of the importance of its sitter versus its significance as an aesthetic object in and of itself. In addition, portraiture (along with landscape painting) was considered an area in the fine arts in which British painters excelled, with Thomas Gainsborough, Joshua Reynolds, and Thomas Lawrence regarded as exceptional practitioners of the genre.

These issues were central to the debates surrounding the British Parliament's establishment in 1856 of the National Portrait Gallery—the first of its kind in Europe.[11] The guiding principle of the museum—the priority of identity and not aesthetics—is encapsulated in the declarations of its promoter, Philip Henry Stanhope, the 5th Earl Stanhope, that only portraits identifiable by "a man of good education" should be included and that its "success... depends on confining the gallery to men of real distinction, of real fame."[12] Along with the explicit male bias of this scheme was the notion that the connoisseurial expertise required for judging old-master paintings was less important than the role of biography and its corollary: provenance. A portrait bought directly from the family that had originally commissioned it possessed a guarantee—in essence, a certification of its genuineness—a fact that Duveen and his firm fully exploited. Although the National Portrait Gallery did not move into its permanent home until 1896, the vogue for exhibitions devoted to portraits began in 1857 and continued into the first decades of the twentieth century.[13] This trend crossed the Atlantic, where exhibitions of portraits took place regularly at museums but were also a staple of commercial art galleries.[14]

Two such exhibitions, both held at the Duveen Brothers galleries in New York, elucidate how the marketing of British portraits to the American audience rested on the conception of provenance as a pedigree of both the portrait's subject and the portrait as an object. By examining the information provided by the catalogs, we will see the prime role of biography and the close connection between the sitter's identity and the painting's provenance, and, by extension, the authenticity of the work of art. Illustrated catalogs accompanied both of these exhibitions. Likewise, in both cases, the portraits were presented as the pinnacle of British painting and the sitters were presented with secure, often aristocratic, identities. However, we will also see that the standards for acquiring portraits for private collections were different from the imperatives governing public institutions. Furthermore, between the first exhibition, held in January 1914, and the second, held in April 1940, the market for British portraits, regardless of their provenance, experienced a sharp contraction.

As Duveen gallery director Edward Fowles noted in his memoirs, British paintings, particularly portraits, were Duveen's specialty.[15] Seventeen portraits by the favored British artists Thomas Gainsborough, John Hoppner, Thomas Lawrence, Henry Raeburn, Joshua Reynolds, and George Romney composed the *Special Loan Exhibition of Old Masters of the British School* held at the New York branch of Duveen Brothers in 1914.[16] As the subtitle of the catalog stated, the works had all been acquired from Duveen "within the last three years" and were part of the celebrated private collections of Frick, George Gould, Huntington, and Edward Stotesbury.[17] This indicates the remarkable rate of transactions that took place in these years as well as the fact that the exhibition was not, on the face of it, assembled as a sales opportunity. Both by providing privileged access to works of art held by private collectors and by including extensive information about the paintings, Duveen Brothers projected an image of public service. The exhibition, in effect, elevated the heretofore somewhat dubious role of the dealer to the status of influential philanthropist, scholar, educator, and tastemaker.[18]

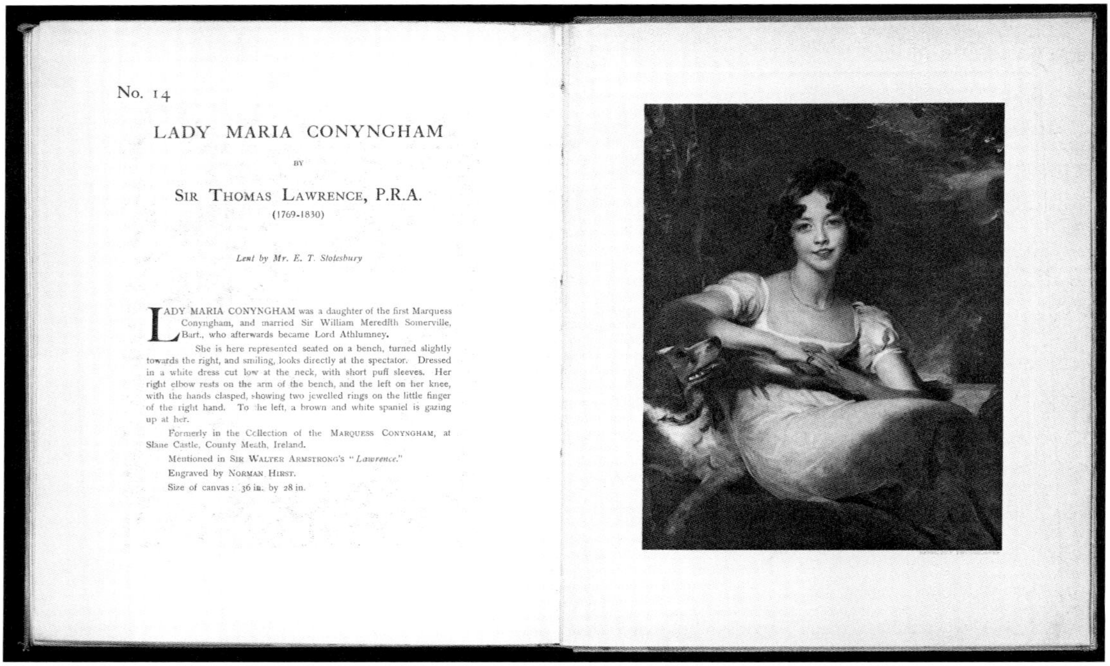
No. 14

LADY MARIA CONYNGHAM

BY

SIR THOMAS LAWRENCE, P.R.A.

(1769-1830)

Lent by Mr. E. T. Stotesbury

LADY MARIA CONYNGHAM was a daughter of the first Marquess Conyngham, and married Sir William Meredith Somerville, Bart., who afterwards became Lord Athlumney.

She is here represented seated on a bench, turned slightly towards the right, and smiling, looks directly at the spectator. Dressed in a white dress cut low at the neck, with short puff sleeves. Her right elbow rests on the arm of the bench, and the left on her knee, with the hands clasped, showing two jewelled rings on the little finger of the right hand. To the left, a brown and white spaniel is gazing up at her.

Formerly in the Collection of the MARQUESS CONYNGHAM, at Slane Castle, County Meath, Ireland.

Mentioned in SIR WALTER ARMSTRONG'S "*Lawrence.*"

Engraved by NORMAN HIRST.

Size of canvas: 36 in. by 28 in.

Fig. 2.
Page spread showing an entry from the 1914 Duveen Brothers catalog.
From *Catalogue of the Special Loan Exhibition of Old Masters of the British School in Aid of "The Artists' Fund" and "Artists' Aid" Societies: Being a Selection from Pictures Acquired from Messrs. Duveen Brothers within the Last Three Years* (New York: Duveen Brothers, 1914), no. 14.

In the Duveen catalog, each painting is introduced with biographical notes, followed by a description of the painting itself (fig. 2). Provenance is then given in a narrative form. Exhibition history and scholarly references are listed in a more cursory way, rounded out by a record of whether the painting was engraved and the size of the canvas. Twelve of the portraits depict members of the aristocracy, signaling the relative importance between the sitter's social standing and the painting's desirability as a work of art. However, the catalog makes clear that secure provenance could compensate for a nonaristocratic subject. Two of the remaining five subjects were famous or notorious figures: Gainsborough's portrait of a virtuoso musician, *Charles Frederick Abel* (no. 4),[19] and Hoppner's portrait of an actress and royal mistress, *Mrs. Jordan* (no. 17).[20] According to the catalog, the portrait of Abel, lent by Gould, had previously been owned by the Earl of Egremont, and the Hoppner had remained in the sitter's family for three generations. Likewise, Raeburn's *Mrs. Andrew Hay* (no. 16) had a sustained connection to the Hay family, having descended through three generations of the sitter's family before being purchased by Stotesbury.[21] Of the two other portraits of non-noble subjects, Reynolds's *Mrs. Otway and Child* (no. 11) had been in the collection of Charles Sackville Bale (1791–1880), the grandson of the sitter and a well-known art collector, before entering the collection of Henry Oppenheim.[22] Although the catalog makes no reference to the provenance of Lawrence's *Mrs. Thomson and Her Child (Afterwards Lord*

Sydenham) (no. 15)[23] lent by Stotesbury, its status as a sanctioned work of British art is secure because it was included, in 1804, in the annual exhibition at the Royal Academy of Arts.

The one other work in the catalog that does not include any information on provenance represents an exception to Duveen's usual practice of confirming the identity and provenance of portraits that came through his dealership. In naming a full-length portrait by Gainsborough *The Hon. Anne Duncombe (Afterwards Countess of Radnor)* (no. 1),[24] Duveen perpetuated the misidentification made by the previous owner, the dealer Charles J. Wertheimer, who had lent the portrait under that title to two important exhibitions—the Royal Academy's annual old-masters exhibition in 1907 and, in Berlin, the Königliche Akademie der Künste's *Aelterer Englischer Kunst* in 1908. Duveen seems to have felt that the association of the sitter (and the painting) with the Earl of Radnor, whose family's art collection at Longford Castle was renowned, conferred enough legitimacy to the portrait to compensate for the lack of detailed ownership history. By this time, however, Frick already knew both the correct identity of the sitter and the painting's provenance. He had purchased the portrait on 3 May 1911, along with Romney's *Lady Milnes.*[25] A month later, having read of Frick's purchase in the *Boston Transcript,* the British art cataloger William Roberts offered, for a fee of "50 or 100 dollars," to provide the industrialist with a "full & exhaustive" history of the portrait, explaining its correct identification as Frances, the elder half sister of Anne.[26] Although this episode shows a rare instance of Duveen's failure to research fully a painting from his gallery, it nevertheless confirms the American collector's interest in acquiring solid information about his purchases.[27]

More often, it was Duveen himself who provided additional documentation about a painting's history. When the publisher William Everts Benjamin purchased Reynolds's *Mrs. Otway and Child* in 1915,[28] Duveen promised to send Benjamin his correspondence with Isabel Oppenheim, who was instrumental in helping Duveen buy the portrait from her husband, Henry.[29] And, when Stotesbury had acquired portraits of two sisters, *Lady Elizabeth Conyngham* (no. 13) and *Lady Maria Conyngham* (no. 14; see fig. 2), Duveen sent him copies of letters written by the artist that were in the possession of the Conyngham family. Duveen noted that the correspondence was important because it showed that "the portrait of Lady Elizabeth was by royal command"—the mother of the sitter, the marchioness Conyngham, was the mistress of George IV.[30]

While these two cases indicate how Duveen supplied additional information to his clients to flesh out details about the portraits they had bought from him, the catalog entries for separate portraits of Viscount Ligonier and Viscountess Ligonier (nos. 5 and 6) by Gainsborough exemplify the way the seemingly dry facts of provenance, exhibition history, and bibliographic references could be used to extrapolate a more expansive narrative of the sitters and their portraits.[31] The full-length pendants had descended through three generations of the latter's family. The viscountess's biography—she was the daughter of George Pitt, who became the first Baron Rivers—makes the connection between the painting's provenance, its subject, and its commission. Although not stated explicitly, the facts as laid out by the catalog suggest that Viscountess Ligonier's father commissioned the pair of portraits on the occasion of the viscount's promotion to colonel.[32] Pitt's commissioning of portraits of his daughter and son-in-law showed the American audience how the portrait functioned as a marker of the increased prestige that could come to a family through an advantageous marriage.[33]

Indeed, throughout the catalog it is intimated that in eighteenth- and nineteenth-century Britain, portraiture performed an important social function by celebrating significant moments in the lives of the sitters. No milestone was more important than marriage, and, just as marriages were arranged to perpetuate the family line, portraits were painted to immortalize this hoped-for continuity. In this context, women, not surprisingly, played a central role.[34] Or rather, as the biographies elaborate, marriage played a pivotal role in the life of women of a certain class. While the biographies of male sitters consider their career accomplishments—Frederick Abel's as a musician, Viscount Ligonier's as a military officer—the lives of female sitters are defined by their parentage, their spouses, and their progeny. The biography of Mrs. Jordan represents the single exception. However, even as the passage makes note of her stage career, it also links her to royalty as the longtime mistress—"from 1790 to 1811"—of the Duke of Clarence, the third son of George III. In many ways, therefore, the twentieth-century trade in female portraits replicated the aristocratic marriage mart of the eighteenth and nineteenth centuries.

Old Masters of the British School opened in January 1914, six months before World War I was triggered by the assassination of Archduke Franz Ferdinand. *Forty British Portraits* opened 9 April 1940, during the early months of the Second World War called the "Phony War"—after Hitler's invasion of Poland but before his invasion of Holland, Belgium, and France. The more local concerns of Depression-era America were reflected in the choice of the Greater New York Fund as the exhibition's beneficiary. In the context of Duveen Brothers' history, it was of great significance that the exhibition opened eleven months after the death of Joseph Duveen. As Edward Fowles, who worked in the gallery's New York office, wrote to his partners in the Paris branch: "It is the first Exhibition we have had for many years and people seem very keen to see what we can do"; at its close, he could report that "it gives life to the house."[35] Amid these bleak circumstances, the exhibition's contents and catalog well illustrate the effervescence of American collecting of British portraits of the previous half-century while also pointing to the post–World War II decline of that taste.

More than twice the size of Duveen's old-masters exhibition in 1914, *Forty British Portraits* continued and expanded on the themes of that earlier display. The majority of the subjects had noble titles, with one duke and one marquis, three marchionesses, three earls, four countesses, one viscountess, three lords, and four ladies. As we have seen, two of the figures represented in 1914 had been connected to royal mistresses. The 1940 exhibit upped the royal ante and included *Queen Charlotte of England* (ca. 1776; no. 12), given to Gainsborough.[36] The primacy of royalty is indicated by the fact that—as an exception to the otherwise alphabetical-by-artist arrangement of the publication—the first painting in the catalog is *Henry, Prince of Wales and Lord Harington,* then ascribed to Isaac Oliver (fig. 3).[37] Once again, female subjects handily outnumbered those

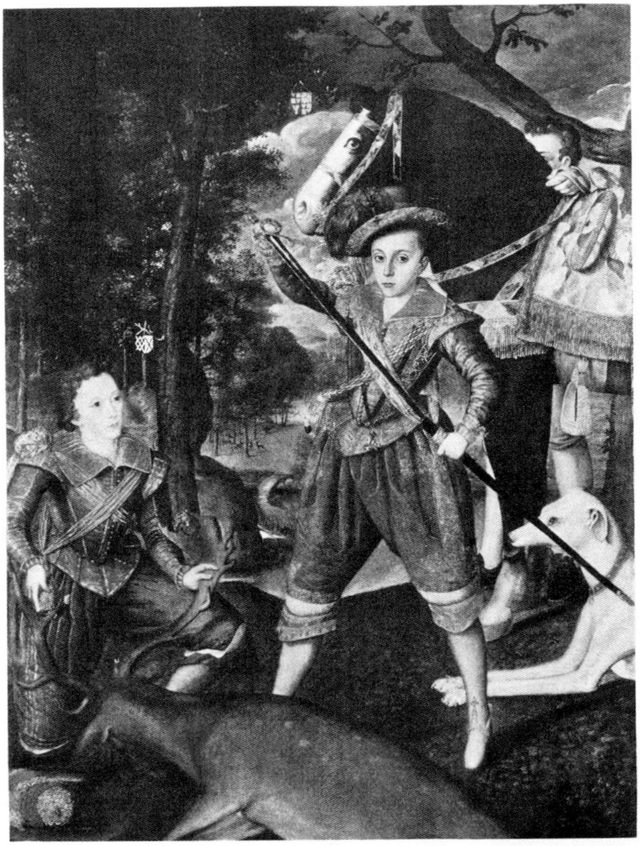

Fig. 3.
Page from the 1940 Duveen Brothers catalog showing *Henry, Prince of Wales and Lord Harington,* then attributed to Isaac Oliver (detail).
From *Forty British Portraits* (New York: Publishers Printing, 1940), no. 1.

of men. As in the 1914 catalog, the biographical passages that dominate the entries emphasize the overwhelming importance of genealogy. However, in 1940, both the time frame and the range of artists represented are much larger. Moreover, the importance of biography extends to the artists, and accounts of their lives highlight official honors, such as Sir William Beechey's appointment in 1793 to the position of portrait painter to George III and John Hoppner's royal patronage. In addition, the 1940 catalog includes an introduction written by W. G. Constable, the dean of art history in Britain, that gives a capsule history of British art.

The most important difference between the two exhibits is that in 1940 the portraits were part of the gallery's stock and were, therefore, for sale. In fact, from the correspondence between Fowles and the Paris branch, we learn that the exhibition was organized with the view to sell one portrait in particular: Arthur William Devis's *Master Simpson* (no. 8; fig. 4).[38] Fowles sets the scene by first reporting that "one of the most important visitors . . . was Miss Frick, who hasn't put a foot in this house for twenty years as she quarreled with your Uncle."[39] His excitement that the industrialist's daughter was "crazy about the *DEVIS picture*" is clear from the tone of the letter. He continues: "Knoedler's have been asking through various channels the price we are quoting on the picture. . . . In fact, it is one of the reasons why we made the Exhibition, as we wanted to find out who really wanted the picture."[40] Fowles's hopefulness is understandable; the *Master Simpson* portrait, a relatively undistinguished subject painted by a lesser known artist, had been on Duveen Brothers' hands for four years.

Before the painting was due to come up at auction in London in 1936, Alec Martin of Christie's had gone to great lengths to interest Duveen. He cabled Duveen several days before the sale: "Most attractive small full length of boy lot 134 in next Fridays sale one I am certain you would like attributed to Devis has all Hoppners charm."[41] Duveen responded that if the portrait were painted by John Hoppner, he would be able to sell it, but "If Devis have no client."[42] Martin followed up Duveen's negative reaction by telephoning him the day before the sale.[43] Martin's oral argument was persuasive; the dealer's London representative acquired the portrait for 3,600 guineas at the auction.[44] That same day, the London office wrote to say that the London *Times* was going to cover the story "as admired Duveen Brothers for buying work [of] art without big name."[45] In this case, the lack of a "big name" referred to the relative obscurity of the artist but could equally be applied to the social status of the sitter. The next day London cabled New York: "All important papers [give] good notices third of column. London Times says most delightful Child Portrait appeared in saleroom many years."[46]

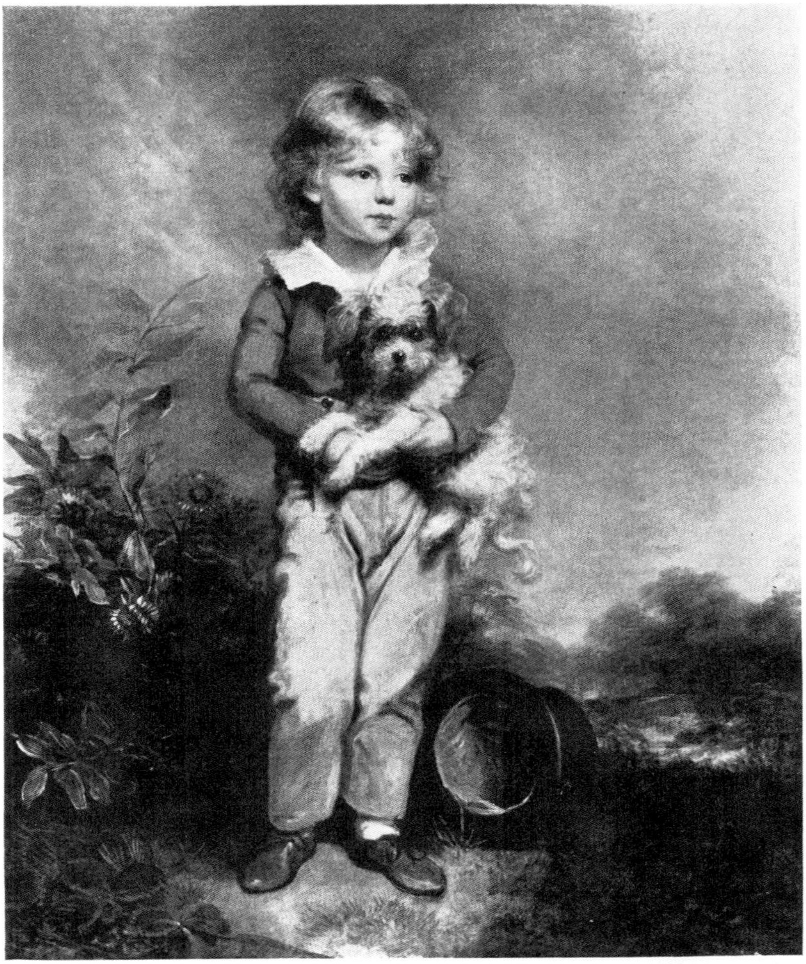

8. DEVIS *Master Simpson*

Fig. 4.
Page from the 1940 Duveen Brothers catalog showing *Master Simpson*, by Arthur William Devis (detail).
From *Forty British Portraits* (New York: Publishers Printing, 1940), no. 8.

After the sale, a Duveen employee "took tea" with the consignor, Mrs. William Simpson, to confirm the identity of the sitter,[47] who was her husband's father, James Alexander Simpson, and the 1940 catalog entry notes the family descent of the portrait. In a rather desperate attempt to elaborate the sitter's biography, the narrative connects the adult achievements of Simpson, who became the attorney to the Foundling Hospital, with that charitable institution's early patrons, the artist William Hogarth and the composer George Frideric Handel. As Joseph Duveen predicted, however, without the imprimatur of a fashionable artist, the portrait proved difficult to sell. Contrary to Fowles's hopes, Helen Clay Frick did not purchase the portrait, and neither did the Huntington trustees, Kay Kimbell, the Putnam Foundation, nor the Nelson-Atkins.[48]

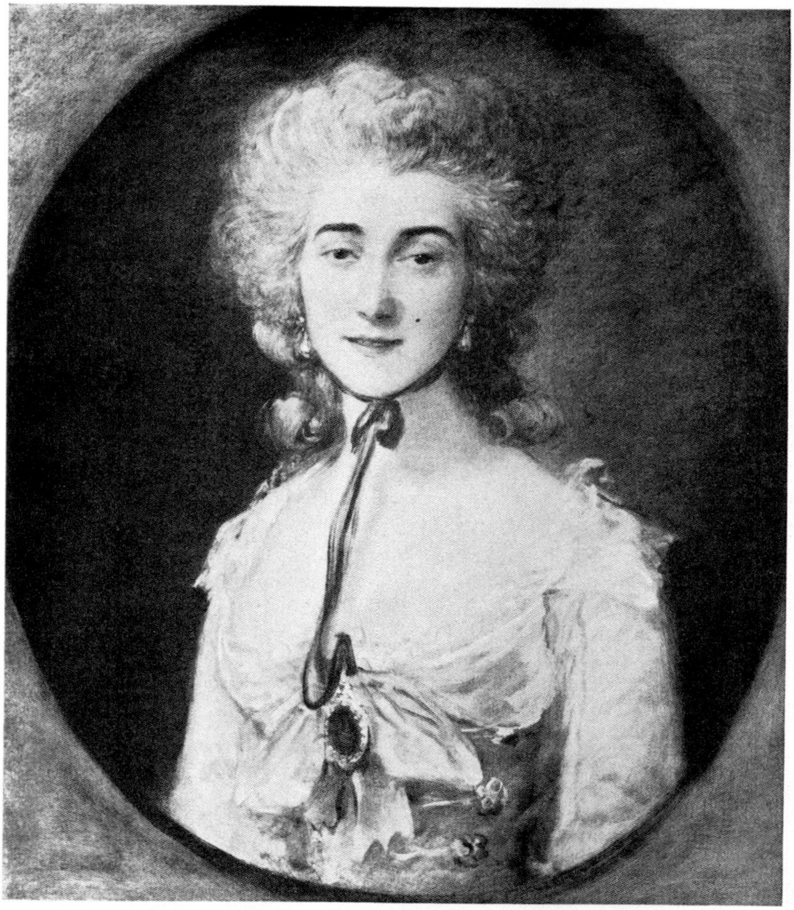

13. GAINSBOROUGH *Mrs. Grace Dalrymple Elliott*

Fig. 5.
Page from the 1940 Duveen Brothers catalog showing *Mrs. Grace Dalrymple Elliott*, by Thomas Gainsborough (detail). From *Forty British Portraits* (New York: Publishers Printing, 1940), no. 13.

In 1946, the Frick Collection purchased two portraits that had been in the 1940 exhibition: *Mrs. Grace Dalrymple Elliott* (no. 13; fig. 5) and *Richard Paul Jodrell, M.P.* (no. 14; fig. 6), both by Gainsborough.[49] In a press release announcing the acquisitions, the portraits' distinction is substantiated by their ownership history. The portrait of Jodrell had "long [been] held in the sitter's family" and that of Elliott had been in the Duke of Portland's famous collection at Welbeck Abbey.[50] The 1940 Duveen catalog had explained the presence of the portrait in that collection by noting that Elliott's daughter, raised by the Earl of Cholmondeley's family, had married the son of the 3rd Duke of Portland, Lord Charles Cavendish Bentinck. However, the press release, in speculating that the duke sold the portrait not because of any aesthetic failing but because the sitter had led a scandalous life, demonstrated that the relationship between biography and provenance is not always a positive one. The press release,

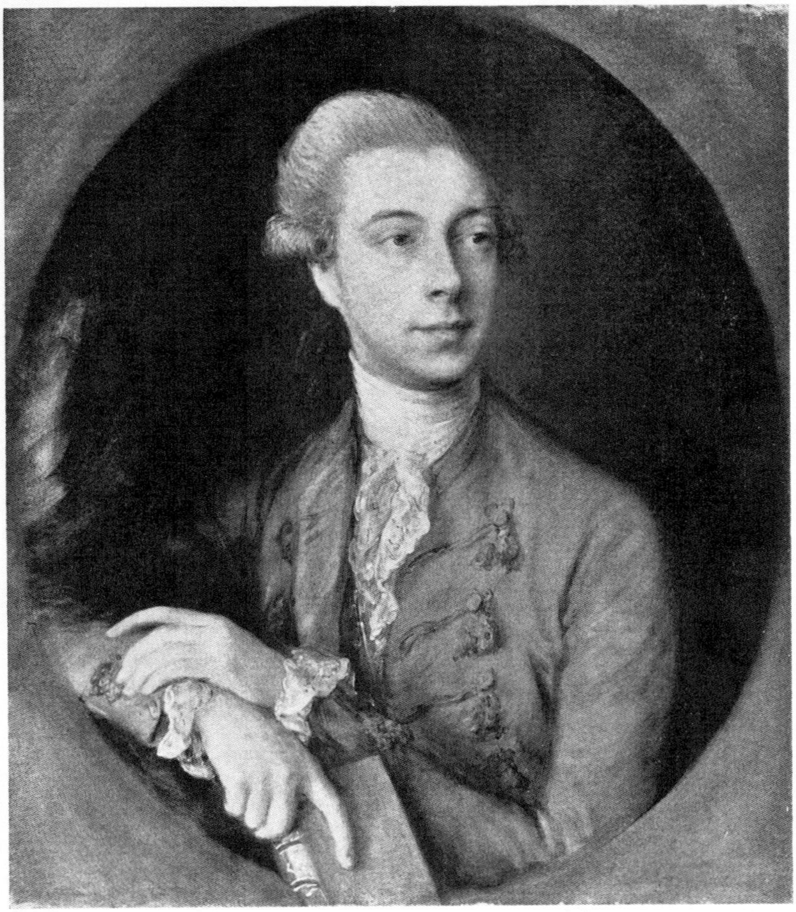

14. GAINSBOROUGH *Richard Paul Jodrell, M.P.*

Fig. 6.
Page from the 1940 Duveen Brothers catalog showing *Richard Paul Jodrell, M.P.*, by Thomas Gainsborough (detail).
From *Forty British Portraits* (New York: Publishers Printing, 940), no. 14.

therefore, broke the centuries-old link between biography and portraiture to emphasize the primacy of aesthetics, noting that the fact that "Gainsborough lavished more than facility" on the portrait was the "only concern" of the acquisitions committee. Not only is Gainsborough's use of color and his ability to capture expression highly praised but his brushwork is seen to anticipate the achievements of impressionism. Thus, a painter associated with the portrayal of the landed elite of pre-industrial England is transformed into a precursor of modernism. The portrait of Jodrell is likewise lauded for displaying the artist's "masterly" technique.

Even as this public pronouncement emphasized the formalist rationale for the acquisitions, the thick typewritten presentation brochures that Duveen Brothers produced for the paintings attest to the continuing and expanding importance of documentation in the transactional process. Not only are bibliographic references listed but the pertinent passages from these books and articles are transcribed in full.[51] Both brochures contain extensive biographical narratives, though only the one for *Mrs. Grace Dalrymple Elliott* includes a short description of the painting itself. A particularly pertinent passage appears in Elliott's biography. Having called into question the details of the sitter's memoir, "Journal of My Life during the French Revolution," the compiler of the brochure notes that Philippe, duc d'Orléans, one of her numerous paramours, had "taught his mistresses the art of fabricating pedigrees for their children."[52] This not-so-subtle warning as to the mutability of facts is at odds with the plethora of data outlined in the first pages of the pamphlet, as well as the 1940 catalog. In fact, the 1968 Frick Collection catalog adds a note of uncertainty to the provenance that, in 1940, is presented as ironclad. Citing the claim in Fairfax Murray's 1894 catalog of the paintings at Welbeck Abbey that the 5th Duke of Portland had acquired the portrait in France, this early provenance is appended with a question mark.[53]

Although the case of *Mrs. Grace Dalrymple Elliott* might be considered an example of how Duveen Brothers massaged provenance information to present a portrait's history as altogether more illustrious and certain than the facts might warrant, it nevertheless provides proof of the intimate connection between the history of the family and that of the painting. The press release's emphasis on the formal achievements of the artist rather than the biography of the sitter points to a paradigm shift in American collecting. The Huntington Library Art Collection's gallery of British Grand Manner portraits is, to this day, the outstanding example of Joseph Duveen's profound influence on American taste and museum-building; the generation of collectors that followed Henry Huntington was less interested in paintings that embodied the Old World's rigid class hierarchies.[54] Thus, while Andrew W. Mellon purchased full-length Grand Manner portraits such as Gainsborough's *Georgiana, Duchess of Devonshire* (1783) (Washington, D.C., National Gallery of Art, 1937.1.93), his son, Paul, turned his attention to smaller-scale conversation pieces such as the artist's early *Gravenor Family* (ca. 1754) (New Haven, Conn., Yale Center for British Art, B1977.14.56).[55]

Much more remains to be uncovered and analyzed in the study of collecting of old-master and British painting in America during the last decades of the nineteenth century and the first half of the twentieth. However, this study of two exhibitions organized and staged at the New York gallery of Duveen Brothers demonstrates how Joseph Duveen and other transatlantic dealers codified the use of provenance as a guarantor of aesthetic authenticity. Duveen, especially, marketed Grand Manner British portraits on the strength of their peerless pedigrees, which functioned on the dual levels of genealogical and art-historical desirability. To strengthen this position, the gallery conducted extensive research and provided documentary evidence to its clients, thereby putting provenance research—something now usually considered an academic pursuit—to commercial use. Furthermore, the two Duveen exhibitions are excellent markers of the shift in American taste that occurred over the course of the first decades of the twentieth century. The social formalities embodied in eighteenth-century British portraits, which made them so popular with collectors of the Gilded Age—Huntington, Morgan, and Frick—were less appealing to collectors who had experienced the horrors of Old World politics as manifested in the First World War and the economic crisis of the Depression. Where once identity—and the social hierarchies inherent in family name and association—had been the standard for evaluating a portrait, after the so-called Great War, American art institutions turned instead to aesthetics as the basis for value.

Notes

I am forever grateful to the staffs of the Frick Art Reference Library, the Thomas J. Watson Library at the Metropolitan Museum of Art, and the Clark Art Institute. At the Frick Archives, Julie Ludwig was an expert guide. In looking at the object files in the Department of European Paintings at the Metropolitan Museum of Art and at the Frick Collection, I was ably assisted by Patrice Mattia and Joanna Sheers. The debt I owe to Shelley Bennett, senior research associate at the Huntington Library, Art Collections, and Botanical Gardens, is unquantifiable.

1. Neil Harris's call for a new approach to the history of collecting in America is conveyed by the title of his keynote paper, "Beyond Biography," presented at the inaugural conference, Turning Points in Old Master Collecting, 1830–1940, held by the Frick's Center for the History of Collecting, 19 May 2007.
2. Duveen's outsized personality, along with his often cloak-and-dagger dealings, inspired numerous biographies. See, for example, Meryle Secrest, *Duveen: A Life in Art* (New York: Alfred A. Knopf, 2005); S. N. Behrman, *Duveen* (New York: Random House, 1951); and Colin Simpson, *The Partnership: The Secret Association of Bernard Berenson and Joseph Duveen* (London: Bodley Head, 1987).
3. Unsigned, "Letter to Knoedler & Co.," 17 May 1915, internal memorandum, M. Knoedler & Co., Frick Collection Object File: Giovanni Bellini, *St. Francis in the Desert* (1915.1.03). The painting is now in the Frick Collection, New York.
4. R. Langton Douglas's account, in 1943, of his rediscovery of this painting and Gerard David's *Descent from the Cross* (ca. 1495–1500) (now at the Frick Collection, New York, and titled *The Deposition* [1915.1.33]) reads like a detective story. R. Langton Douglas to Miss Margaret E. Gilman, Fogg Art Museum, 30 November 1943, Frick Collection Object File: Giovanni Bellini, *St. Francis in the Desert* (1915.1.03). See my "From Manchester to Manhattan: The Transatlantic Art Trade after 1857," *John Rylands Bulletin* 87 (2005): 79–80.

5. Bernard Berenson to Joseph Duveen, 2 March 1913, Department of European Paintings, Metropolitan Museum of Art, Object File: Cosmè Tura, *Portrait of a Young Man* (14.40.649).
6. Before Berenson assigned the portrait to the Ferrarese artist, it was, in 1857, considered the work of Piero della Francesca and subsequently that of Francesco Cossa. See Federico Zeri with Elizabeth E. Gardner, *Italian Paintings: A Catalogue of the Collection of The Metropolitan Museum of Art, North Italian School* (New York: Metropolitan Museum of Art, 1986), 62–63.
7. John Wilson, review of *British Paintings at the Huntington,* by Robyn Asleson and Shelley M. Bennett, and of *Great British Paintings from American Collections: Holbein to Hockney,* by Malcolm Warner et al., *Burlington Magazine* 144 (2002): 303. Cynthia Saltzman uncritically repeats this outdated interpretation in explaining the rise of prices for English portraits around the turn of the century; see Saltzman, *Old Masters, New World: America's Raid on Europe's Great Pictures 1880–World War I* (New York: Viking, 2008), 104.
8. Malcolm Warner, "Anglophilia into Art," in idem et al., *Great British Paintings from American Collections: Holbein to Hockney* (New Haven, Conn.: Yale Center for British Art, 2001), 7.
9. Warner, "Anglophilia," 8.
10. The Settled Land Act freed works of art from the legal restrictions of heirloom status; the Payne-Aldrich Tariff Act rolled back the 20 percent import duties on artworks.
11. Giles Waterfield, "The Development of the Early Art Museum in Britain," in *The Genesis of the Art Museum in the 18th Century: Papers Given at a Symposium in Nationalmuseum Stockholm, June 26, 1992, in Cooperation with the Royal Academy of Letters, History, and Antiquities,* ed. Per Bjurström (Stockholm: Nationalmuseum, 1993), 84. For a general account of the foundation of the National Portrait Gallery, see Charles Saumarez Smith, "Introduction," in idem, *The National Portrait Gallery* (London: National Portrait Gallery, 1997), 9–13.
12. See Sir George Scharf, *Historical and Descriptive Catalogue of the Pictures, Busts, &c. in the National Portrait Gallery, St. Martin's Place, W.C.,* ed. Lionel Cust (London: printed for H.M. Stationery Office by Eyre & Spottiswoode, 1896), v. More than a century later, on the founding of America's National Portrait Gallery, primacy was placed on the subject rather than its means of depiction: "The criterion of admission shall be the national significance of the person portrayed and to a lesser degree the competence and skill of the artist." See *National Portrait Gallery . . . a New Bureau of the Smithsonian Institution* (Washington, D.C.: The Gallery, 1965), n.p.
13. The British Portrait Gallery at the 1857 Manchester *Art Treasures Exhibition* initiated the trend with nearly four hundred works arranged roughly according to reign; see *Catalogue of the Art Treasures of the United Kingdom: Collected at Manchester in 1857,* exh. cat. (London: Bradbury & Evans, 1857). For more on the circumstances surrounding that groundbreaking exhibition, see my dissertation, "'Waking the Soul': The Manchester Art Treasures Exhibition of 1857 and the State of the Arts in Mid-Victorian Britain" (PhD diss., Institute of Fine Arts, 2001), and my book *The Manchester Art Treasures Exhibition of 1857: Entrepreneurs,*

Connoisseurs and the Public (Surrey, U.K.: Ashgate, 2011). The Manchester exhibition was followed by a series of exhibitions of national portraits held at the South Kensington Museum between 1866 and 1868.

14. See, for example, Wilhelm Reinhold Valentiner and L. J. Waltherr, *Loan Exhibition of Fifty Paintings by Anthony Van Dyck,* exh. cat. (Detroit, Mich.: The Detroit Institute of Arts, 1929).
15. Edward Fowles, *Memories of Duveen Brothers* (New York: Times Books, 1976), 112.
16. The *New York Times* review concentrated on the characters of the artists represented. See "Art at Home and Abroad: Works of Great British Portrait Painters on View at the Duveen Galleries," *New York Times,* 11 January 1914, SM 15.
17. See *Catalogue of the Special Loan Exhibition of Old Masters of the British School in Aid of "The Artists' Fund" and "Artists' Aid" Societies: Being a Selection from Pictures Acquired from Messrs. Duveen Brothers within the Last Three Years* (New York: Duveen Brothers, 1914). Two paintings by Reynolds—*Mrs. Otway and Child* (ca. 1775, now in a private collection) and *Lady Sarah Bunbury* (present location unknown; David Mannings does not list any copies of the original version of this full-length portrait now at the Art Institute of Chicago; see Mannings, *Sir Joshua Reynolds: A Complete Catalogue of His Paintings* [London: Yale University Press, 2000], 111–12, cat. no. 279)—were still part of the dealer's stock. A draft of Joseph Duveen's letter to the Huntingtons thanking them for lending their portraits to the exhibition is preserved in the Duveen Brothers Records, 1876–1981 (960015), reel 323, box 468, folder 1, Getty Research Institute, Los Angeles; hereafter Duveen Archives.
18. The topic of the Victorian art dealer has recently been explored by Pamela Fletcher, "Creating the French Gallery: Ernest Gambart and the Rise of the Commercial Art Gallery in Mid-Victorian London," *Nineteenth-Century Art Worldwide* 6 (2007), and Aviva Bronfels, *The Deceivers: Art Forgery and Identity in the Nineteenth Century* (Ithaca, N.Y.: Cornell University Press, 2006).
19. Currently Thomas Gainsborough, *Karl Friedrich Abel,* ca. 1777, San Marino, Huntington Library Art Collections (25.19).
20. The sitter's real name was Dorothea Bland, but she was widely known by her stage name, Mrs. Jordan. The portrait was sold at the Stotesbury Sale, Parke-Bernet, New York, 18 November 1944, lot 11, for $4,000.
21. Now at the Joslyn Art Museum in Omaha, Nebraska: Henry Raeburn, *Portrait of Mrs. Andrew (Elizabeth Robinson) Hay,* ca. 1795 (1941.40).
22. Joseph Duveen acquired the portrait through the machinations of Isabel, Henry Oppenheim's wife, over the course of September 1911. Their correspondence exemplifies the extensive negotiations and backdoor dealings in which Duveen engaged in pursuit of fine art. Isabel refers to the financial plight that led to the eventual auctioning of the rest of the Oppenheim collection on 13 June 1913; see Isabel Oppenheim to Joseph Duveen, 8 September 1911, 12 September 1911, 13 September 1911, and 30 September 1912, Duveen Archives, reel 136, box 281, folder 16. The painting is now in a private collection; see Mannings, *Sir Joshua Reynolds,* 359, no. 1371.
23. Thomas Lawrence, *A Portrait Group of Mrs. John Thomson and Her Son Charles Edward Poulett Thomson, later Baron Sydenham of Sydenham, Kent, and Toronto,*

and Governor-General of British North America, Fredericton, N.B., Canada, Beaverbrook Art Gallery (1990.04).

24. Thomas Gainsborough, *The Hon. Frances Duncombe,* ca. 1777, New York, Frick Collection (1911.1.61).
25. George Romney, *Charlotte, Lady Milnes,* 1788–92, New York, Frick Collection (1911.1.106). The cost of the two portraits totaled $550,000; see Joseph Duveen to Henry Clay Frick, 3 May 1911, Henry Clay Frick Art Collection Files, Frick Collection/Frick Art Reference Library Archives, New York; hereafter Henry Clay Frick Art Collection Files.
26. William Roberts to Henry Clay Frick, 16 June 1911, Henry Clay Frick Art Collection Files.
27. Frick paid Roberts £20 for the six-page typescript that gave a full biography of Frances and her family, as well as the history of the portrait, where it had been exhibited, engraved, and illustrated. See Henry Clay Frick to William Roberts, 27 June 1911, Henry Clay Frick Art Collection Files.
28. Benjamin bought the portrait at the Duveen Brothers sale held at the American Art Association on 29 April 1915; see Mannings, *Sir Joshua Reynolds,* 359, no. 1371.
29. The painting, having been damaged in a fire aboard the steamship *Mississippi* in November 1914, was sold at auction on 29 April 1915. See "Injured Paintings on View," *New York Times,* 25 April 1915, C2, and "Painting by Cuyp Sold for $73,000," *New York Times,* 30 April 1915, 13. Because of legal issues deriving from the settlement of the insurance from the fire, it was several years before Duveen was able to send Benjamin copies of the letters on 4 April 1918; see Duveen Archives, box 281, reel 136, folder 16.
30. Joseph Duveen to Edward T. Stotesbury, 21 September 1913, Duveen Archives, box 513, reel 368, folder 4. *Lady Elizabeth Conyngham* (1824) is now in the Museu Calouste Gulbenkian, Lisbon, and *Lady Maria Conyngham* (ca. 1824–25) is now at the Metropolitan Museum of Art, New York (55.89).
31. Both paintings are now in the Huntington Library Art Collections, San Marino, Calif.: *Edward, Viscount (later Earl) Ligonier*, 1770 (11.30), and *Penelope (Pitt), Viscountess Ligonier*, 1770 (11.29).
32. Pitt had commissioned the paintings shortly after his son-in-law's succession to his uncle's title of viscount; see Robyn Asleson and Shelley M. Bennett, *British Paintings at the Huntington* (New Haven, Conn.: Yale University Press, 2001), 130.
33. What neither the viscount nor the viscountess's biographies relate, however, is that their marriage was short lived because of the viscountess's infidelity. See Asleson and Bennett, *British Paintings,* 134.
34. For the preponderance of portraits of beautiful women in Henry Huntington's collection, see Shelley M. Bennett, "The Formation of Henry E. Huntington's Collection of British Painting," in Robyn Asleson and Shelley M. Bennett, *British Paintings at the Huntington* (New Haven, Conn.: Yale University Press, 2001), 1–15.
35. New York office [Edward Fowles] to Paris office, 8 April 1940 and 7 May 1940, Duveen Archives, reel 272, box 416, folder 3. Internal documents record that 963 catalogs were bought during the exhibition's duration. An additional 214 catalogs were sent at no charge to journalists and important collectors such as Joseph Widener and Robert Lehman; see Duveen Archives, reel 272, box 416, folder 3.

Fowles does not mention the exhibition in his *Memories of Duveen Brothers.*

36. Current whereabouts unknown. This bust-length portrait is more likely a reduced version after William Beechey's portrait of Queen Charlotte in the Royal Collection (inv. 405423).
37. The painting is now in the Metropolitan Museum of Art, New York, with a different attribution and slightly different title: Robert Peake the Elder, *Henry Frederick (1594–1612), Prince of Wales, with Sir John Harington (1592–1614), in the Hunting Field,* 1603 (44.27). In the catalog, this portrait is followed by four examples by Anthony van Dyck; after that, however, the catalog proceeds with entries in alphabetical order by artist: Beechey, Devis, Hoppner, Lawrence, Raeburn, Reynolds, and Romney; see *Forty British Portraits* (New York: Publishers Printing, 1940). By 1953, Roy Strong had convincingly reattributed the portrait to Robert Peake the Elder; see Roy Strong, "Elizabethan Painting: An Approach through Inscriptions; I: Robert Peake the Elder," *Burlington Magazine* 105 (1953): 54.
38. The attention to the Devis portrait is indicated by the fact that it is the only work also illustrated in color and tipped in as the frontispiece. The painting's current whereabouts are unknown.
39. New York office [Edward Fowles] to Paris office, 11 May 1940, Duveen Archives, reel 272, box 417, folder 3. Although the recipient is not specified, Fowles was probably writing to Armand Lowengard, Joseph Duveen's nephew, who ran the Paris branch.
40. New York office [Edward Fowles] to Paris office.
41. Alec Martin to Joseph Duveen, 2 March 1936, Duveen Archives, reel 91, box 236, folder 15.
42. Joseph Duveen to Alec Martin, 3 March 1936, Duveen Archives, reel 91, box 236, folder 15. There were six Hoppner portraits (nos. 15–20) in the 1940 exhibition: *Miss Harriet Ann Seale as "Bo-Peep"* (ca. 1780); *Lady Louisa Manners, Countess of Dysart* (ca. 1782); *Elizabeth, Countess of Mexborough* (1783); *Lady Georgina Buckley* (ca. 1785); *Mrs. George Mowbray* (ca. 1795); and *The Hon. Mrs. Jerningham as "Hebe, Goddess of Youth"* (ca. 1800–1805). I have not been able to locate the present whereabouts of any of these portraits.
43. From a cable that same day, we know Martin and Duveen spoke about the portrait. Alec Martin to Joseph Duveen, 5 March 1936, Duveen Archives, reel 91, box 236, folder 15.
44. London office to New York office, 6 March 1936, Duveen Archives, reel 91, box 236, folder 15. An annotated copy of the sales catalog at the Frick Art Reference Library indicates that no other work fetched nearly as high a price as the Devis—the second highest price achieved was £588 for lot 119, James Stark's painting *Sheep Washing at Thorpe;* see *Catalogue of Ancient and Modern Pictures and Drawings of the British Continental Schools... the Properties of Major George R. Benson, Howard Bliss, Esq., Mrs. Simpson, R. W. Cater, Esq., Deceased, and Others*, Christie's, Manson & Woods, London, 6 March 1936. Arthur William Devis (1762–1822) was the son of Arthur Devis, the portrait painter who specialized in conversation pieces; see Stephen Whittle, *Arthur William Devis, 1762–1822*, exh. cat. (Preston: Harris Museum & Art Gallery, 2000).

45. London office to New York office, 6 March 1936, Duveen Archives, reel 91, box 236, folder 15.
46. London office to New York office, 7 March 1936, Duveen Archives, reel 91, box 236, folder 15.
47. London office to New York office, 31 March 1936, Duveen Archives, reel 91, box 236, folder 15.
48. B. S. Boggis to curator of the Henry Huntington Library, 26 February 1953, Duveen Archives, reel 91, box 236, folder 15; B. S. Boggis to Frederick S. Parker, Putnam Foundation, 4 May 1954, Duveen Archives, reel 91, box 236, folder 15; B. S. Boggis to Patrick Kelleher, curator, Nelson Gallery of Art, 18 February 1954, Duveen Archives, reel 91, box 236, folder 15; Kay Kimbell to Duveen Brothers, 20 April 1953, Duveen Archives, reel 91, box 236, folder 15; and unsigned internal memorandum, 26 April 1954, Duveen Archives, reel 91, box 236, folder 15.
49. The Frick Collection now lists them as follows: *Grace Dalrymple Elliott,* ca. 1782 (1946.1.153), and *Richard Paul Jodrell,* ca. 1774 (1946.1.154).
50. "Additions to the Frick Collection," 2 October 1946, press release, Frick Collection Object File: Thomas Gainsborough, *Richard Paul Jodrell* (1946.1.154).
51. "A Life-Size Bust Portrait in Oils Representing *Mrs. Grace Dalrymple Elliott,* 1753–1823, Painted in 1778 by *Thomas Gainsborough, R.A.*, 1727–1788, English School," 1946 (Frick Collection Object File: Thomas Gainsborough, *Grace Dalrymple Elliott* [1946.1.153]); "An Oil Painting on Canvas Representing the Portrait of Richard Paul Jodrell, M.P., Classical Scholar and Dramatist (1745–1831), Painted about 1785 by Thomas Gainsborough, R.A., 1727–1788, British School," 1946 (Frick Collection Object File: Thomas Gainsborough, *Richard Paul Jodrell* [1946.1.154]).
52. According to the preface of the 1859 publication of *Journal of My Life during the French Revolution*, Grace Dalrymple Elliott wrote the memoir on her return from France at the express wish of George III. Grace Dalrymple Elliott, *Journal of My Life during the French Revolution* (London: Richard Bentley, 1859), ix–x.
53. *The Frick Collection: An Illustrated Catalogue,* vol. 1, *Paintings: American, British, Dutch, Flemish and German* (New York: distributed by Princeton University Press, 1968), 56.
54. See Bennett, "Formation."
55. Warner, "Anglophilia," 3.

PART FOUR

Provenance Research Instrumentalized

TILMANN VON STOCKHAUSEN

THE FAILURE OF PROVENANCE RESEARCH IN GERMANY

Introduction

Provenance research in Germany first took off after the Washington Declaration of 3 December 1998[1] obliged museums to revisit recent history and examine the unjust National Socialist rule of 1933–45. Since the signing both of that declaration, on the "general principles applicable to artworks confiscated by the Nazis," and of the still more explicit Joint Declaration[2] (signed by the German federal government, the German state governments, and the local and regional authorities), publicly funded museums have been obliged to carry out provenance research proactively. The object of the investigations is to identify works of art sold under duress, or even stolen, during the National Socialist era. This would include any work of art acquired by German museums after 1945 that had been sold or relinquished by a previous owner as a consequence of persecution. Through the Joint Declaration, the Federal Republic, all its federal states, and the local and regional authorities undertook to abide by the Washington Declaration and signaled their intention to investigate all of the cultural assets in question. If a work of art proves to have been disposed of under the National Socialist regime as a consequence of persecution, it must be returned to the descendants who have title to it, or be made the subject of a financial settlement. There is no direction as to how such restitution or financial compensation is to be made: that has been left to the museums to decide.

However, the call by political leaders for a comprehensive provenance history of all works acquired since 1933 met with little response from German museums, partly because of lack of staff, but partly also because provenance investigation was seen as a laborious and not particularly purposeful type of research. Accordingly, renewed impetus for provenance research came not from museum curators but from scholars engaged specifically for this research, most of them on fixed-term contracts. The Hamburger Kunsthalle led the way in 2000 by creating a permanent post in provenance research; it was here that Ute Haug followed up the history of works acquired since 1933 in particular.[3]

Relatively little interest was shown at the time in various provenance research projects that had been running for years, for example in the United

Kingdom, the Netherlands, France, and, above all, at the Getty Research Institute in the United States. The many years of research built up in the Getty Provenance Index®, under the leadership of Burton B. Fredericksen, have at no time attracted much interest in Germany, except from historians, who recognized the significance of this research and of the voluminous accumulated sources of social history. In the Benelux countries and France, the same phenomenon can be observed: the basic research carried out for the Getty Provenance Index® attracted more interest from social historians than from art historians or museum staff.[4] In Germany, it tended to be economic historians who availed themselves of the data in the Getty Provenance Index, most notably the Greifswald-based economic historian Michael North, who has specialized in art collecting and the art market from a historical perspective.[5] The Getty Research Institute's own project on provenance research in Germany, which focused on the eighteenth century, was carried out between 1990 and 1999 in collaboration with the Hamburger Kunsthalle. Over the course of this research program, a total of 298 eighteenth-century auction catalogs from German-speaking countries were systematically evaluated.[6] The political configuration of eighteenth-century Germany renders research difficult in this area, as the legal context in which art trading took place varied widely from state to state. While Paris and London had hitherto generally been regarded as the principal art markets, in the eighteenth century Frankfurt and Hamburg also became players of some significance. Regrettably, the comprehensive research efforts underpinning the Getty Provenance Index coverage of the German eighteenth century are no longer ongoing, so that even today very little is known about the art trade or auction practice in Germany in the nineteenth and early twentieth centuries. Happily, research has now recommenced, at least into the most recent past. In a collaborative research project involving the Getty Research Institute, Kunstbibliothek–Staatliche Museen zu Berlin, and Universitätsbibliothek Heidelberg, details of all auction sales held in Germany, Austria, and Switzerland between 1933 and 1945 are currently being fed into the pooled data of the Provenance Index. For museums coping with the problem of illegally acquired artworks, and for their provenance research in particular, this project will provide an important database.

The politically instigated provenance research that took place in Germany itself following the Washington agreement (1998) was confined to the post-1933 period and as a rule focused on specific individual cases. Here it was usually important to research the history of individual works of art in minute detail, as fine nuances might often prove decisive in determining whether a sale really had resulted from persecution and therefore warranted recommending restitution. The museums' first priority was to create a preliminary overview of acquisitions made between 1933 and 1945; their second priority was to review all purchases from 1945 to the present, as it was always possible that owners further back had sold under the pressures of persecution. To this end, the museums combed methodically through the entire inventory of acquisitions they had made since the National Socialists seized power in 1933. However, museums focused attention only on those cultural assets that gave grounds for suspecting that a sale had been motivated by persecution. In the long run, this meant that the provenance research was limited to a small number of artworks, leaving no prospect of comprehensive knowledge or of comparable data for research purposes. In most museums, moreover, the research was purely reactive. On receipt of a restitution claim, a museum would be required to respond by endeavoring to establish the precise provenance of the work in question.

In some cases, the major German museums would engage specialists on fixed-term contracts to carry out provenance research, though they were always motivated either by fear of restitution claims and/or by the directives imposed by the Washington agreement. A provenance research working group would meet regularly to exchange and review relevant experience. Alongside the institutional research activity at the museums, a new development occurred: a free-market research scene arose, with active participants either hired by the museums to resolve particular provenance issues or commissioned by lawyers acting on behalf of restitution applicants. This latter type of research was often driven by substantial monetary expectations on the part of the lawyers, who take a percentage of the subsequent sale proceeds. For this reason, the resulting research scenario had closer affinities with the work of private detective agencies than with conventional research, which has an ethos of maximum objectivity and broad focus. Research undertaken hitherto, whether on behalf of the restitution claimants or on behalf of the museums, has often been merely reactive actionism, a series of responses to fresh restitution demands and continuing heavy political pressure. The expectation is generally that research will produce unambiguous findings that ideally will dictate a solution. In reality, this often proves impossible because the precise details of provenance between 1933 and 1945 cannot be definitively ascertained, and because the issue of restitution ultimately needs to be decided on ethical and political criteria.

As there is no routinely available arbitration panel to help with difficult cases—the so-called Limbach Commission proposed in the Berlin Declaration has been invoked only a few times to date and lacks the power to do more than recommend—the research must be worked through again and again for the benefit of a media-led public that chooses to subsume the complex and difficult field of persecution-motivated property losses under the one-word headline "Raubkunst" (looted art) and that obstructs rational debate. Since only public museums are affected by restitution claims, decisions on artwork restitution usually end up with politically affiliated administrators occupying what is effectively a museum trustee role. However, subcommittees of municipal councils or state legislatures have become increasingly involved in discussions of these cases, because in property disputes where more than a certain sum is at stake the normal practice is for the final decision to rest with the legislature, and any decision in favor of restitution amounts to putting public property back in private hands.

Inventory Issues

The findings from provenance research enhance the data resources and state of knowledge relating to individual works of art. Provenance is often included in the record when cultural assets are listed. In Germany, however, standards in modern inventory listings are extremely variable, since there are still no national quality standards governing this fundamental museum work. While initially the HiDA inventory system, developed in collaboration with the Bildarchiv Foto Marburg at the Philipps-Universität Marburg, found widespread acceptance, a large number of museums subsequently opted for a motley range of inventory programs. Those adopted in Germany included, for instance, MuseumPlus, Primus, Faust, and IMDAS-Pro—among many others. Alongside the listing process and as a result of ongoing technological advances, digitization of the holdings came to play an increasingly important role. Computer programs often have a useful life of no more than a few years, while libraries commit to their chosen systems at widely varying points in time, often going through expensive and long, drawn-out decision-making processes before settling on their own local software solution. At present, there is no easy way to compare systems, and only very limited facilities exist for networking data. The transfer of knowledge is thus impeded, and the exchange of information relating to collections and collectors—which are of major importance, for example, in the provenance research found in the Getty Provenance Index—is consequently almost impossible. There are only isolated instances of efforts to standardize how information is stored: one example is the German *Land* (state) of Baden-Württemberg, where all state museums and several major municipally run museums use the IMDAS-Pro inventory system under the guidance of a state-owned research institute, the MuSIS museum information system administered by the Konstanz-based Baden-Württemberg

Bibliotheksservicezentrum (Library services center), which is responsible for standardization and compatibility of the data held. Generally speaking, it has been the exception rather than the rule that central funding at *Land* level be made available for these concerns. One exception is the Daphne research project linked to the Staatliche Kunstsammlungen Dresden: this project, supported by the Free State of Saxony with a subvention of 15 million euros, made it possible to engage sixty scholars, who will have the task of systematically documenting the entire art holdings of the Dresden museums. However, the project has been based on a specially devised inventory program,[7] which means that yet another chance to establish compatibility has been lost. Even so, in a few years' time, the Staatliche Kunstsammlungen Dresden will be among the handful of German museums to have compiled a systematic scholarly catalog of their entire collection of artworks and to be able to provide information on the provenance of a work of art. However, the restitution claims arising out of the period from 1933 to 1945 are by no means the only issue at stake here in Dresden: much more substantial issues arise from the claims put forward by former princes and royal houses, and from the loss of works seized and removed by the Soviet military after 1945 and held to this day by Russian museums.

The Global Perspective

The relatively backward state of research in Germany, its disparateness and lack of coordination, grow ever more apparent as global standards are increasingly applied. When Internet companies such as Google take over the field of artworks, providing documentation and precise locations, as is now the case in the Museo del Prado in Madrid, or the field of libraries, with book holdings and, in some cases, the complete text made available on the Internet, museums relinquish the power to determine for themselves how listing and documentation are handled. The Europeana project may be regarded as a European riposte to the global endeavors of Google. Looking at the unitary polities within the European community, such as the policies of France and the United Kingdom, the work of digitally encoding the entire cultural record is much further advanced than in Germany, to the extent that the first moves can now be made toward pan-European or even global networking. One outcome is the Europeana project, under which books and physical artworks are to be made universally available by way of the Internet. Aside from legal issues—the two issues of most concern to the museums being reproduction rights for artwork and data protection of ownership details—the problem that now has to be faced is feeding holdings that have been listed using different programs into a new common database.

Center for Provenance Research and Coordination Office for Lost Cultural Assets

Under Germany's federal structure, support for culture has, for all practical purposes, devolved to the *Länder* (federal states) and municipal authorities. This prevents the establishment of national standards and any buildup of cooperation between *Länder,* as each *Land* follows its own rules. While it is true that a Federal Commissioner for Culture and the Media (Bundesbeauftragte für Kultur und Medien), with headquarters in the Federal Chancellery itself, has existed since 1998 and enjoys a measure of policy control nationwide, efforts made so far to strengthen provenance research have been only modest. Since 2008, the Bundesbeauftragte für Kultur und Medien has indeed been supporting the Arbeitsstelle für Provenienzforschung (Center for Provenance Research), which is located in the Institut für Museumskunde der Stiftung Preussischer Kulturbesitz (Institute of Museum Studies, Prussian Cultural Heritage Foundation) and is responsible for helping German museums individually in matters of provenance research. This program is supported by a grant of one million euros per year. All German museums are free to apply for funding from this budget for provenance research expressly aimed at clarifying the status of post-1933 acquisitions. The program was initiated primarily as a response to numerous complaints from smaller and midsized, municipally owned museums whose curators had pointed out again and again that the Berlin Declaration requirements with regard to proactive provenance research could for the most part not be fulfilled with their existing resources.[8] Simultaneously, and following the restitution, from the Brücke-Museum in Berlin, of Ernst Ludwig Kirchner's 1913 painting *Berlin Street Scene,* and its sale at auction a few months after the restitution for 38 million dollars, a debate on current restitution practice took off. The debate has continued; it was given fresh impetus in 2009 by remarks made by Norman Rosenthal calling for an end to restitutions.[9]

Essentially, there has been no change in restitution practice in Germany since the Joint Declaration of 1999, but the audit of holdings is proceeding at an extremely slow pace. The museums and their sponsoring bodies still have no basis in established property law for transactions involving restitution of artworks, as such restitutions continue to be based solely on the Joint Declaration and on a chain of precedents leading back to the same source.[10]

American museums faced with restitution claims have accordingly switched to a proactive role, filing actions in American courts aimed at securing their ownership rights.

Back in 2001, the German federal government and state governments together set up the Koordinierungsstelle für Kulturverluste (Coordination Office for Lost Cultural Assets) in Magdeburg, which is similarly intended to provide assistance both to museums and to restitution applicants in the course of its provenance researches. In addition, a series of academic papers and conferences have disseminated new knowledge and new questions; one example was the conference "Provenance research in German art museums: an international comparison."[11] The Coordination Office offers the Lost Art Internet Database as a platform both for holdings of works of art confiscated in the context of National Socialist persecution and for others that were lost or looted from museums during the upheavals caused by the Second World War. This register is thus more a listing of lost and nonassigned art than a platform for provenance research.[12] The Staatliche Kunstsammlungen Dresden alone has entered more than 10,000 items in this database, most of them missing since World War II. The Lost Art Internet platform brings home the point that in Germany the constantly reiterated property rights in works of art that went missing from German museums during World War II, which are stored for the most part in archives and museums on former Soviet Union territory, must be seen from the same perspective as the recognition of restitution claims relating to property once owned by Jews.

Historical Provenance Research

An interest in the history of specific artworks is a phenomenon that can be traced all the way back to the Renaissance. Initially, it reflected the need to document a work's originality. As the academic study of art became professionalized during the second half of the nineteenth century, research on historical source material rose to full recognition, alongside connoisseurship, as a scholarly resource for analyzing an artwork's authenticity and historical importance. Theoretically, on this basis, an artwork can be traced back from the present to the time of its creation. Apart from enabling originality to be proven, research along these lines would also illuminate the history of a work's reception, thus opening up exciting new avenues for research in the history of culture. A major turning point in provenance research occurred in 1873 with the debate over the two Holbein Madonnas. For many years, Hans Holbein the Younger's *Madonna of Mayor Meyer* of 1526 (Dresden) had been believed to be the original. Only after close comparison with its counterpart at the

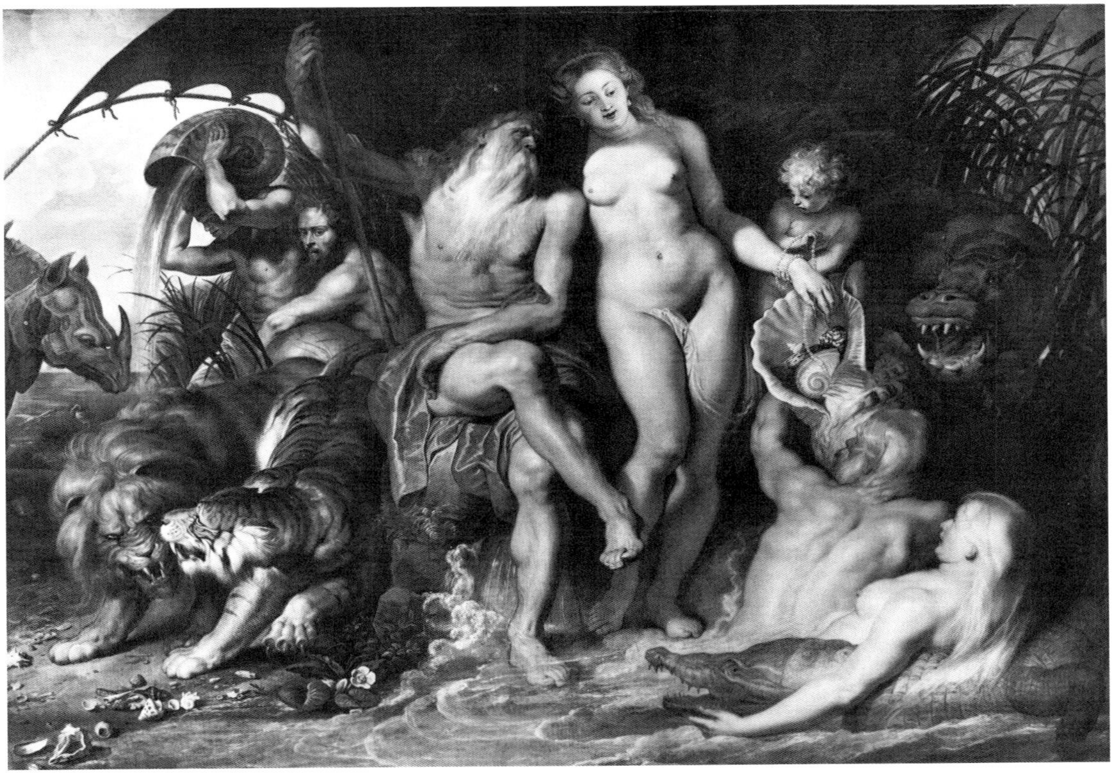

Fig. 1.
Peter Paul Rubens (Flemish, 1577–1640).
Neptune and Amphitrite, ca. 1620, oil on canvas, 230 × 305 cm (90⅝ × 120⅛ in.). Probably destroyed in 1945; formerly: Berlin, Gemäldegalerie.
The issue of provenance played an important role in the debate over the work's authenticity.

Schlossmuseum Darmstadt and analysis of the provenances did it emerge that the Darmstadt painting (today, Schwäbisch Hall, Sammlung Würth, Johanniterhalle) was in fact the original and the Dresden painting a copy by Bartholomäus Sarburgh (Dresden, Gemäldegalerie Alte Meister).[13] The controversy over the Peter Paul Rubens painting *Neptune and Amphitrite* (fig. 1), acquired for the Berlin Gemäldegalerie by Wilhelm von Bode in 1881, followed a similar pattern.[14] The attribution to Rubens was disputed by critics, especially in artistic circles, and a lengthy debate over the picture's authenticity ensued. It took a rigorously conducted study of the painting's provenance to establish beyond doubt that it was in fact a Rubens.[15] The issue of the authenticity of artworks also led to the first petition for a common standard at the First International Congress on the academic study of art, held in Vienna in 1873: agreement was reached on standards to be observed in the cataloging and exhibiting of artworks—including a requirement that provenances, complete with source documentation, should be supplied.[16] It needs to be noted that these early examples also constitute evidence that provenance research was often undertaken only in response to pressure—in other words, when arguments based on connoisseurship had failed.

Even so, the slowly awakening interest in the origins and history of artworks led to the inclusion, in the majority of late-nineteenth- and early-twentieth-century collection catalogs, of information on the provenance of the works listed, though such information was never given a standardized format. The Berlin museums, whose collection catalogs set standards for others to follow, took the lead and provided a firm foundation for later scholarly publications. The index for the Berlin Gemäldegalerie, first compiled in 1830, includes some early guidance as to the works' origins; however, this is confined to indicating the broad sources from which the gallery's pictures came. By contrast, the collection catalogs from 1870 onward include precise information on provenance. Remarkably, catalogs of the post-1945 period fall short of this standard: they fail to further expand knowledge and the availability of information. In fact, the origin of new acquisitions after 1945 was often left entirely open; the then-current level of information was reduced, with the result that research can produce significant new knowledge only if it is based on older catalogs. For example, the provenance of Albrecht Dürer's *Portrait of Jacob Muffel* (fig. 2) is reported in detail in the catalog published in 1906, but compilers of the Gemäldegalerie's index in 1968 merely noted that the picture had been "acquired in 1883" and had been transferred from a wooden panel to canvas in 1870.[17] The fact that the painting had come from the Gräflich Schönbornsche collection at Pommersfelden no longer seemed worthy of mention. The practice of neglecting provenance information in museum catalogs went hand in hand with the ignorant way that auction catalogs themselves were handled: in many cases, they were not systematically preserved, and they were not always correctly entered in library catalogs. However, as part of a collaborative research and digitization project undertaken by several organizations, an inventory of German sales catalogs for the period 1930–45 is now being assembled, and representative catalogs are being scanned by the Universitätsbibliothek Heidelberg. The Getty Provenance Index will maintain a database of the results and provide online access to all the relevant catalog information.These catalogs often include handwritten annotations that may supply valuable research evidence.

For the Getty Provenance Index's research on eighteenth-century auction catalogs, a project the Getty undertook in the 1990s, the special challenge was to trace the few catalogs still preserved. The potential importance of catalog annotations as a research source met with little interest in Germany outside the context of the Getty Provenance Index project.

Most notably, the role of Germany in the art trade overall was underrated and misunderstood. In the 1990s, there was some astonishment over the results

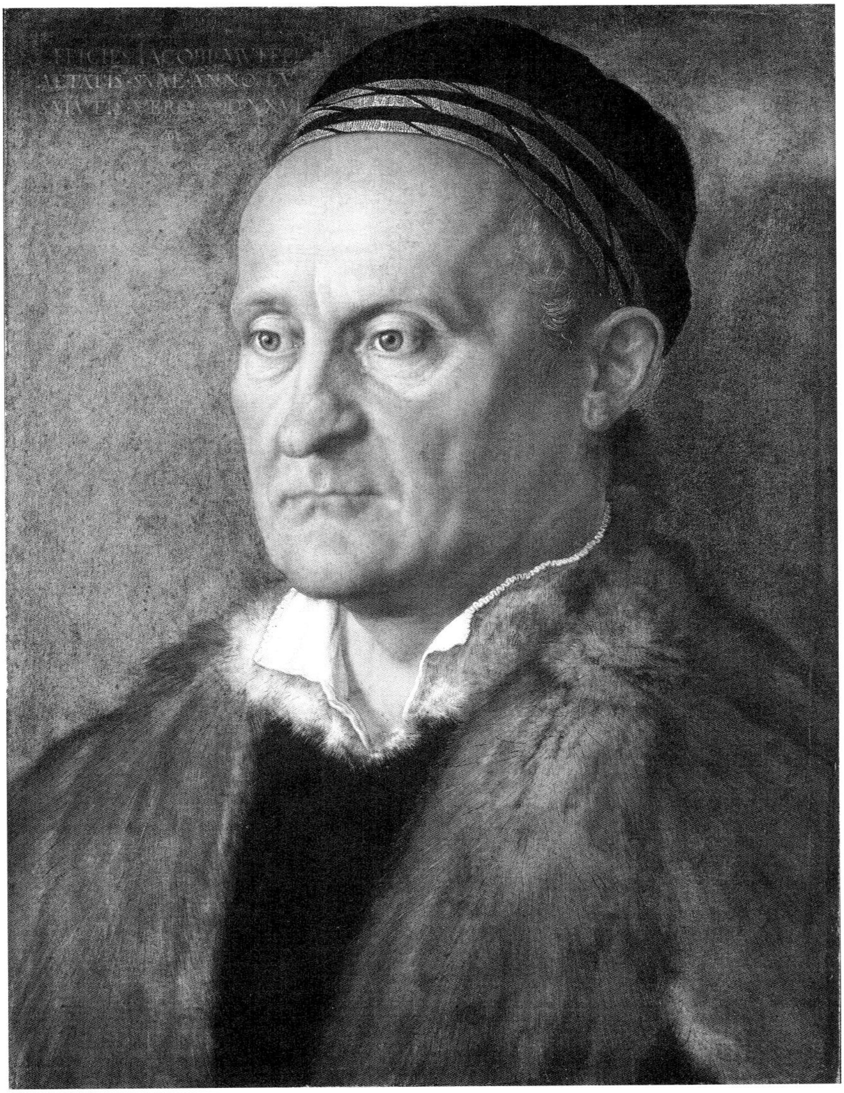

Fig. 2.
Albrecht Dürer (German, 1471–1528).
Portrait of Jacob Muffel, 1526, oil on canvas, 48 × 36 cm (19 × 14¼ in.). Berlin, Gemäldegalerie, Staatliche Museen zu Berlin.

of the research project on the eighteenth century, which documented the intensive trading activity on the Hamburg and also Frankfurt art markets.[18] Dealing remained extremely brisk on the Hamburg market through the early part of the nineteenth century, with many French collections being diverted there for auction because of the political situation in France. After 1870, the Berlin art trade grew in importance; auctions were frequent, and substantial quantities of art changed hands. It is regrettable that research efforts so far have focused on post-1933 auctions: study of auction activity throughout the preceding period will make an essential contribution to comprehensive provenance research.

Concluding Observations

It is natural to wonder why there was virtually no sign of provenance research, and no advocacy of such research, in the first postwar years from 1945 onward and in the early years of the Federal Republic. Given that unresolved ownership issues and claims for restitution were anticipated in connection with at least some of the works concerned, one explanation that cannot be discounted is that there was a conscious intent to veil the origins of artworks. In the first few years after the war ended, representatives of former owners could still demand the return of their artworks under normal property law. In light of this possibility, silence might often have seemed the best policy, at least until the statutory period of limitations expired. Yet, at the same time, German museums were working to restore losses suffered under the National Socialists' Entartete Kunst (degenerate art) campaign; they were once again buying up classical modernist works, including expressionist ones. Most acquisitions were made without asking about a work's provenance; indeed, provenance was generally left unresearched even after acquisition. Until just a few years ago, auction catalogs of the major art dealers in Germany—and abroad—continued to provide only sparse information on the origins of the artworks described.

In addition to a lack of interest—either consciously or subconsciously generated by the instinct to obscure over the past—another important factor came into play. Art history had lost a higher proportion of trained personnel than virtually any other discipline. Large numbers of art experts and museum curators had been forced to emigrate; today it would be called a brain drain. Between 1933 and 1945, about 250 art scholars left Germany—many of them widely recognized, even leading, figures in the academic world.[19] Many of the art historians and museum staff working during the early Federal Republic had been at their jobs during the National Socialist years, and there was little interest, after the collapse of National Socialism, in coming to terms with the past. A shortfall in basic academic research also had a significant impact. During the early years of the Federal Republic, up to the 1980s, few publishers produced new academic catalogs; for decades on end, the practice was to draw on the knowledge amassed and results achieved by the academic colleagues of the years before 1933. Any systematic stocktaking was confined mainly to documenting wartime losses—and this documentation, too, was inadequately handled for the most part. It took the advent of electronic data processing to inject some stimulus into this branch of art-historical research; hitherto, the traditional inventory books and card indexes had been continued and, at best, updated. In Germany, the first fresh impetus in inventory work came not from museums but, above all, from those working in the preservation of monuments. Memorials and monuments were systematically listed using electronic databases and staff members were told to prioritize projects with a view to their completion. While it is true that provenance research now receives more support, due to the pressure from the Washington agreement, there is reason to fear that attention will focus exclusively on the complex provenance issues of the period beginning in 1933, leaving the systematic pursuit of basic research on provenance as an unfulfilled need. Indeed, there is still a danger that a one-sided fixation with the post-1933 period and with the fortunes of individual works will preclude any comprehensive study of the provenances of cultural assets. Research for the period between 1800 and 1933 remains a gaping void. Only the systematic, well-coordinated study of provenances and related source material will at some point in the future illuminate the history of art dealing and art markets to a degree of detail not hitherto achieved for Germany.

Notes

This essay and all quoted passages were translated from the German by James Michael Loughridge.

1. *Principles of the Washington Conference with Respect to Nazi-Confiscated Art, Published in Connection with the Washington Conference on Holocaust-Era Assets, Washington, D.C., 3 December 1998.* The text is available online in English and German at http://www.lostart.de.
2. *Statement by the Federal Government, the Länder (Federal States) and the National Associations of Local Authorities on the Tracing and Return of Nazi-confiscated Art, Especially from Jewish Property* (1999); reprinted in original German in *Museumskunde* 73 (2008): 35–36.
3. Ute Haug, "Schicksale von Kunstwerken—Provenienzforschung an der Hamburger Kunsthalle," *Im Blickfeld,* 2003, 20–23.
4. Observable, for instance, at a conference held at The Hague in 1996. See Tilmann von Stockhausen, "Symposium on the Use of Archival Inventories in Art History. Den Haag, Rijksbureau voor Kunsthistorische Documentatie, 6.–9.6.1996," *Kunstchronik* 51 (1998): 58–61. The Getty Provenance Index® can be accessed online at http://www.gettty.edu/research/tools/provenance/search.html.
5. Michael North, *Das Goldene Zeitalter: Kunst und Kommerz in der niederländischen Malerei des 17. Jahrhunderts* (Cologne: Böhlau, 2001); translated by Catherine Hill as *Art and Commerce in the Dutch Golden Age* (New Haven, Conn.: Yale University Press, 1997); Michael North, "Kunstsammlungen und Geschmack im ausgehenden 18. Jahrhundert," in *Kunstsammeln und Geschmack im 18. Jahrhundert,* ed. Michael North (Berlin: Berlin Verlag A. Spitz, 2002), 85–103.
6. Tilmann von Stockhausen, "Kunstauktionen im 18. Jahrhundert: Ein Überblick über das *Verzeichnis der verkauften Gemälde im deutschsprachigen Raum vor 1800,*" *Das 18. Jahrhundert: Zeitschrift der Deutschen Gesellschaft für die Erforschung des Achtzehnten Jahrhunderts* 26 (2002): 63–78.

7. The Daphne inventory program was specially developed by the company Robotron for the Staatlichen Kunstsammlungen Dresden. See press release issued by the Staatlichen Kunstsammlungen Dresden, 1 October 2008, with the headline: "Ten years on from the Washington Declaration of 1998, in a large-scale and unique research project, the Dresden State Art Collections are researching the provenance of every artwork they hold."
8. Federal Press Office, "Provenienzforschung wird deutlich verstärkt," press release no. 436, 14 November 2007.
9. Ulrike Knöfel, "Raubkunst: Die zornige Debatte," *Der Spiegel,* 6 April 2009, 128–29 and Ulrike Knöfel, "Spiegel-Gespräch: 'Wir müssen im Heute leben': Der britische Kunstexperte Sir Norman Rosenthal, 64, über seine umstrittene Forderung, die Rückgabe von NS-Raubkunst zu stoppen, den kritischen Zustand des Kunstmarktes und seine jüdischen Wurzeln," *Der Spiegel,* 6 April 2009, 130–32.
10. *Eine Debatte ohne Ende? Raubkunst und Restitution im deutschsprachigen Raum,* 22–24 April 2007, Potsdam, Altes Rathaus; proceedings published by *H-Soz-u-Kult,* 25 May 2007; available online at http://hsozkult.geschichte.hu-berlin.de/tagungsberichte/id=1576.
11. Ulf Häder, Katja Terlau, and Ute Haug, eds., *Museen im Zwielicht: Ankaufspolitik 1933–1945, Kolloquium vom 11. und 12. Dezember 2001 in Köln / Die eigene Geschichte: Provenienzforschung an deutschen Kunstmuseen im internationalen Vergleich, Tagung vom 20. bis 22. Februar 2002 in Hamburg,* 2nd ed. (Magdeburg: Koordinierungsstelle Magdeburg, 2007).
12. See the Internet platform http://www.lostart.de. The Koordinierungsstelle (Coordination Office) is also the headquarters of the Beratende Kommission (Advisory Commission), which has powers of recommendation in connection with the return of cultural assets lost in circumstances of National Socialist persecution, especially those whose former owners were Jewish.
13. Heinrich Dilly, *Kunstgeschichte als Institution, Studien zur Geschichte einer Institution* (Frankfurt am Main: Suhrkamp, 1979), 165–68.
14. Wilhelm von Bode, *Mein Leben,* ed. Thomas W. Gaehtgens and Barbara Paul (Berlin: Nicolai, 1997), 1:80, 2:156–57.
15. Tilmann von Stockhausen, *Geschichte der Berliner Gemäldegalerie und ihrer Erwerbungspolitik 1830–1904* (Berlin: Nicolaische Verlagsbuchhandlung, 2000), 60–64.
16. Uwe Hartmann, "Provenienzforschung: Anmerkungen zu aktuellen Anforderungen an einen historischen Gegenstandsbereich," *Museumskunde* 73 (2008): 9.
17. Wilhelm von Bode, *Beschreibendes Verzeichnis der Gemälde im Kaiser-Friedrich-Museum,* 6th ed. (Berlin: G. Reimer, 1906), 105; and *Verzeichnis der ausgestellten Gemälde des 13. bis 18. Jahrhunderts im Museum Dahlem* (Berlin: Staatliche Museen, Gemäldegalerie, 1966), 42.
18. Thomas Ketelsen and Tilmann von Stockhausen, *Verzeichnis der verkauften Gemälde im deutschsprachigen Raum vor 1800: Mit einer Einführung zum Kunsthandel im 18. Jahrhundert,* 3 vols. (Munich: K. G. Saur, 2002).
19. Karen Michels, *Transplantierte Kunstwissenschaft: Deutschsprachige Kunstwissenschaft im amerikanischen Exil* (Berlin: Akademie, 1999).

UWE FLECKNER

MARKETING THE DEFAMED
On the Contradictory Use of Provenances in the Third Reich

Knowledge of the often devious paths by which an artwork has come forward through space and time, of the rank and name of its successive owners, has for centuries now constituted one of the standing resources of art history. Princely collectors added paintings, sculptures, drawings, and also illuminated manuscripts, acquired by purchase or by force of arms, to their hoard of art treasures like *spolia,* but not without indicating their provenance; collectors among the moneyed middle classes could look on every documented record of unbroken lineage as a form of letters patent, ennobling the possession by bestowing the certainty that here was the authentic work of a respected artist. And a further consideration applies: for the new owner of an artwork, the fact that it had once passed through the hands of some illustrious personage—a king, perhaps, or an artist or a scholar—was, and often still is, of greater significance than the work itself. Art-historical research, too, has benefited from archived documentation of the provenance of individual works. Scholars have used this information to tackle problems of ascription and questions relating to the history of reception, such as the contemporary and subsequent standing of an artist or an era, historical changes in tastes and preferences, the social framework in which collecting took place, and where and in what form artworks were presented.

Research into the provenance of twentieth-century collections in particular has become an important and sensitive art-historical concern.[1] As an era of dictatorships and armed conflict, the century is one of malign memory for transactions, most of them involuntary, involving artworks: in National Socialist Germany, for instance, not long after the handover of power to Adolf Hitler in 1933, Jewish collectors were forced to dispose of paintings, graphic art, sculptures, and other objets d'art, in many cases so that they could pay the so-called *Reichsfluchtsteuer* (Reich emigration tax) that was extorted from them. In the occupied territories, collections were stolen by the German forces, while works of contemporary art belonging to German museums were seized by order of the country's own government on grounds of "degeneracy," many of them to be sold abroad, some simply destroyed. Later, in the chaos surrounding the end of the war, Allied troops removed artworks from museums and repositories in Germany, sometimes as official spoils of war, sometimes for personal—and hence criminal—gain. For several decades now, researchers in international provenance have been increasingly seeking to reconstruct these historical events and to establish the whereabouts of expropriated and stolen artworks, with the object not simply of examining the injustice done when art was taken from emigrants, stolen, or captured by occupying forces but of establishing a legal basis for restitution or for compensating former owners. Items that the National Socialists confiscated from German museums on grounds of "degeneracy" have likewise been subjected to intensified research by art historians.[2]

Relative to the legal and ethical aspects of the knowledge gained through research on the art transfers—official and clandestine—of the 1930s and 1940s, it may ultimately prove a still more important outcome, from the point of view of historical scholarship, that the motives and mechanisms of totalitarian art policy are coming to light. Reich Field Marshal Hermann Goering, for instance, in the grip of collector mania, had tried to use artworks in his personal possession—many of them pilfered from various sources—to fashion himself as an art-loving Renaissance princeling; Hitler intended his museums policy, in particular the so-called *Sonderauftrag Linz* (special mission Linz), to demonstrate German cultural hegemony.[3] Yet, at the same time, the goal of suppressing modern art was to eradicate the wider impact of the denounced works and their potential to evoke the democratic past—just as ruthlessly as they eradicated political opponents or the Jewish population of Germany and occupied countries. The forced liquidation of an entire generation of contemporary works from the public holdings of German museums, which was one of the direct consequences of the National Socialist arts policy, also falls within the sphere of provenance research; however, analysis of the processes involved must go far beyond the predominantly positivist approach of the research studies published so far in this field. The task of charting the individual histories of "degenerate" artworks is still overshadowed by the forensic investigation of the circumstances of the cases involving emigrant art, stolen art, and looted art, the high market value of which has tended to make them the subject of flamboyant or even sensationalist reporting. One phenomenon that has not yet attracted the notice of art historians is the distinct interest that National Socialist enemies of modern and avant-garde art showed in the origins of the works they confiscated. This essay focuses on how the arts policy of the Third Reich handled the provenances of "degenerate" art and on the eloquent contradictions that emerge.

Provenances Pilloried

During 1937, a commission appointed by Joseph Goebbels, the Reich's minister of public enlightenment and propaganda, confiscated some 20,000 works of art from the holdings of German museums. No fewer than 1,400 painters, sculptors, and graphic artists were affected; they included such major figures as Ernst Barlach, Max Beckmann, Lovis Corinth, Otto Dix, Ernst Ludwig Kirchner, and Emil Nolde. In order to provide a legal cover for this unprecedented action, the commission—consisting of artists and art consultants of doubtful reputation—was furnished with terms of reference. In these, we can see a first indication that artworks representing modernism and the avant-garde were not simply to be gathered indiscriminately: "Acting on the express authority of the Führer, I hereby empower the President of the Reich Chamber of Art, Professor [Adolf] Ziegler, of Munich, to select for purposes of an exhibition, and to impound, such works of German decadent art in the fields of painting and sculpture since 1910 as are at present in the possession of the German Reich or of its constituent states or municipalities."[4] The sequestration order thus applied only to artworks that were no longer in private possession, having passed definitively out of the hands of artists, gallery owners, or collectors and into public ownership; paintings and sculptures that had been loaned to a museum but still belonged to private individuals or *Kunstvereine* (art societies) were not subject to confiscation; in a number of cases, such works, after having been taken away in error, were restored in response to their owners' protests. The wording of Ziegler's order also specified the program's immediate purpose: the works seized were to be subjected to defamatory public display in the *Entartete Kunst* (Degenerate art) exhibition that first opened in Munich as early as July 1937 (fig. 1). A second round of confiscations—much more extensive and also more efficiently implemented than the first—was to follow during the autumn of that year.

In contrast to the confiscation of art from Jewish collectors and the theft of artworks in the occupied countries, the Entartete Kunst program and its consequences were not criminalized after the war, neither by the Allied Control Commission nor by the legislators of the young German Federal Republic (Bundesrepublik Deutschland). Retrospectively legitimized by the National Socialist government on 31 May 1938 by a law "providing for the impoundment of products of degenerate art," the confiscations retained this status after the war, on the grounds that they had not been carried out on a racially or politically discriminatory basis and so failed to meet the legal definition of a "lawful injustice."[5] The key passage in the law's wording makes further reference to the public ownership of the confiscated works:

> Those products of degenerate art that prior to the coming into force of this law were officially impounded from museums and public collections and declared by an appointed representative of the Führer and Reich

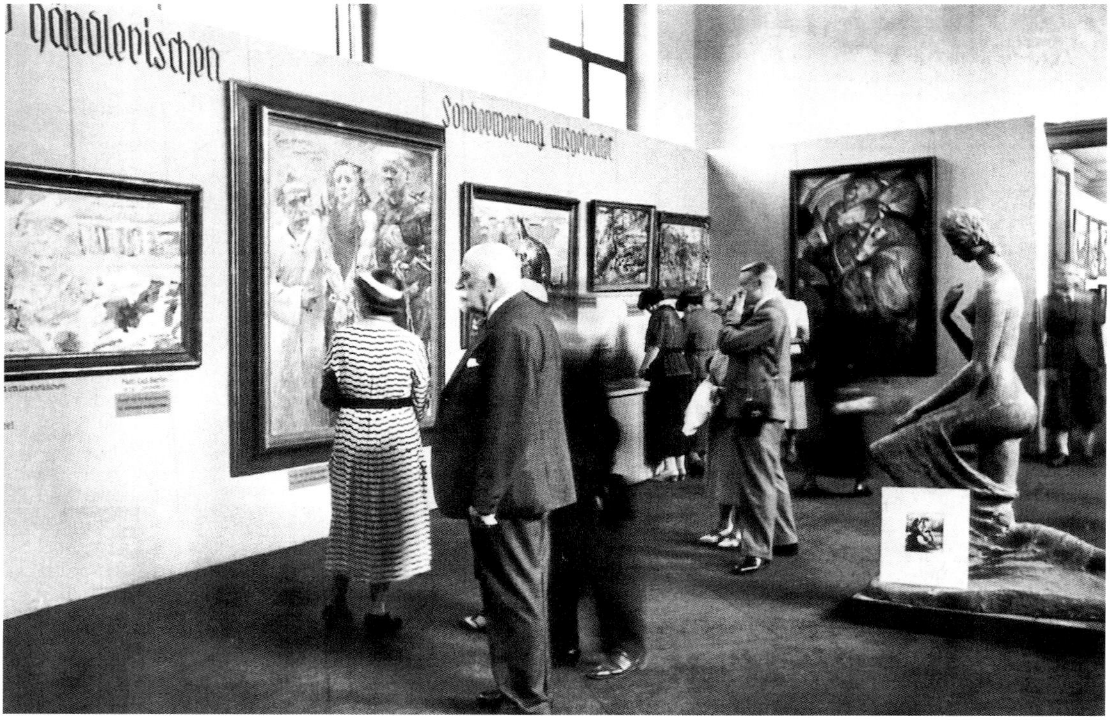

Fig. 1.
View of a room in the exhibition *Entartete Kunst*, 1937, Munich, with works by Lovis Corinth, Franz Marc, and Wilhelm Lehmbruck.
Berlin, Zentralarchiv der Staatlichen Museen zu Berlin—Preussischer Kulturbesitz.

> Chancellor to be products of degenerate art may be held for the benefit of the Reich and without compensation, provided that at the time of impoundment they were the property of Reich subjects or of legal persons within the Reich.[6]

Through these provisions, information on the provenance of an artwork that not only localized it to a museum collection but also indicated its status as public rather than private property now became the legal basis for its impoundment and defamatory display, and ultimately also for the sale of modernist works on behalf of the National Socialist government.

And that was not all. Commission members who descended on German museums in summer and autumn 1937 in order to identify and confiscate works of "degenerate" art began with provenance research, for they were instructed to document the proof of origin and circumstance of acquisition of every item sequestered. The information required was:

1. The cost at which each piece was acquired
2. The date of acquisition
3. The name of the museum curator responsible at the time.[7]

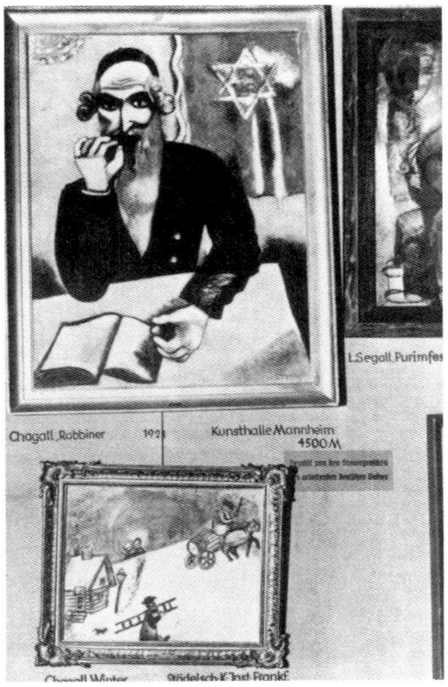

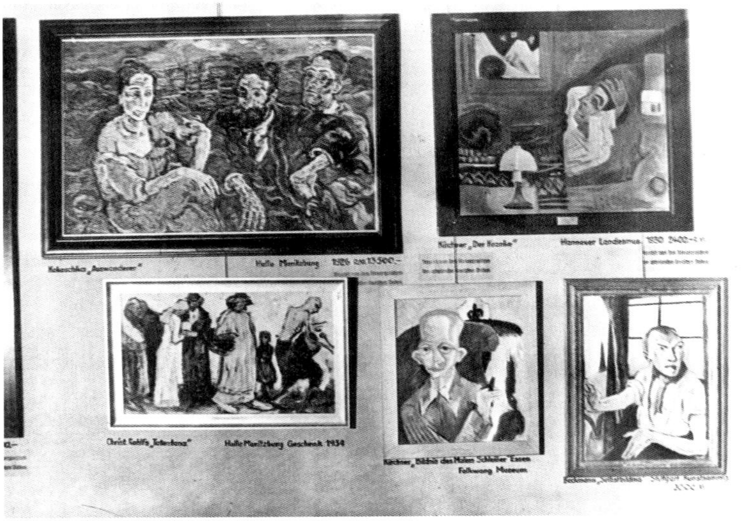

Of course, the data compiled was not intended to serve as scholarly cataloging of the work concerned: it was used solely, and perfidiously, to enable the works in question to be pilloried by the *Entartete Kunst* exhibition that first opened in Munich on 19 July 1937 and toured many towns and cities in Germany and the annexed territory of Austria up until 1941. The exhibition curators, who included the painter Adolf Ziegler, had put substantial effort into how these works would be presented. This included mixing diverse genres and media, varying display schemes (some of them pseudo-avant-garde in character), and juxtaposing artworks with slanderous quotations: devices uniformly calculated to generate a strident polemic and heap obloquy on the artworks presented.[8]

Fig. 2.
View of a wall in the exhibition *Entartete Kunst,* 1937, Munich, with works by Marc Chagall and Lasar Segall.
Berlin, Zentralarchiv der Staatlichen Museen zu Berlin—Preussischer Kulturbesitz.

Fig. 3.
View of a wall in the exhibition *Entartete Kunst,* 1937, Munich, with works by Oskar Kokoschka, Ernst Ludwig Kirchner, Christian Rohlfs, and Max Beckmann.
Berlin, Zentralarchiv der Staatlichen Museen zu Berlin—Preussischer Kulturbesitz.

In the exhibition, provenance information was usually displayed on the wall directly below the artworks and in arrestingly large type, so that the public could not fail to register which museum had bought a particular condemned work and how much it had paid (figs. 2, 3). Superficially factual in tone, in reality the notes manipulated the viewer into reacting negatively, as in the following examples: "Nolde: 'Christus und die Sünderin' Nationalgalerie Berlin 1929 M. 25.000"; "Chagall, Rabbiner 1928 Kunsthalle Mannheim 4.500 M"; "Gross 'Abenteurer' Städt[isches]. Mus[eum]. Dresden 1921 10.000 M"; "Kokoschka 'Auswanderer' Halle, Moritzburg 1926 RM 13.500."[9] In many cases, the prices noted were high figures from the inflation period, designed to elicit further aggressive responses from the viewers. For instance, the 1923 purchase price of Emil Nolde's painting *Young Oxen* (1909; Saarbrücken, Saarlandmuseum) paid by the Kaiser-Friedrich-Museum, Magdeburg, was given as 680,000 Reichsmark; Kurt Schwitters's *Merz Picture* from 1919 (location unknown) was shown as bought in 1920 by the Stadtmuseum in Dresden for 14,000 Reichsmark. Next to the price there would often be a sticker telling the visitor that the artwork had been "bought with tax revenues taken from the hard-working German people."[10] Ultimately, the aim in presenting the works to the public in this manner was, first, to insinuate that they were inferior as art and had been purchased at exorbitant cost and, second, to make it clear that the works had not been in the possession of the artists themselves, their dealers, or private collectors, but had actually been purchased by public museums—including even the modern section of the Berlin Nationalgalerie, located in the Kronprinzenpalais—and thus, in short, had received an official seal of approval.[11] The provenance information supplied in this manner deliberately brought all progressively run museums into discredit, and with them the emerging cultural identity of the Weimar Republic, the democratic state that had sanctioned the purchasing policy in the first place.

In the brochure published—although not until early 1938—to accompany the *Entartete Kunst* exhibition on tour, this particular criticism was directed

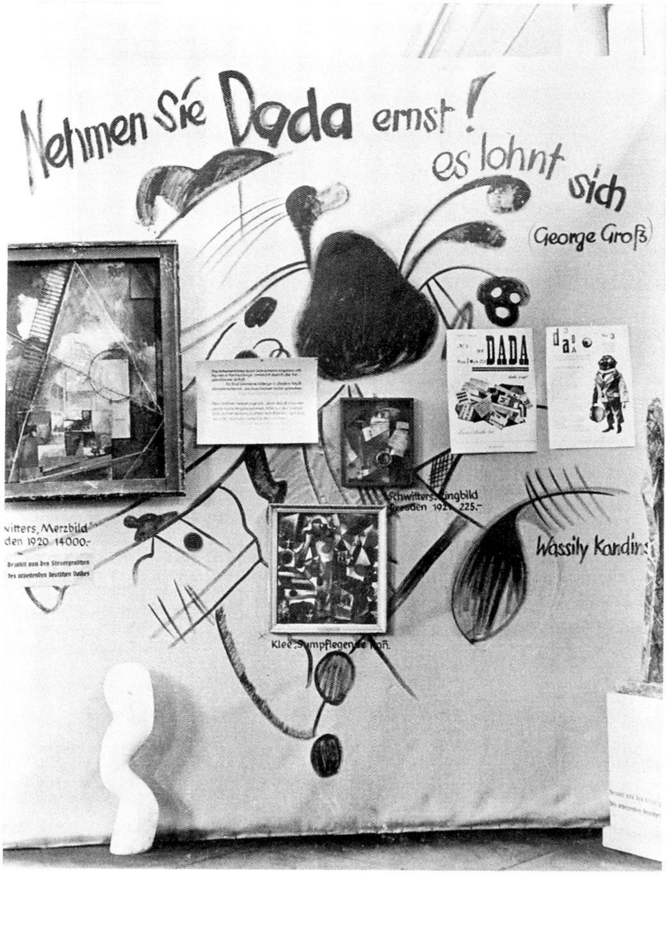

Fig. 4.
View of the "Dada wall" in the exhibition *Entartete Kunst*, 1937, Munich, with works by Kurt Schwitters and Paul Klee.
Munich, Stadtarchiv.

openly at Schwitters's *Merz Picture* (fig. 4).[12] This assemblage, a significant work, had already been made the victim of a particularly dishonest kind of exposure on the so-called Dada wall when the exhibition opened in Munich, and was held up for the scorn and mockery of the visiting public until the bitter end, at Chemnitz in 1941, the last showing of the undivided exhibition; now, in the official publication accompanying the exhibition, *Merz Picture* was ridiculed in a manner that made it impossible for the reader to view it with any degree of detachment. A banner heading designed for impact proclaimed: "Even these things were once taken seriously—and good money was paid for them!" The work was displayed next to pieces by Johannes Molzahn and Jean Metzinger, and its creator was derisively styled as an "artist" in quotation marks (fig. 5).

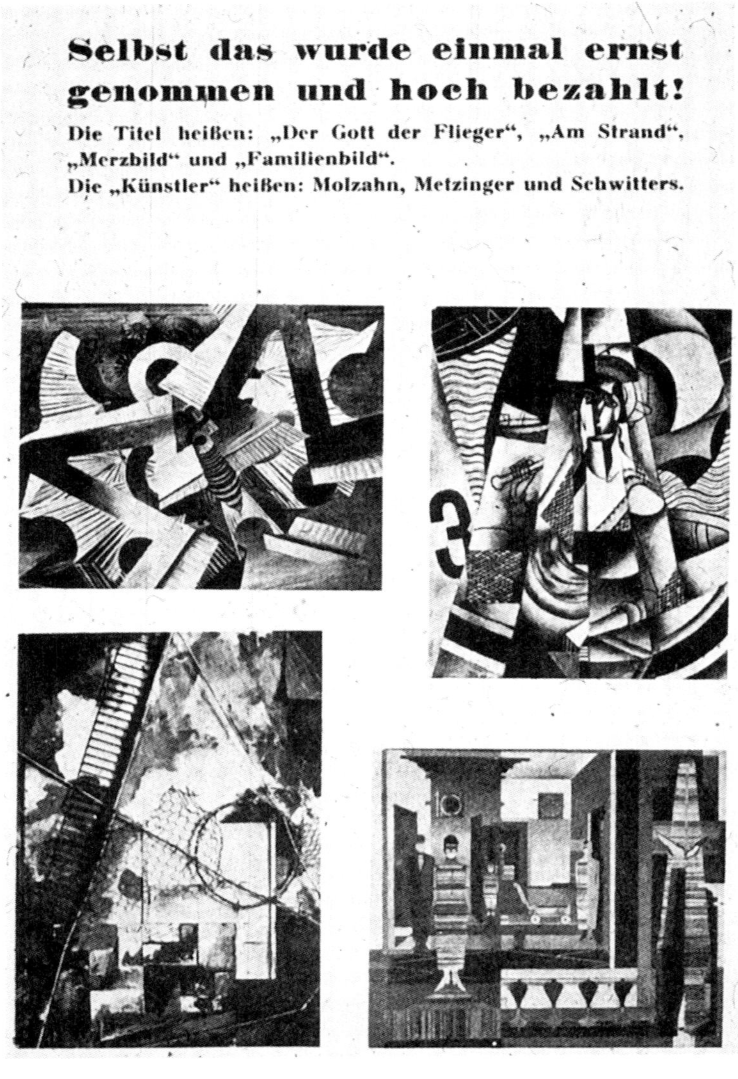
Selbst das wurde einmal ernst genommen und hoch bezahlt!

Die Titel heißen: „Der Gott der Flieger", „Am Strand", „Merzbild" und „Familienbild".
Die „Künstler" heißen: Molzahn, Metzinger und Schwitters.

Fig. 5.
Page 23 from *Führer durch die Ausstellung Entartete Kunst* (Berlin: Verlag für Kultur- und Wirtschaftswerbung, [1938]), official brochure for the touring exhibition *Entartete Kunst*, 1937–41, showing works by Johannes Molzahn, Jean Metzinger, and Kurt Schwitters.
Hamburg, Universität Hamburg, Kunsthistorisches Institut.

The detailed commentary that followed was even more venomous. Its unidentified author—thought to be Wolfgang Willrich, a failed artist and author of a 1937 polemic titled *Säuberung des Kunsttempels* (Cleansing of the art temple)—gave the entire portfolio of this category of the denounced artworks the generic title "Vollendeter Wahnsinn" (Sheer insanity). The author did not hesitate to attack Schwitters personally; although he was not actually named here, he was bound to be identified without hesitation by every reader: "From the pictures and drawings in this chamber of horrors it is usually impossible to work out what might have been envisioned by the sick mind when the hand took up brush or pencil. One of these people, by the end, would 'paint' only with what he could find in trash cans."[13] The verbal attack was intended to suggest that the artworks on view simply did not merit serious consideration and could be treated as a joke were it not for the dumbfounding fact of their provenance from German museums:

> When they reach this "Insanity" section of the exhibition, visitors generally react only with headshaking and laughter. And not without reason. However, when one stops to think that all these so-called works of art have been brought here not from dusty recesses in abandoned studios, but from the art collections and museums of the great German cities, where some of them indeed even stayed on the walls during the first few years after the seizure of power and were flaunted there to the astonishment of the contemporary public, then the laughing really stops; then one is left choking with fury at the thought that a people as decent to the core as the German people could be made the victim of such scandalous abuses.[14]

Stigma Equals Market Value

It is striking that, for all the conspicuous pains taken to sequester and subsequently exhibit the artworks in a manner suggesting respect for the rule of law, the perpetrators nevertheless were fully aware of the heinous nature of what they were doing. When the National Socialists set out to dispose of the outlawed masterpieces, in most cases abroad, with the help of four accredited art dealers—Bernhard A. Böhmer, Karl Buchholz, Hildebrand Gurlitt, and Ferdinand Möller—the order was given, significantly, that no reference should be made to the museum provenance of the paintings, graphic art, and sculptures concerned, and that any identifying marks on the works were to be removed. The directive to this effect from the Reich Ministry of Public Enlightenment and Propaganda was received by the participating dealers on 15 December 1939: "The white slips bearing inventory numbers and any stamps or labeling indicating the museum from which the works have come must be removed or rendered illegible before delivery to the prospective purchaser."[15]

However, an operation of this kind, aimed at concealing the provenance of the paintings and sculptures as they changed hands, conflicted with the revenue-raising objectives behind the planned disposal of these museum holdings. It had been explicitly established that the condemned works were to be sold abroad to raise urgently required foreign currency. The art dealers appointed to oversee the sales sometimes disobeyed this prescription; indeed, continuing into the early 1940s, they were able to find a supply of German collectors interested in their consigned goods and would also buy such works themselves. It was thus not the case—as often assumed—that the artworks brought into disrepute by the state were always to be sold off indiscriminately at knockdown prices. On the contrary, the ministry consulted in detail with a commission appointed for the "valorization" of condemned art on the prices to be obtained for specific lots. The statement of provenance was inherently a selling point in that German museums had gained worldwide and fully deserved recognition during the 1920s and early 1930s as leaders in the connoisseurship and acquisition of contemporary art; as a result, this very provenance was now needed to maximize the selling prices. Here again, the contradictory nature of National Socialist arts policy is exposed, and, as was only logical, the directive of 15 December 1939 was frequently ignored. Indeed, in one instance, probably the most significant case of disposal abroad, the state itself expressly turned the previously stigmatized provenance of the works into a selling point.

On 30 June 1939 at Galerie Fischer in the Swiss city of Lucerne, a famous—and infamous—art sale took place. It was a relatively small-scale auction with only 125 paintings and sculptures on offer, but the international resonance was considerable, albeit divided.[16] The Third Reich authorities saw this auction as an experiment designed to gauge what kind of returns might be expected, and the works put forward were accordingly of the first rank. All had been among the now-available mass of "degenerate" artworks. They included Vincent van Gogh's *Self-Portrait* (1888; Cambridge, Mass., Fogg Art Museum) and Pablo Picasso's *Acrobat and Young Harlequin* (1905; Merion, Pa., Barnes Foundation)—that is, works by non-German artists that dated from before 1910, the year specified in the sequestration edict. As expected, these works fetched the highest auction prices.[17] Even the wording chosen to announce the auction in Lucerne—"paintings and sculptures by modern masters from German museums"—advised the public of the museum provenance of the works up for auction, flagrantly disregarding the earlier order that any and all indications of the works' origins should be "removed or rendered illegible." That the works on auction were represented as being by "modern masters"

April 29, 1939 3

Fischer Gallery, Lucerne

(Switzerland)

IMPORTANT AUCTION SALES IN 1939

Auction in Lucerne June 30, 1939

PAINTINGS & SCULPTURE BY MODERN MASTERS
from GERMAN MUSEUMS

Braque, Chagall, Derain, Ensor, Gauguin, Van Gogh (Self-portrait), Laurencin, Modigliani, Matisse, Pascin, Picasso, Vlaminck, Marc, Nolde, Klee, Hofer, Rohlfs, Dix, Kokoschka, Beckmann, Pechstein, Kirchner, Hecke, Grosz, Schmidt-Rottl, Müller, Moderson, Macke, Corinth, Liebermann, Amiet, Baraud, Feininger, Levy, Lehmbruck, Mataré, Marcks, Archipenko, Barlach.

EXHIBITION in ZURICH: Zunfthaus z. Meise, May 17 to 27, 1939.

EXHIBITION in LUCERNE: Fischer Gallery, May 30 to June 29, 1939.

AUCTION in LUCERNE: Fischer Gallery, June 30, 1939.

Auction in Zurich May 10, 11, 12, 13, 1939

SPITZER COLLECTION OF PARIS
FURNITURE FROM MR. L., PARIS
PAINTINGS BY OLD & MODERN MASTERS

Furniture, tapestries, carpets, stained glass, silver, porcelain, sculpture, pewter, antiquities.

EXHIBITION in ZURICH: Zunfthaus z. Meise, April 30 to May 9, 1939.

AUCTION in ZURICH: Zunfthaus z. Meise, May 10, 11, 12, 13, 1939.

Auction in Zurich May 10, 1939

IMPORTANT ARMS AND ARMOR
FROM A WELL KNOWN AMERICAN COLLECTION
AUSTRIAN ARISTOCRACY

Gothic horse armor, complete historical suits of armor, fine guns and pistols.

EXHIBITION in ZURICH: Zunfthaus z. Meise, April 30 to May 9, 1939.

AUCTION in ZURICH: Zunfthaus z. Meise, May 10, 1939.

Separate Illustrated Catalogue

Auction in Zurich May 15, 16 & 17, 1939

LIBRARY of the PRINCE OF ESSLING
DUKE OF RIVOLI, (Part I)

Illustrated books of the XV, XVI and XVII centuries.

EXHIBITION in ZURICH: Zunfthaus z. Meise, May 10 to 14, 1939.

AUCTION in ZURICH: Zunfthaus z. Meise, May 15, 16, 17, 1939.

Auction in Lucerne August 18 & 19, 1939

Collection of The Late Dr. ROMAN ABT, Lucerne

Important religious works from the XII to the XVIII centuries. Silver collection. Mediaeval jewelry. Stained glass. Paintings by old and modern masters.

EXHIBITION in LUCERNE: Fischer Gallery, July 10 to August 17, 1939.

AUCTION in LUCERNE: Fischer Gallery, August 18 and 19, 1939.

Five Illustrated Catalogues in preparation. Price 20 Swiss Francs each. Please apply to:

FISCHER GALLERY, LUCERNE, Switzerland

Catalogues may be seen, in the near future, at the offices of The Art News, 136 East 57th Street, New York.

rather than by "art dwarfs," "art abusers," "art manufacturers," "art swindlers," and "art stutterers," as Hitler styled them, was likewise incompatible with the National Socialists' aesthetic doctrine and evidently stemmed solely from considerations of financial gain.[18]

A letter written to Joseph Goebbels on 21 October 1938 by Franz Hofmann, a senior official in the propaganda ministry and chair of the Commission for Valorization of Products of Degenerate Art, contains a revealing slip, as Hofmann uses the term *Spitzenwerke* (outstanding works) to describe some of the paintings by foreign artists that were intended for auction, thus documenting that at least some of the National Socialist spokespersons were fully aware of the artistic—as distinct from financial—value of the condemned works, irrespective of the demagogic rhetoric to the contrary.[19] In addition, a number of art trade announcements of the auction in specialist periodicals in the United States, France, and Britain openly indicated the provenance of all the works concerned from museum holdings (fig. 6), and in the auction catalog itself each lot number had a note identifying by name the previous owner of the painting or sculpture, thus ruling out any possibility that the public might remain ignorant of a work's background. American collectors and museum curators, and especially the German critic Paul Westheim, then living in exile in Paris, were prominent among the internationally respected figures from the art world who responded by calling for the auction to be boycotted.[20] The German authorities had read a draft of the catalog before it went to press and had given their explicit consent, approving not only the detailed itemization of the works and the use of some illustrations for promotional purposes but also the identification, throughout the catalog, of the public collections that had held the paintings and sculptures at the time of confiscation (fig. 7).[21] Finally, there is at least one piece of evidence to indicate that the future provenance was also of interest to the Berlin regime: on 26 June 1939, the auctioneer was notified by Karl Haberstock, art dealer and member of the valorization commission, that the authorities wished the proceedings' report to include the names of purchasers, "at least of the most important pieces."[22]

The National Socialist enemies of art had calculated correctly: the auction was the financial success that they had hoped for, and there were, even among the leftover remnants of "degenerate" art that had not been considered worth including in the special auction, a number of pieces that subsequently found their way into exile abroad—often, once the war had begun, at extremely low prices. In this way, private and public collections throughout the world were able to acquire works of early modernist and avant-garde art through a flush of sales that was never again matched for either quantity or quality. It is important to note that what ultimately rescued some works from the clutches

Fig. 6.
Advertisement for the auction *Gemälde und Plastiken moderner Meister aus deutschen Museen*, Lucerne, Galerie Fischer.
From *Art News*, 29 April 1939, 3a.
Los Angeles, Getty Research Institute.

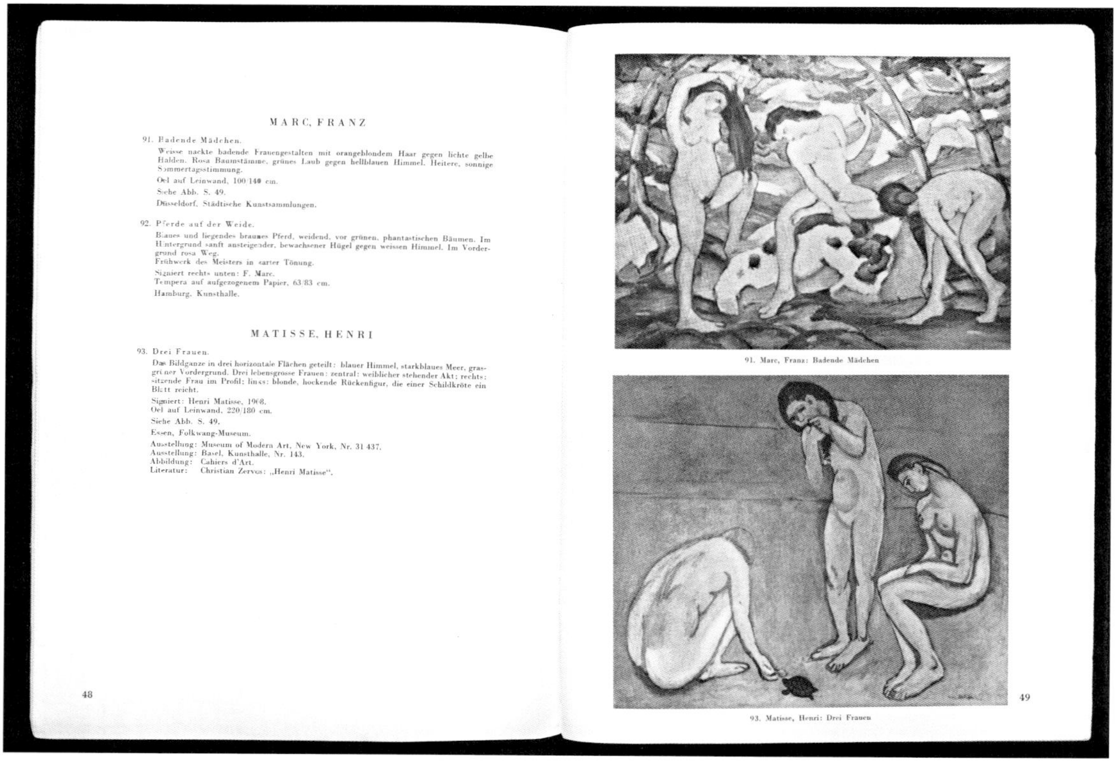

MARC, FRANZ

91. Badende Mädchen.

Weisse nackte badende Frauengestalten mit orangeblondem Haar gegen lichte gelbe Halden. Rosa Baumstämme, grünes Laub gegen hellblauen Himmel. Heitere, sonnige Sommertagsstimmung.

Oel auf Leinwand, 100/140 cm.

Siehe Abb. S. 49.

Düsseldorf, Städtische Kunstsammlungen.

92. Pferde auf der Weide.

Blaues und liegendes braunes Pferd, weidend, vor grünen, phantastischen Bäumen. Im Hintergrund sanft ansteigender, bewachsener Hügel gegen weissen Himmel. Im Vordergrund rosa Weg.
Frühwerk des Meisters in zarter Tönung.

Signiert rechts unten: F. Marc.
Tempera auf aufgezogenem Papier, 63/83 cm.

Hamburg, Kunsthalle.

MATISSE, HENRI

93. Drei Frauen.

Das Bildganze in drei horizontale Flächen geteilt: blauer Himmel, starkblaues Meer, grasgrüner Vordergrund. Drei lebensgrosse Frauen: zentral: weiblicher stehender Akt; rechts: sitzende Frau im Profil; links: blonde, hockende Rückenfigur, die einer Schildkröte ein Blatt reicht.

Signiert: Henri Matisse, 1908.
Oel auf Leinwand, 220/180 cm.

Siehe Abb. S. 49.

Essen, Folkwang-Museum.

Ausstellung: Museum of Modern Art, New York, Nr. 31 437.
Ausstellung: Basel, Kunsthalle, Nr. 143.
Abbildung: Cahiers d'Art.
Literatur: Christian Zervos: „Henri Matisse".

48

91. Marc, Franz: Badende Mädchen

93. Matisse, Henri: Drei Frauen

49

Fig. 7.
Page from the auction catalog *Gemälde und Plastiken moderner Meister aus deutschen Museen* (Lucerne: Galerie Fischer, 1939).
Los Angeles, Getty Research Institute, 84-P13730.

of the German authorities and thus saved them from the fate either of further defamation or of destruction was their market value. As early as 1939, Oskar Kokoschka, whose *Portrait of the Publisher Robert Freund* (1909; location unknown) had been slashed in his Vienna studio by the Gestapo, was wondering, at once presciently and from bitter experience: "Why don't the Swedes and Danes at least buy my pictures now in Lucerne?—to save them from destruction and oblivion, given that the one and only argument that counts in Berlin is foreign currency."[23]

In an outcome totally unintended by the National Socialist demagogues, the Entartete Kunst campaign contributed in some measure to publicizing the condemned masterpieces and thus bringing international recognition to early-twentieth-century German art. Paul Westheim was not alone in his assessment: "The auction at Fischer's in Lucerne may well help to provide so-called degenerate modern German art with the thing it has for various reasons lacked so far: market value outside Germany."[24] Today, almost one hundred works from that auction are still preserved, as are a large number of confiscated pieces that were disposed of in other ways or bartered against old masters. Most of the rescued paintings, sculptures, and graphic works are now once again universally accessible in public galleries in Germany and elsewhere. And for twelve of the works auctioned at Lucerne, the story of their provenance actually came full circle after the war, when they were returned to those same museums that had once had the courage to buy them as exemplars of the vibrant art production of the time.[25]

The Schizophrenia of National Socialist Policy on the Arts

The chasm of contradiction running through the Third Reich's arts policy is deep and wide: the National Socialists defamed modern art yet systematically arranged for the confiscated artworks to be sold to foreign collectors and museums at the highest possible prices. And no ideological chicanery could help conceal that glaring inconsistency. The National Socialist leadership found itself in a schizophrenic situation vis-à-vis the works it had so scorned and derided, obliged to communicate to the German public that the works were worthless while placing a high valuation on the same works when negotiating with accredited art dealers and their clients, foreign gallery owners, and museum curators. It was under these constraints that Franz Hofmann wrote, in a letter from December 1939, to the dealers commissioned to handle the disposal of the "degenerate" artworks: "The paintings, sculptures and graphic works placed in your hands for sale on the basis of offers made or as consigned goods are products of 'decadent art' and have been categorically rejected and rooted out as 'degenerate' by the German Reich. Accordingly, any indication of a positive view of these items on Reich territory in the form of exhibition etc. must be rigorously avoided."[26] The chairperson of the valorization commission evidently felt that one strong argument for viewing the works positively would be the presence of any evidence of their distinguished provenance: his letter urged—in a passage already quoted—that all such identifying marks should be obliterated. The Third Reich's remarkable handling of the provenance issue in relation to condemned artworks reflects the inherent contradiction between malice and marketing, which in this context appears to be a simple clash between ideology and profit: "For purposes of sale abroad the commercial aspect takes priority, regardless of the different view taken in Germany."[27]

Even after 1937, with the party's internal dissensions over policy in the visual arts seeming to have been broadly resolved, the National Socialists did not have anything approaching a defined party line on aesthetic issues. The actual sequestering followed no consistent principles; how works were removed might in practice take any form, ranging from a furtive raid to a state-regulated bureaucratic procedure. The inclusion of individual painters and sculptors within the definition of "degenerate" artists was subject to constant review and amendment; several works had to be withdrawn from the

Munich exhibition after it had opened, and the exhibition itself used modern and avant-garde modes of presentation to defame precisely those art forms. The ostensibly rock-hard ideological rejection of modernism likewise proves, on inspection, to contain its share of inconsistencies. For example, some leading National Socialists continued until far into the 1930s to seriously consider whether expressionism, as a supposedly Nordic-Germanic art, could serve their political aims. Adolf Hitler believed art was his vocation, and there are good reasons to argue that his invective represented the obsessive grudge harbored by a failed painter against the envied figures of an art scene from which he had been excluded. This view appears to be substantiated by the way he stereotyped and denounced the "whole art and culture babble of cubists, futurists, and Dadaists."[28] Time and again, Hitler felt compelled to renew his vituperative attacks on early-twentieth-century art, and he appears to have had a true love-hate relationship with Dadaism in particular.[29]

From a broader perspective, the very irrationalism invoked by Hitler and his National Socialist Party comrades ("Art is a sublime mission and demands fanaticism") is wholly incompatible with the cold-blooded financial calculation behind the marketing of the condemned works to foreign collectors and museums.[30] In light of historical events, the dictum of the Reich chancellor on art and policy can be recognized as pure demagoguery, its rhetoric cut to the ground by the market-aware rationality of the program of selling off "degenerate" artworks. That the National Socialist authorities could impound paintings, sculptures, and graphic art from German museums as allegedly worthless products of cultural decay and then proceed to sell these artifacts while—at least in several important instances—achieving high market value by citing their provenance may itself serve as evidence of the fundamental incoherence of the Third Reich's policies on art and culture.

Notes

This essay and all quoted passages were translated from the German by James Michael Loughridge.

1. See Nancy H. Yeide, Konstantin Akinsha, and Amy Walsh, *The AAM Guide to Provenance Research* (Washington, D.C.: American Association of Museums, 2001); and *Vitalizing Memory: International Perspectives on Provenance Research* (Washington, D.C.: American Association of Museums, 2005).
2. See Uwe Fleckner, ed., *Das verfemte Meisterwerk: Schicksalswege moderner Kunst im "Dritten Reich,"* Schriften der Forschungsstelle "Entartete Kunst" (Berlin: Akademie, 2009). This volume of essays was produced under the aegis of the Forschungsstelle "Entartete Kunst" (Freie Universität Berlin and Universität Hamburg); since 2003 the center has focused on the study of National Socialist

policy in the arts and has started to compile a full index of the approximately 20,000 sequestered artworks.

3. See Birgit Schwarz, *Hitlers Museum: Die Fotoalben "Gemäldegalerie Linz," Dokumente zum "Führermuseum"* (Vienna: Böhlau, 2004); Hanns Christian Löhr, *Das Braune Haus der Kunst: Hitler und der "Sonderauftrag Linz"; Visionen, Verbrechen, Verluste* (Berlin: Akademie, 2005).
4. Quoted in Peter-Klaus Schuster, ed., *Nationalsozialismus und "Entartete Kunst": Die "Kunststadt" München 1937*, 3rd ed. (Munich: Prestel, 1988), 219; cf. Christoph Zuschlag, *"Entartete Kunst": Ausstellungsstrategien im Nazi-Deutschland* (Worms: Wernersche Verlagsgesellschaft, 1995), 178, doc. 18.
5. See Carl-Heinz Heuer, "Die eigentumsrechtliche Problematik der 'entarteten' Kunst: Ein Fall 'gesetzlichen Unrechts?'" in Uwe Fleckner, Andreas Hüneke, and Christoph Zuschlag, *Forschungsstelle "Entartete Kunst,"* descriptive brochure, Freie Universität Berlin and Universität Hamburg, 2004, n.p.
6. Quoted in Zuschlag, *"Entartete Kunst,"* 207, doc. 30.
7. See Uwe Fleckner, "Montierte Reproduktionen—demontierte Kunst: Nationalsozialistische Versuche, die Avantgarden mit avantgardistischen Mitteln zu schlagen," *Fotogeschichte: Beiträge zur Geschichte und Ästhetik der Fotografie* 123 (2012): 63–73.
8. Quoted in Schuster, *Nationalsozialismus und "Entartete Kunst,"* 219; cf. Zuschlag, *"Entartete Kunst,"* 178, doc. 18.
9. The works in question here are: Emil Nolde's *Christ and the Sinner* (1926; private collection; formerly Berlin, Nationalgalerie); Marc Chagall's *The Pinch of Snuff* or *Rabbi* (1912; Basel, Kunstmuseum; formerly Mannheim, Kunsthalle); George Grosz's *The Adventurer* (1916; location unknown; formerly Dresden, Stadtmuseum); and Oskar Kokoschka's *The Emigrants* (1916–17; Munich, Pinakothek der Moderne; formerly Halle, Städtisches Museum für Kunst und Kunstgewerbe).
10. Quoted in Mario-Andreas von Lüttichau, "'Deutsche Kunst' und 'Entartete Kunst': Die Münchner Ausstellungen von 1937," in *Nationalsozialismus und "Entartete Kunst": Die "Kunststadt" München 1937*, 3rd ed., ed. Peter-Klaus Schuster (Munich: Prestel, 1988), 83–118, 104. The sticker can be seen in many documentary photographs taken of the exhibition.
11. On the fate of the contemporary art collection housed in the Nationalgalerie, see Annegret Janda and Jörn Grabowski, eds., *Kunst in Deutschland 1905–1937: Die verlorene Sammlung der Nationalgalerie im ehemaligen Kronprinzen-Palais*, exh. cat. (Berlin: Gebr. Mann, 1992).
12. See Uwe Fleckner, "Sie nahmen Dada ernst: Das 'Merzbild' von Kurt Schwitters und seine Inszenierungen als Werk 'entarteter' Kunst," in *Das verfemte Meisterwerk: Schicksalswege moderner Kunst im "Dritten Reich,"* Schriften der Forschungsstelle "Entartete Kunst," ed. Uwe Fleckner (Berlin: Akademie, 2009), 75–101.
13. Anonymous, *Führer durch die Ausstellung Entartete Kunst* (Berlin: Verlag für Kultur- und Wirtschaftswerbung, [1938]), 22.
14. Anonymous, *Führer durch die Ausstellung Entartete Kunst*, 22.

15. Franz Hofmann to Ferdinand Möller, 15 December 1939; quoted in Eberhard Roters, *Galerie Ferdinand Möller: Die Geschichte einer Galerie für Moderne Kunst in Deutschland, 1917–1956* (Berlin: Gebr. Mann, 1984), 174; cf. Paul Ortwin Rave, *Kunstdiktatur im Dritten Reich* (Berlin: Gebr. Mann, 1949), 66.
16. See Stefan Frey, "Die Auktion der Galerie Fischer in Luzern am 30: Juni 1939—ein Ausverkauf der Moderne?," in *Überbrückt: Ästhetische Moderne und Nationalsozialismus; Kunsthistoriker und Künstler, 1925–1937,* ed. Eugen Blume and Dieter Scholz (Cologne: Walther König, 1999), 275–89; and Gesa Jeuthe, "Die Moderne unter dem Hammer: Zur 'Verwertung' der 'entarteten' Kunst durch die Luzerner Galerie Fischer 1939," in *Angriff auf die Avantgarde: Kunst und Kunstpolitik im Nationalsozialismus,* Schriften der Forschungsstelle "Entartete Kunst," ed. Uwe Fleckner (Berlin: Akademie, 2007), 189–305.
17. The Picasso painting came from the Städtische Galerie, Wuppertal; the painting by Van Gogh was taken from the Neue Staatsgalerie in Munich on 27 March 1938, having been selectively targeted because it was expected to fetch a high price; see Stephanie Barron, ed., *Degenerate Art: The Fate of the Avant-Garde in Nazi Germany* (Los Angeles: Los Angeles County Museum of Art, 1991), 140; and Gesa Jeuthe, "'... der arme Vincent!': Van Goghs Selbstbildnis von 1888 und die 'Verwertung' der 'entarteten' Kunst," in *Das verfemte Meisterwerk: Schicksalswege moderner Kunst im "Dritten Reich,"* Schriften der Forschungsstelle "Entartete Kunst," ed. Uwe Fleckner (Berlin: Akademie, 2009), 445–62.
18. Adolf Hitler, "'Programmatische Kulturrede des Führers': Rede zur Eröffnung der Großen Deutschen Kunstausstellung in München" [1937], in *Reden zur Kunst- und Kulturpolitik: 1933–1939,* ed. Robert Eikmeyer (Frankfurt am Main: Revolver, 2004), 123–43, 128, 132, 141; cf. "Adolf Hitler weiht den Tempel für wahre und ewige deutsche Kunst," *Völkischer Beobachter,* 19 July 1937, 1–4.
19. Franz Hofmann to Joseph Goebbels, 21 October 1938; quoted in Jeuthe, "Die Moderne unter dem Hammer," 285.
20. See Paul Westheim, "Bilderraub," *Die neue Weltbühne* 35 (1939): 559–62; Paul Westheim, "Auktion in Luzern," *Die neue Weltbühne* 35 (1939): 758–59; Paul Westheim, "Propaganda für 'Entartete,'" *Die neue Weltbühne* 35 (1939): 871–74.
21. See Jeuthe, "Die Moderne unter dem Hammer," 289.
22. Karl Haberstock to Theodor Fischer, 26 June 1939; quoted in Frey, "Die Auktion der Galerie Fischer," 281.
23. Oskar Kokoschka to Joseph Paul Hodin, summer 1939; quoted in Georg Kreis, *"Entartete" Kunst für Basel: Die Herausforderung von 1939* (Basel: Wiese, 1990), 30; cf. Christina Feilchenfeldt, "'... meine Bilder zerschneidet man schon in Wien': Das Porträt des Verlegers Robert Freund von Oskar Kokoschka," in *Das verfemte Meisterwerk: Schicksalswege moderner Kunst im "Dritten Reich,"* ed. Uwe Fleckner (Berlin: Akademie, 2009), 259–79.
24. Westheim, "Propaganda für 'Entartete,'" 871.
25. See Jeuthe, "Die Moderne unter dem Hammer," 250 and 282–83.
26. Franz Hofmann to Ferdinand Möller, 15 December 1939; quoted in Roters, *Galerie Ferdinand Möller,* 174.
27. Roters, *Galerie Ferdinand Möller,* 174.

28. Adolf Hitler, "'Kunst verpflichtet zur Wahrhaftigkeit': Rede auf der Kulturtagung des Parteitags der NSDAP in Nürnberg" [1934], in *Reden zur Kunst- und Kulturpolitik: 1933–1939,* ed. Robert Eikmeyer (Frankfurt am Main: Revolver, 2004), 63–79, esp. 74; see also, for example, Adolf Hitler, "'Kein Volk lebt länger als die Dokumente seiner Kultur': Rede auf der Kulturtagung des Parteitags der NSDAP in Nürnberg" [1935], in Eikmeyer, *Reden zur Kunst- und Kulturpolitik,* 81–97, esp. 90; Adolf Hitler, "'Das Bekenntnis des Führers zu Kunst und Künstler': Rede zur Eröffnung der Großen Deutschen Kunstausstellung in München" [1938], in Eikmeyer, *Reden zur Kunst- und Kulturpolitik,* 179–87, esp. 183.
29. The formulation "eine besondere Haßliebe" (a special love-hate relationship) with reference to Hitler and Dadaism was coined by Lüttichau, "'Deutsche Kunst' und 'Entartete Kunst,'" 105; cf. Uwe Fleckner, "Sie nahmen Dada ernst," 80.
30. Adolf Hitler, *Die deutsche Kunst als stolzeste Verteidigung des deutschen Volkes* (Munich: Eher, 1934), 14. The maxim quoted was displayed on a bronze plaque erected in 1937 at the Haus der Deutschen Kunst in Munich. On the National Socialist use of the concept of fanaticism, see Victor Klemperer, *LTI: Notizbuch eines Philologen* (Leipzig: Reclam, 1946), 62–64.

ROGER E. STODDARD

TRANSFIGURED BOOKS

Notes on Some Marks Left by Owners in Books of American Poetry Printed from 1610 to 1820

> The bibliographer's ideal would be to compel each
> and every volume to tell its own history.
> —Seymour de Ricci[1]

Early and late in my career as an acquisitions librarian in historical collections, I considered provenance to be an added value in the books I chose to acquire. For instance, in 1958 I purchased for the Houghton Library at Harvard University, Cambridge, an extensively annotated set of the works of Jean de La Bruyère (London, 1713) from the library of the English poet William Shenstone (1714–63), whose own works had been assiduously collected by generations of Harvard librarians. Thirty-one years later, in 1989, I added the unrecorded sales catalog of the bookseller Thomas Davies (London, 1764); that catalog includes the library of Shenstone, and the La Bruyère figures as item 1390: "with a few Ms. Notes, and a Character of the Work by Mr. Shenstone." Copies of classical French books often show extensive provenances from their bookplates and sales records, as in the Chaponay–La Roche Lacarelle–de Backer–Bodmer copy of an early book by Clément Marot or the Naurois–Lignerolles–Guyot de Villeneuve–Millot copy of Jean Racine's first book. Once, I fitted together into provenance strings the recorded owners of Jean de La Fontaine's first book, only to discover that I had just acquired the second copy known to exist. Conversely, some copies of early books travel down the centuries without a single clue about the identification of those who have preserved them. The Paris book dealer Georges Heilbrun once advised Harvard's librarian William Jackson to buy a book from a competitor instead of his own copy because "it is a bit cheaper than mine, and I think it is more interesting as it has a provenance."[2] This essay is a demonstration piece on the recording and indexing of provenance data for practical use—what you might call applied provenance.

When we create a bibliography, we establish a laboratory for future experimentation. It goes without saying that we record the texts and reveal where they may be found; however, we also make it possible to discern how printers and publishers treated the material—with their types and papers and pictures and bindings—as well as how recipients responded to that material. Did owners bind their books or leave them in paper? If they bound the texts, did they expend care and funds to make them look stylish? Did they sign the books or mark ownership in other ways? Did they annotate the books? Did they create elaborate presentations? Did they abuse the books?

Many of these questions are addressed in my recently published bibliography of early American poetry printed from 1610 to 1820.[3] Sixteen-ten was the year that R. Rich, gent., published his "Virginia Tract" called *Newes from Virginia,* the first published poem written in the English colonies; by 1820, the wily Samuel G. Goodrich had published in two illustrated octavo volumes *The Poetical Works of John Trumbull, LL. D.* Goodrich had misjudged the timing of that publication and lost his shirt: by 1820, American readers had forgotten Trumbull and the Hartford Wits, and they were ready and waiting for fiction, such as J. F. Cooper's *The Spy,* published in 1821. From 1610 to 1820, however, poetry was king of American literature, so my bibliography—my "laboratory"—can support representative experiments such as provenance studies.

Altogether, I have examined and described more than 6,900 copies of 1,327 editions. My "provenance index" amounts to thirty pages of printout, something more than 1,300 names literally transcribed. Here is half a page of it:

Wallcut, Thomas, 29, 37, 84, 188, 259, 276, 330, 356, 453, 454, 481.
Waller, Henry, 488.
Walsh, John S., 434.
War Department Library, 830.
Ward, Chas. A., 1247.
Ward, William, 1052.
Ware, Harriet, 1119.
Ware, Henry, 1119.
Warren, Henry, 425.
Warrenn, Ruth, 35.
Washburn, Dolly, 455.
Washburn, J., 659.
Washington, Mrs., 417.
Washington, George, 65, 243, 274, 301, 303, 355, 358, 362, 369, 389, 410, 510.
Washington, Martha, 301.
Waterman, Elijah, 448.
Watson, Richard, 440.
Watterston family, 929, 1046.
Watterston, R. C., 236.
Way, Geo. B., 830.

This segment begins with Thomas Wallcut, a squirrel of a bookhunter at the turn of the nineteenth century, whose collections enriched the American Antiquarian Society in Worcester, Massachusetts (he often inscribed the source of his copy), and ends with three Websters, among them Daniel, many of whose books came to the Massachusetts Historical Society in Boston, and Noah, to whom manuscript notes are attributed in a copy of Joel Barlow's *A letter to the National Convention of France* (New York, 1793) at the New York Public Library. In the middle of the list are books from the family of George Washington, most of them now in the Boston Athenæum.

My first copy-specific note includes the library location symbol, height of the leaf, and defects in a tally of examined copies for entry number one, *Newes from Virginia,* 1610:

> *Copies examined.* BL: 17.3cm., -B4, F. W. Caulfeild, 2nd Earl of Charlemont (11 Aug. 1865 sale, lot 128)—A. H. Huth copy (*Catalogue of the fifty manuscripts & printed books bequeathed to the British Museum by Alfred H. Huth* (London, 1912), no. XLIX, p. 81), F. Bedford binding. CSmH: 16.7cm., -B4, S. G. Drake—C. H. Kalbfleisch—M. C. Lefferts (G. H. Richmond, *A check-list,* New York, 1901, p. 18)—E. D. Church copy, binding signed by "S David" and "Domont." University of Durham: 17.5cm., John Cosin's copy. NjP: 17.5cm., Henry Percy, 9th Earl of Northumberland—Lord Leconfield (23 Apr. 1928 sale, lot 123)—Cyrus McCormick copy. RPJCB: 17.8cm., stitched, unbound, "6742" inscribed on title-page, A Nobleman (Sotheby's, 25 July 1930 sale, lot 66)—A. S. W. Rosenbach and Lathrop C. Harper—John F. Fleming—Paul Mellon copy.

You can see from the list that English noblemen (Charlemont and Northumberland) owned copies in the seventeenth century, no doubt in order to watch an English colony from the beginning. The list also includes a nineteenth-century book scout (Samuel G. Drake) of Boston, twentieth-century American book dealers (Rosenbach, Harper, and Fleming), and several connoisseurs (Huth, Kalbfleisch, Lefferts, and Church). Only five copies survive, and each is tucked away now in a library. Owners of each copy are listed in my "provenance index," and all are quite refined, with no evidence of unidentified owners.

The unrefined? The Library Company of Philadelphia copy of Michael Wigglesworth's *The day of doom: or, a poetical description of the great and last judgment* (Boston, 1715) is signed "Nathaniel Hall," "Susanah Hall," "Joseph Hall," and "Nehemiah Hall His Book 1756"; the American Antiquarian Society copy of Benjamin Colman's *Reliquiae Turellæ, et lachrymae paternæ* (Boston, 1735) is inscribed "For the Reverend Mr. President Willia[ms] Newhaven," "Anne Williams her Book," and "E Williams"; and the Harvard copy of William Munford's *Poems, and compositions in prose on several occasions* (Richmond, [Va.], 1798) is signed "Mr Arthur Millikin," "Mary Millikin," and "Tommy Millikin." Here is work for the genealogists; they can tell us where, when, and who these Halls, Williamses, and Millikins were; perhaps they can tell us why such folks owned our books, marking their names generation after generation, as if in a family Bible. Could such a book have been the only one in the household other than the family Bible?

Let's look at samples of what awaits investigation, starting with some bookbindings commissioned by their owners. After that, we will consider valuable or amusing annotations, presentation inscriptions, surprising owners, very special copies, and presentation bookbindings.

Some Bookbindings Commissioned by Their Owners

A copy of *A Hymn of St. Bernard's to the Holy Jesus* translated from Saint Bernard of Clairvaux (Boston, 1744) at the Massachusetts Historical Society bears a typographic bookplate in a frame of fleurons reading "James Foster, His Book. 1744" (fig. 1) and the inscription "Given to Sarah Foster by her Father—Nov.13.1800." The hymn is bound—in lined heavy magenta paper wrappers printed in a green-gilt floral design—as an addendum to a sermon by Benjamin Colman, *Jesus Weeping over His Dead Friend. . . .* (Boston, 1744). American bookplates are a rarity at this early date; this one is unrecorded, and the binding material is unlike any other I have ever seen.

There is not much evidence of American poets indulging themselves with special copies of their books, but Fitz-Greene Halleck is an exception. A copy of his popular poem *Fanny* (New York, 1819) that figured in the auction sale of his library[4] after his death is bound in straight-grain citron morocco, gilt extra, all edges gilt, with his manuscript notes. The manuscript identification of that copy is signed "Fred," the *nom de vente* of C. W. Frederickson, in whose sale[5] it figured,[6] later entering the Huntington Library with the collection of Frederick R. Halsey in 1915.[7]

The book collector John Carter Brown had his copy of Anne Bradstreet's *The Tenth Muse lately Sprung up in America* (London, 1650)—the first collection of

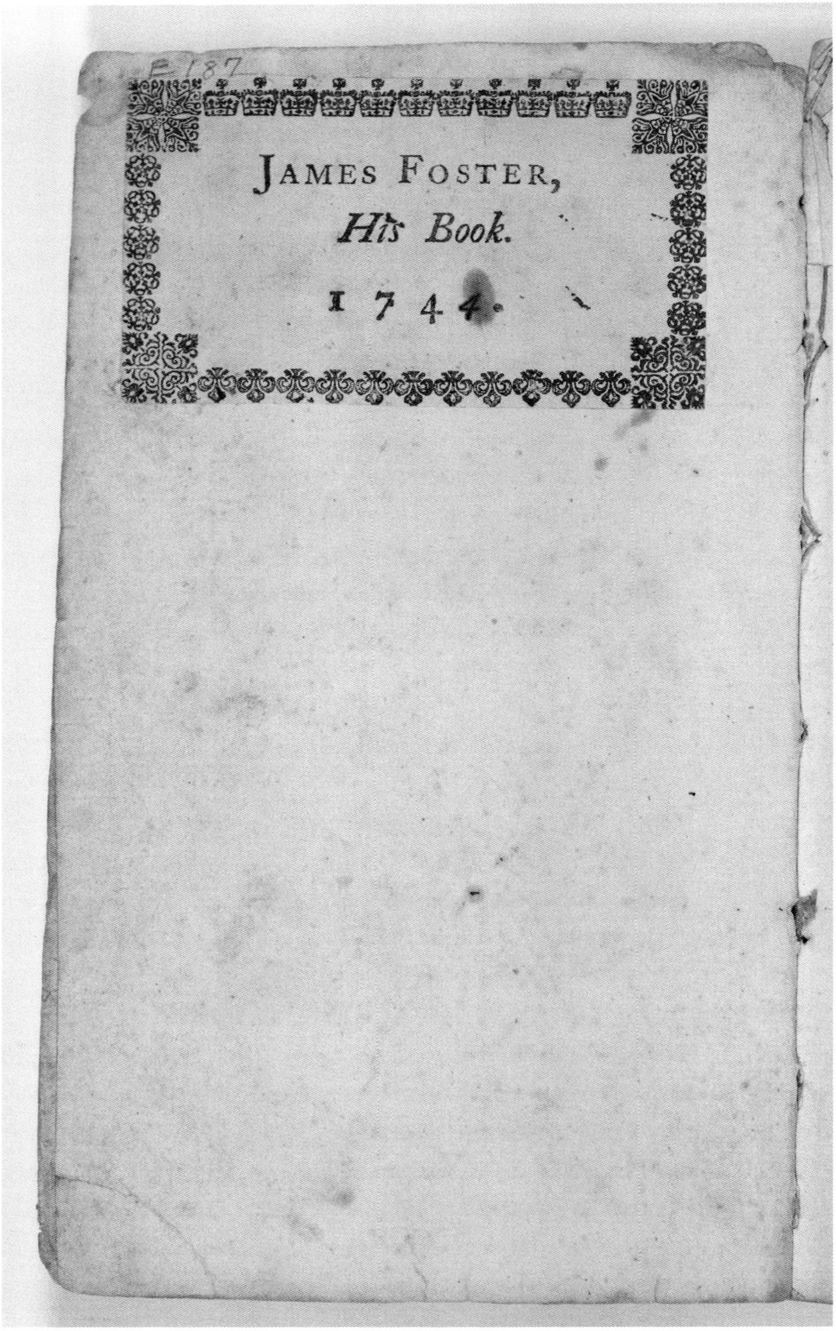

Fig. 1.
Unrecorded typographic bookplate in *A Hymn of St. Bernard's to the Holy Jesus* (Boston: Printed by B. Green . . . for D. Gookin, 1744), bound with Benjamin Colman, *Jesus Weeping over His Dead Friend*. . . . (Boston: printed by Rogers and Fowle, for J. Edwards in Cornhhill, 1744), inside front cover.
Boston, Massachusetts Historical Society, box 1744.

verse from the English colonies and the fourth collection to be published by an Englishwoman—bound in blue straight-grain morocco with his crest and initials gold-stamped on the covers, in imitation of Henri Ternaux-Compans's bindings, several of which he had acquired.[8]

Some Valuable or Amusing Annotations

William Livingston's *Philosophic solitude: or, the choice of a rural life. A poem. By a gentleman educated at Yale College* (New York, 1747) was one of the most popular poems of the period. It was published five times and collected in the anthologies, so we may expect that annotations by owners will abound attributing authorship of the poem and of its commendatory verses. Several copies correctly attribute authorship of the latter (signed in print "N. W." and "W. P. S.") to the author's Yale schoolmates Noah Welles and William Peartree Smith. The copy at the John Carter Brown Library (Providence, Rhode Island)—much worn, stitched, and repaired, in homemade paper wrappers—was, according to an inscription, "Read and Admired by Edward Kinnicutt." It is also inscribed "By Wm Livingston," "Donum Amici Ann francis Lippitt," "James Fitch," "Abram Francis," "By William Livingston of N. York," "Ann Francis," and "The gift of Mrs Ann Francis to her Neice [*sic*]-Ann Francis Lippitt." The Brown University copy is inscribed "Noah Welles's Ex Dono Authoris D: G: Livingston. 1747," and two errata are added in manuscript.

Bishop Thomas White's copy of William Smith's *A Poem on Visiting the Academy of Philadelphia, June 1753* (Philadelphia, 1753) in the John Carter Brown Library discloses inside information in this inscription: "The Author of this Poem was ye well known Divine, who was so long ye Provost of ye College[.] At ye Time of writing ye Poem he was Tutor in ye Family of Col. Martin of Long Island. M[ ] 9.1826 W. W."

A copy of Thomas Godfrey's *Juvenile poems on various subjects. With The prince of Parthia, a tragedy* (Philadelphia, 1765) at Harvard is inscribed "This Volume of Poems, the Offspring of an American Bard, is presented as an Evidence, 'that Harvard College has Reputation & Friends in Pensilvania [*sic*],'" "From Jona: Smith, Mercht. Philadelphia." It was received in Cambridge on 4 April 1768. The book, celebrated for containing the (posthumous) first publication of a play composed by a native-born American and first to be performed professionally, exists in other remarkable copies, another of them at Harvard inscribed "For Doctor [Benjamin] Franklin from his very oblig'd and most obedient humble servt. N[athaniel]. Evans." Another copy, at the Huntington Library (San Marino, California), was signed by an original subscriber, Moore Furman, and then made its way to Leeds, where it was labeled

"J. Milligan Book-Seller 13 Blenheim Place Leeds" before turning up in the auction of R. G. Wilberforce's library on 11 December 1903; it finally entered the Huntington Library in the purchase of F. R. Halsey's collection in 1915.

Saint George Tucker's anonymous *The knight and friars, an historical tale* (New York, 1786), inspired by a poem of the same title by Richard Paul Jodrell (London, 1785), has survived in a copy at the Beinecke Rare Book and Manuscript Library at Yale inscribed "The Author of this Version was Mr: Saint George Tucker, a Native of America, & Resident in Virginia. He sent me this Poem in a parcel from Mr. Wythe of Williamsburg; & it arrived in London on March the 21st. 1787. Richard Paul Jodrell-."

The John Carter Brown Library possesses a copy of Peter Markoe's *The times, a poem* (Philadelphia, 1788), which is inscribed "This was the Copy of Tench Coxe Esq. who has marked (new) the passages not published in the newspapers. The names are taken from a Copy formerly that of Gen. Jonathan Williams. A Copy appears for sale in Thorpe's Catal. part 2 for 1848, at 8s." The manuscript key to the names should be compared with those in the British Library and Brown University Library copies.

A vital statistic was inspired by a copy of Jane (Fenno) Ames's *Original compositions, in prose and verse. On subjects moral and religious* (Boston, 1791) at the American Antiquarian Society. A woman who owned the book gives us not only her name and two places of abode but also her date of birth: "Rachel Guilds Book Walpole Born June the 9 1769," "Rachel Guild her book Stoughtton."

Elhanan Winchester's epic, *The process and empire of Christ; from his birth to the end of the mediatorial kingdom; a poem, in twelve books* (London, 1793), fruit of his temporary residence in London, is illustrated with a portrait of this handsome American, an idol of the pulpit. Like Winchester's extremely popular elegy on the death of John Wesley, *The process and empire of Christ* was entered for copyright in England's Stationers' Register by the poet himself. The Huntington Library copy, which has the portrait of Winchester, is inscribed "Peter Keyser his Book bought of the author in the year 179[?4]," "P Keyser 1796," and "Philada March 15th 1806 Peter Keyser," showing that its possessor followed the author back to America.

A copy of Timothy Dwight's *Greenfield Hill: a poem, in seven parts* (New York, 1794) at the Library of Congress tells a different story. On page 45, line 477, an anonymous owner has identified a "female worthy" in manuscript as "Mrs. Eleanor Bradley Sherwood," a neat clue for a researcher.

The American Antiquarian Society copy of Brockholst Livingston's *Democracy: an epic poem, by Aquiline Nimble-Chops, Democrat* (New York, [1794]) contains a manuscript key to the characters as well as the notice "The meeting which is the subject of this Canto was on Thursday Feb: 27th 1794 and on Tuesday the fourth of March following the Poem was printed," "[ ]uby Esq. from TMumf[ord]."

"Revd. Jedediah Morse" is inscribed at the end of the (unsigned) preface in the State Library of Massachusetts (Boston) copy of Richard Devens's anonymous *A paraphrase on some parts of the book of Job* (Boston, 1795), and several members of the Devens family have signed their names. Copies at the American Antiquarian Society and Massachusetts Historical Society are inscribed by Devens.

Abiel Holmes's unique family anthology of verse, *A family tablet: containing a selection of original poetry* (Boston, 1796), features poems signed with pseudonyms, such as Myron, Myra, Cecilia, and so on; in a copy at the Beinecke Rare Book and Manuscript Library, however, all authors are identified in manuscript. A copy at the Massachusetts Historical Society includes this puzzling, unrelated inscription: "John Henfield's book presented to him by his father for a new years present in the year of our lord 1831 aged ten years."

John "Walking Stewart" Stewart (1749–1822) produced a long poem, *The revelation of nature, with the prophesy of reason,* during his peregrinations in the United States; the book is undated, but we are encouraged to find helpful inscriptions dated by early owners ("1796 Thos Chapman") in the Harvard copy and ("Saml. Paine's from the Author John Stewart, the Traveller. Newport August 1796") in the American Antiquarian Society copy.

Henry Maurice Lisle's anonymous poem *Milton Hill* (Boston, 1803) is dedicated "To Miss H...... [*sic*] of Milton Hill," but in the Huntington Library copy an early owner—either the author or Thaddeus M. Harris, who signed his name—identifies her as H "olbrook." That copy was later owned by the historian Charles Deane.

The Huntington Library copy of Joseph Story's *The power of solitude. A poem. In two parts. By Joseph Story... A new and improved edition* (Salem, [Mass.], 1804), inscribed by the author to his future wife, identifies Story's collaborator on page [4] ("Written by Mary Lynde Fitch Oliver") and "M. O." in manuscript for verses on pages 206–9 and 209–10.

William Sullivan's anonymous political salvo, *The Demos in council: or 'Bijah in pandemonium. Being a sweep of the lyre, in close imitation of Milton* (Boston, 1799), names the principals using pseudonyms, but the anonymous original owners of both the American Antiquarian Society copy and the Brown University Library copy have identified all of them in manuscript.

Winthrop Sargent's anonymous poem, *Boston,* published in Boston in 1803 and "Corrected and enlarged" later in the year, has accumulated interesting annotations. Daniel Webster's copy at the Massachusetts Historical Society identifies "Court Street" on page 10 as "Meaning the Chronicle," and

E. B. Winthrop's copy, also at the Massachusetts Historical Society, is marked "cost 1/6 much too dear!!!" A copy of the reprint at the American Antiquarian Society, signed "Jennison Jr 1803 1/6" (thereby confirming the price) bears a long and useful manuscript note: "Mr. Sargent graduated at Harvard University in 1804. This poem of 'Boston' was reviewed in the National Aegis soon after its publication—This review was attributed to Mr. D. W Lincoln."

An inscription in *Poems, on various subjects. By Isabella Oliver, of Cumberland County, Pennsylvania* (Carlisle, [Pa.], 1805) states that the author, "not being a ready writer herself, [...] dictated them to another person, who wrote them down. These Poems, therefore, have come, not so properly from the pen, as from the memory and the heart of the Poetess." A page headed "To the editor" states that "R. D." transcribed the poems from dictation and that the publisher Archibald Loudon edited them for publication. An anonymous owner of the Library of Congress copy has identified "R. D." in manuscript as Robert Davidson, president of Dickinson College.

Poems, by the late George Heartwell Spierin, of Charleston, South-Carolina, student of law (Charleston, [S.C.], 1805) poses several questions. Anonymous owners have identified the editor as "Lucius Bellinger Esqr" (in the Library of Congress copy) and the author of the unsigned poem on page [V] as "W. Simmons.—" (in the Brown University Library copy).

Manuscript notes in the Library of Congress, American Antiquarian Society, and University of Virginia Library copies of *Poems by the Late Doctor John Shaw. To which is prefixed a biographical sketch of the author* (Philadelphia, 1810) reveal the identity of the book's anonymous editor: J. E. Hall. The Library of Congress and Brown University Library copies include an aquatint engraving of the author (from a physionotrace) by Charles Balthazar Julien Fevret de Saint-Mémin (fig. 2).

The edition of Michael Wigglesworth's steady-selling poem *The Day of Doom* published by E. Little & Co. of Newburyport in 1811 seems unaccountably rare—until you encounter notes by the antiquary John Ward Dean in the New York Public Library and Brown University Library copies stating that most of the edition was lost in the Newburyport fire of 31 May 1811. Dean adds helpfully in the New York copy that the 1 June 1759 inventory of the T. Fleet estate includes ninety copies of his 1751 edition of the poem valued at "22s. 6d. or 3p." each.

In the University of Virginia copy of Henry Bliss, *The genius of Federalism, a poem, in three cantos* (Pittsfield, [Mass.], 1813), an inscription cites the date and price of purchase—a bibliographer's dream come true: "Ebenezer Hollis' Book price 20 Cents Bought July 19th,, [*sic*] 1813."

The inscription on the envelope containing the Connecticut Historical Society copy of Joseph Chapman's *Poems, on various subjects, religious and*

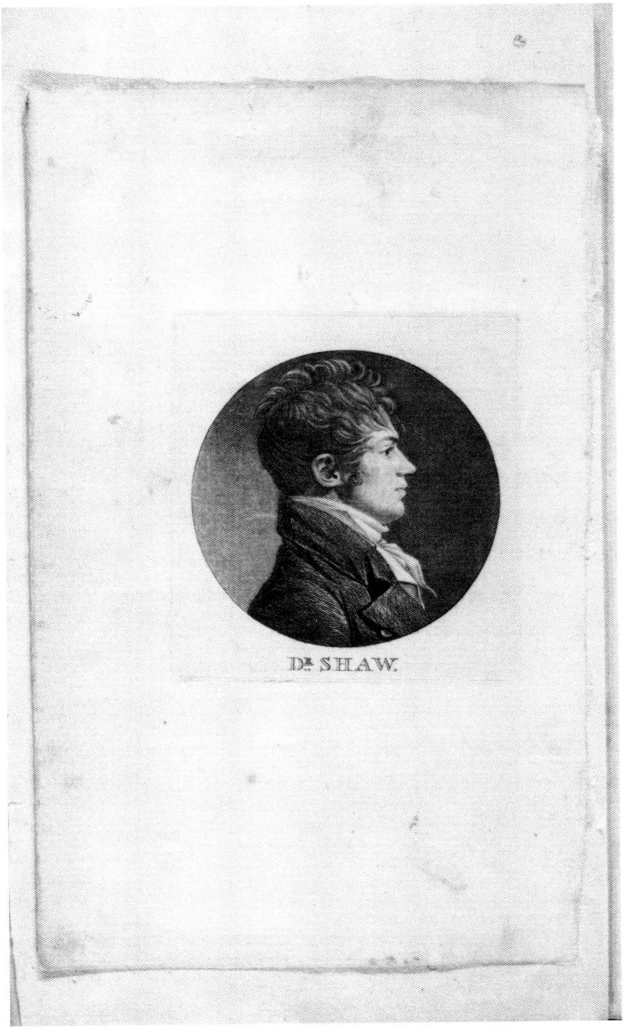

Fig. 2.
Charles Balthazar Julien Fevret de Saint-Mémin (French, 1770–1852).
Portrait of John Shaw, 1810, aquatint physionotrace.
From John Shaw, *Poems by the Late Doctor John Shaw* (Philadelphia, 1810).
Providence, Brown University Library.

moral (n.p., 1813) is even better: "Joseph Chapman, a resident of Jewett City, in the town of Griswold, Conn., had a private printing press on which he printed this, and other, small items."

Oliver Evans's important annotated poem on patent law, *Patent right oppression exposed; or, knavery detected. In an address, to unite all good people to obtain a repeal of the patent laws. By Patrick N. I. Elisha, Esq. poet laureate [pseud.]. To which is added, an alarming law case; also, reflections on the patent laws. Illustrated with notes and anecdotes, by the editor* (Philadelphia, 1813), is rendered slightly less mysterious thanks to an inscription in the Historical Society of Pennsylvania copy by L. Byllesby dated November 1853 that acknowledges authorship of the verses: "I was accordingly consulted, the documents, papers, &c. put in my hands, and, in due course, the ensuing book the result."

Rebecca Hammond Lard's anonymous *Miscellaneous poems on moral and religious subjects. By a lady* (Woodstock, [Vt.], 1820) includes a dedication "To the Hon. J. D. H*****d," identified in the New-York Historical Society copy as Jabez D. Hammond.

Some Presentation Inscriptions

Poems on several occasions. By Mr. Byles (Boston, 1744) is one of the rarest of the early poem collections. The copy at the Rosenbach Museum and Library, Philadelphia, is inscribed to the president of Harvard College, "Edwd. Holyoke Don. Authoris," and it includes a presentation poem. The copy in the American Antiquarian Society, still in its original gray paper wrappers, is inscribed "Mather Byles. The Gift of his Father."

David Humphreys was one of the greatest self-promoters of the Federal era, reminding everyone that he had served as "aide-de-camp to Gen. Washington." He inscribed his *A poem, addressed to the armies of the United States of America. By a gentleman of the army* (New Haven, Conn., 1780) "To M[rs.] Washington from her Most Obedie[nt] and most devoted Serva[nt] The Auth[or]" (in a copy in a tract volume in the Boston Athenæum); he inscribed copies of the Paris reprint of 1785 "To Monsr. le Duc de Rochefoucault from His Most obedient & Most humble Servant The Author" (in the Huntington Library) and "To His Excellency Dr Franklin from his humble Servt The Author," (at the Historical Society of Pennsylvania, Philadelphia).

Not to neglect George Washington himself, Humphreys inscribed the Boston Athenæum copy of *A poem, on the happiness of America; addressed to the citizens of the United States* [London, 1786] "To His Excellency Gen Wash[ington] from His Friend and most hu[mble servant] The Autho[r]." However, the promotion of Humphreys's *Poems by Col. David Humphreys, late aid-de-camp to his excellency General Washington*, 2nd ed. (Philadelphia: Printed by Mathew Carey, 1789) seems to have fallen to his publisher, who inscribed "The gift of M. Carey to the Blockley + Merrion Ag[ri]cultural Society" in a copy now at the American Antiquarian Society and "Presented to the City Library Company by M. Carey" in not one but two copies at the Library Company of Philadelphia.

The great American bluestocking Mercy Otis Warren published her *Poems, dramatic and miscellaneous* at Boston with "I. Thomas and E. T. Andrews," in 1790, dedicating the work to President Washington. Her copy, with manuscript corrections and identifications throughout, is in the Boston Athenæum, a gift of "Henry Warren Esq." Proud of his publication, Isaiah Thomas acquired a very fancy bound copy in first-quality calf with gilt-rolled board edges, gilt red spine label (centered), with three gilt squares above and below, with loops, stars, and other embellishments, to donate to the American Antiquarian Society; Thomas added his bookplate, which was engraved by Paul Revere, and noted the value as "1.25."

The spirit of The Farmers' Museum, and Lay Preacher's Gazette. Being a judicious selection of the fugitive and valuable productions, which have occasionally appeared in that paper, since the commencement of its establishment. Consisting of a part of the essays of the Lay Preacher, Colon and Spondee, American biography, the choicest efforts of the American muse, pieces of chaste humour, the easy essays of the Hermit, the most valuable part of the weekly summaries, nuts, epigrams, and epitaphs, sonnets, criticism, &c. &c. (Walpole, N.H., 1801), anonymously selected by the editor, Joseph Dennie, is as lively an anthology of anonymous pieces as you could want. A copy in the Boston Public Library is inscribed "This Volume was presented to James Abercrombie, Dec[r] 26th 1801 By His learned & facetious Friend Joseph Dennie Esq[ ]," and attributions are inscribed in manuscript, providing the basis for all subsequent work. The Massachusetts Historical Society copy is shattered and defective, no doubt evidence that it was abused in school by "Laskett J C Sweet Ph[ilips] E[xeter] Academy 1819."

An elaborate inscription graces the Huntington Library copy of Oliver Whipple's pseudonymous *The historic progress of civil and rational liberty, and order, triumphant over faction: a poem ... By a farmer* (Portsmouth, [N.H.], 1802): "The Farmer presents his Compliments to Mr. John Carter and begs his acceptance of his little Book, the Effort of a Leisure hour; his Patronage, and Candour, to its Just Merits, will amply repay The Farmer for his Labours. Hampton (N. H.) August 6th, 1802."

In a copy of *A leisure hour; or, a series of poetical letters: mostly written during the prevalence of the yellow fever. By a citizen of Philadelphia* (Philadelphia, 1804) at the Brown University Library, John Purdon reveals, in his presentation inscription, that he himself is the work's pseudonymous author: "Mr. Porter his friend the author J Purdon."

The poems of Philip Freneau. Written chiefly during the late war (Philadelphia, 1786) was the first collection of the prolific poet's works, so presentations should have been the order of the day. So far, two have been discovered: a copy at the Boston Public Library is inscribed "Col. Wadsworth will do Mr. Freneau the honour to accept of [*sic*] this Volume of his writings—," and a copy at the New York Public Library has this inscription: "General Washington will do the author the honour to accept a copy of his poems, as a small testimony of the disinterested veneration he entertains for his character—Philip Freneau." The former is bound simply in acid-stained sheepskin, but the latter is in calf with gilt borders and dentelles, red spine onlay, green label, yellow stained edges, and blue ribbon place-marker.

Some Surprising Owners

Narcissus Luttrell (1660–1730), the prodigious English book collector, owned one of only two copies known of Benjamin Tompson's anonymous account of the Indian Wars, *New-Englands tears for her present miseries* (London, 1676), as well as Ebenezer Cooke's *The sot=weed factor: or, a voyage to Maryland* (London, 1708), also surviving in two copies. The former passed into two other great collections, Richard Heber's and the library at Britwell Court, in Buckinghamshire, before entering the Huntington Library. The second copy was owned by the French collector Henri Ternaux-Compans before John Carter Brown purchased it. Luttrell's copy of the Cooke is now in the British Library; another copy of it, now at the New York Public Library, was once owned by the English bishop White Kennett, who recorded it in the first bibliography of English Americana in 1713.[9]

The only known copy of William Dawson's pseudonymous *Poems on several occasions... By a gentleman of Virginia* (Williamsburg, [Va.], 1736) owes its survival to George Washington and came to the Boston Athenæum with Washington's library in 1848.

Some Very Special Copies

John Parke's *The lyric works of Horace, translated into English verse: to which are added, a number of original poems. By a native of America* (Philadelphia: Eleazer Oswald, 1786) marks the first serious influence of the classics on American literature. The publisher's bindings, available both in plain sheep and in red sheep gilt with a pomegranate on the spine, are known as the work of Caleb Buglass. (Dr. James Rush's copy, now at the Library Company of Philadelphia, is inscribed "Presented by Caleb Buglass Book-Binder.") The allegorical frontispiece, *Ut pictura poesis alter et idem,* designed by the poet Peter Markoe and crudely engraved by James Peller Malcom, is the most creative illustration in all of early American literature. A copy was discovered in 2009 with delicate, perhaps professional, hand coloring, a feature rare in early American book culture. The only clue to the origin of this new copy comes from the signature Maria or Marian Francis inscribed on the title page. It has been purchased as a gift to the Library Company by Michael Zinman. Several copies in the red sheepskin binding have survived: Robert Morris's (previously owned by E. D. Ingraham, Daniel E. Kennedy, and Michael Papantonio), now at the Antiquarian Society, and George Washington's, now at George Washington's Mount Vernon Estate, Museum and Gardens.

Books printed on different grades of paper such as *grand papier* and *papier ordinaire* are usually associated with France, but one was produced in Portland, Maine, in 1800: Jonathan Ellis's *An eulogical poem, on General George Washington, who died at his seat at Mount-Vernon, December 14, 1799. Pronounced at Topsham, February 22d. 1800. The day assigned by authority, for the citizens of the United States to testify their grief for his death.* (Portland, Maine: Published at the Request of the hearers, 1800). Most copies of the book are printed on regular wove paper, but the copy inscribed "Revd Alden Bradford from his friend th[e] Author" at the Massachusetts Historical Society, with manuscript corrections and notes, is printed on imported paper watermarked "J WHATMAN 1794."

The poem *The complete coiffeur; or an essay on the art of adorning natural, and of creating artificial, beauty. (Ornamented with plates.) By J. B. M. D. Lafoy, ladies' hair-dresser* (New York, 1817), ghostwritten by Samuel Woodworth, is a sumptuous production: stereotyped on superior wove paper with elegant engraved vignette title pages for the English and French texts, two pages of engraved music, and four stipple-engraved fashion plates. The work is best enjoyed in the Antiquarian Society copy, in which the vignette titles are engraved on the covers and the fashion plates are decorated in bright watercolors, a feature that was virtually unknown in early American bookmaking.

Some Presentation Bookbindings

A so-called presentation binding is a fancy, perhaps gilt-extra binding commissioned by a donor as a gift. Sometimes the donor is the author or publisher. For instance, I commissioned emblematic red-morocco bindings of my selected writings for presentation to my wife and to my editor.

The most celebrated presentation binding on a volume of early American literature graces copies of a Harvard College confection of poems in Latin and Greek titled *Pietas et gratulatio collegii Cantabrigiensis apud Novanglos* (Boston, 1761 [i.e., 1762]). The colonial governor pressed the college to mourn the passing of King George II of England and celebrate the coronation of George III in a work similar to those customary in Oxford and Cambridge. Presentation copies to the English court were bound by the London binder Richard Montagu,

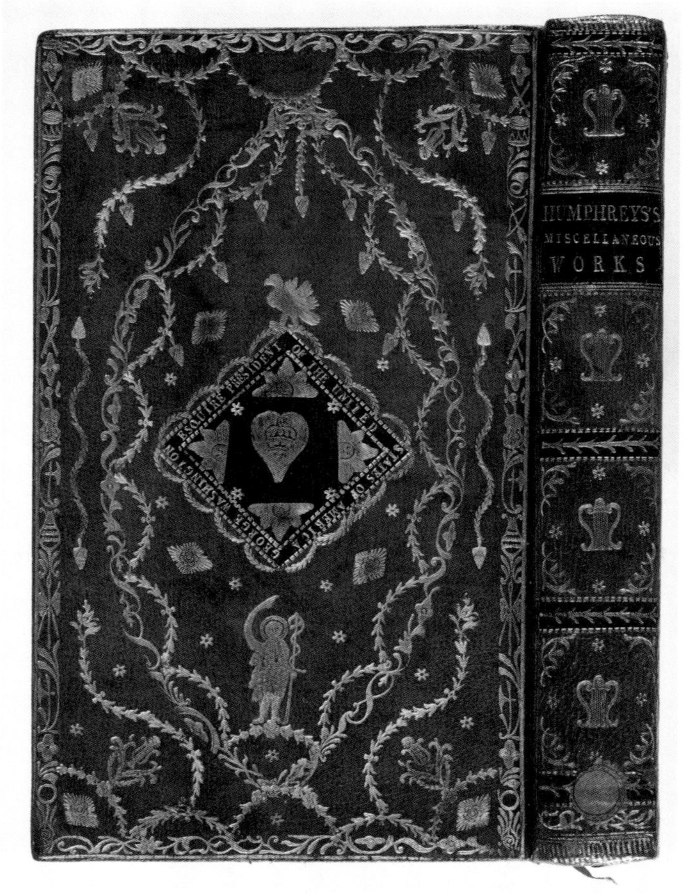

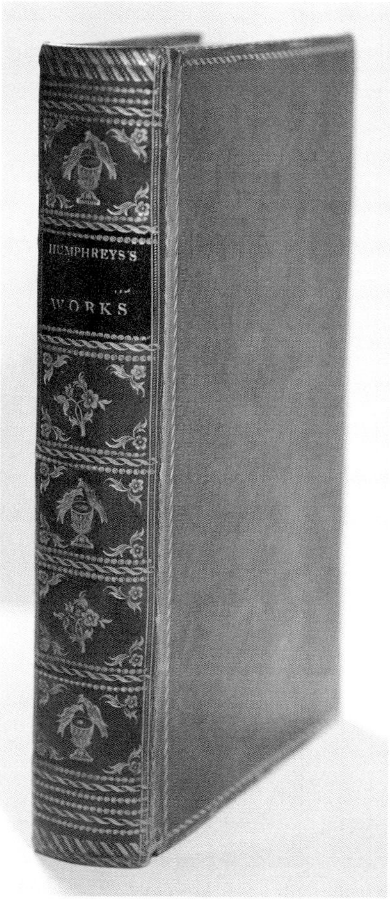

Fig. 3.
Unidentified presentation binding, front board and spine, of a copy of David Humphreys, *The miscellaneous works of Colonel Humphreys* (New York, 1790).
Boston, Boston Athenæum.

Fig. 4.
Presentation binding by Henry Bilson Legge (American, d. 1804) on David Humphreys, *The Miscellaneous Works of David Humphreys, Late Minister Plenipotentiary from the United States of America to the Court of Madrid* (New York: printed by T. & J. Swords, 1804).
Boston, Massachusetts Historical Society.

through the good offices of Harvard's great friend Thomas Hollis of Lincoln's Inn, in red morocco gilt with the royal arms. Such copies can be found in the British Library, Harvard (2), and the Huntington Library.

David Humphreys commissioned presentation bindings for his collected works. The most outlandish example is a copy of Humphreys's *The miscellaneous works of Colonel Humphreys* (New York, 1790) in George Washington's library now at the Boston Athenæum (fig. 3). It is bound in red morocco gilt extra, with green leather onlays on the spine and sides, red-paste-decorated edges with gilt gauffered center panels—a Spanish touch?—and endpapers; "George Washington Esquire President of the United States of America" is gold-stamped on the covers.

Boston bookbinder Henry Bilson Legge's commissions on copies of *The Miscellaneous Works of David Humphreys, Late Minister Plenipotentiary from the United States of America to the Court of Madrid* (New York: printed by T. & J. Swords, 1804) are a bit more tasteful than the previous example. A copy inscribed "Presented to the Library of the University at Cambridge by The Author" is bound in gilt, grained red sheepskin, with a blue leather spine label, marbled endpapers, and yellow edges. The copy given to the Massachusetts Historical Society on 27 August 1805 is similarly bound (fig. 4). The library bookplate in the Harvard copy is printed in red, a warning that the book should not be circulated for outside use.

Prize bindings—special bindings on books presented as trophies to students in recognition of academic excellence—are often marked with an inscription or book label, but Henry W. Longfellow's grammar school offered copies of Enoch Lincoln's *The village; a poem* (Portland, [Maine], 1816) bound in brown russia by the Portland binder David Buxton. Young Longfellow took the prize in both 1818 and 1819, winning two copies of the same book in the same binding; both copies are now part of his library at Harvard.

When the Russian consul Alekseĭ Grigor'evich Evstafiev published *Demetrius, the hero of the Don. An epick poem* (Boston, 1818), he dedicated the book "To the Empress of all the Russias, Elizabeth Alexievna," and he applied to the great Boston binder John Roulstone for a masterwork of red morocco, gilt extra, marbled endpapers, all edges gilt, to mark the dedication copy. That copy, bearing the ink stamp "Bibliothèque de Tsarskoe Selo," has returned to the United States. Purchased by Michael Papantonio, the premier collector of American bookbindings, it is now in the American Antiquarian Society as his gift.

The foregoing offers a taste of the way that proper names of concealed authors, editors, dedicatees, printers, and bookbinders are revealed or at least suggested by inscriptions.[10] Every proper name we can connect with the making of a book enhances our understanding. Portraits of an author are revealed. Hidden comments by readers are shown. The peregrinations of books from collection to collection and from place to place are documented. Long dead owners can still "speak" to us. One cannot "compel each and every volume to tell its own history," but, under gentle but sustained interrogation, some of them will talk.

Notes

1. Seymour de Ricci, *English Collectors of Books and Manuscripts (1530–1930) and Their Marks of Ownership* (Cambridge: Cambridge University Press, 1930), 3.
2. Quoted in Roger E. Stoddard, "'More Valuable to Us than All the Books in the World': Georges Heilbrun and His Harvard Library Friends," in idem, *A Library-Keeper's Business: Essays by Roger E. Stoddard,* ed. Carol Z. Rothkopf (New Castle, Del.: Oak Knoll Press, 2002), 295.
3. Roger E. Stoddard, comp., and David R. Whitesell, ed., *A Bibliographical*

Description of Books and Pamphlets of American Verse Printed from 1610 through 1820 (University Park: Published by the Pennsylvania State University Press for the Bibliographical Society of America, 2012).

4. Leavitt, N.Y., *Library,* 12 October 1868, lot 134.
5. Bangs, N.Y., *Books, Autographs, &c. Part 1,* 12 April 1886, lot 968.
6. Frederickson owned also Halleck's copy of the second edition, 1821. See his sale at Bangs, N.Y., *Library, Manuscripts and Autographs,* 24 May 1889, lot 671.
7. A celebrated extra-illustrated Halleck volume is at Houghton Library, Harvard University (F*94-285). The extra-illustrator, Charles Moreau, completed his work on the two-volume *Poetical Works* in 1852, and it became noticed in the press.
8. See Susan Danforth, *A Matter of Taste . . . Catalogue of an Exhibition of Rare Books from the John Carter Brown Library* (Providence, R.I.: John Carter Brown Library, 2008), 8–9.
9. See his *Bibliothecæ americanæ primordia: an attempt towards laying the foundation of an American library, in several books, papers, and writings, humbly given to the Society for the propagation of the Gospel in foreign parts, for the perpetual use and benefit of their members, their missionaries, friends, correspondents, and others concern'd in the good design of planting and promoting Christianity* (London: J. Churchill, 1713), 200. Such flattering attention by major European collectors deserves study. What other "American" books did they seek out? Is there a pattern to their "American" collecting?
10. For a more comprehensive treatment of the books cited here, including additional library locations, see my new bibliography, Stoddard and Whitesell, *A Bibliographical Description of Books and Pamphlets of American Verse.*

JEANNINE TANG

FUTURE CIRCULATIONS
On the Work of Hans Haacke and Maria Eichhorn

> You are working with a view to the future circulation of your work.
> —Daniel Buren to Maria Eichhorn[1]

Strategic Provenance

If *provenance* is broadly defined as an art object's history of ownership—a contingent afterlife of evolutions in social taste, values, and accumulations of institutional legitimations both private and public—provenance may be understood as a process that secures the object's authentication, aiding the commercial work of the art market and the scholarly work of the art historian. This essay suggests a different basis for understanding provenance: it considers the use of provenance when performed and motivated by the artist, who folds the object's futurity into a work of art's anteriority, in *preparation* for provenance, calculating how art will be inserted into future relations and exchange values. The global postwar conceptual-art movement of the 1960s and '70s ejected the artist's practice from the studio and displaced the art object's site of production, no longer contained but displaced into future circuits of dissemination, publication, and collection in an attempt to defy the market and forge a democratic public sphere. The ostensible failure of this enterprise nonetheless laid the groundwork for the tools, strategies, legacies, and genealogies of artmaking, display, ownership, and study that, several decades later, were recalibrated in the present tense. The future circulation of the art object is embedded within these legacies, with its consequent pressure upon the ethics and politics of ownership, to suggest the transformation of their current conditions. This raises the question: who and what principles govern the right to art?

In the postwar period of the 1960s and '70s, forms of medium-specific modernism criticism proposed that the discursive field of aesthetic experience, criticism, and display was distinct from the politico-economic realm, assuming the aesthetic's purity, functionlessness, disinterestedness, transhistoric, and ahistoric essence through a privileging of opticality.[2] Pierre Bourdieu argues that the experience of art is one of misrecognition, because the accumulation of symbolic capital hinges on disavowing economic capital to guarantee profit

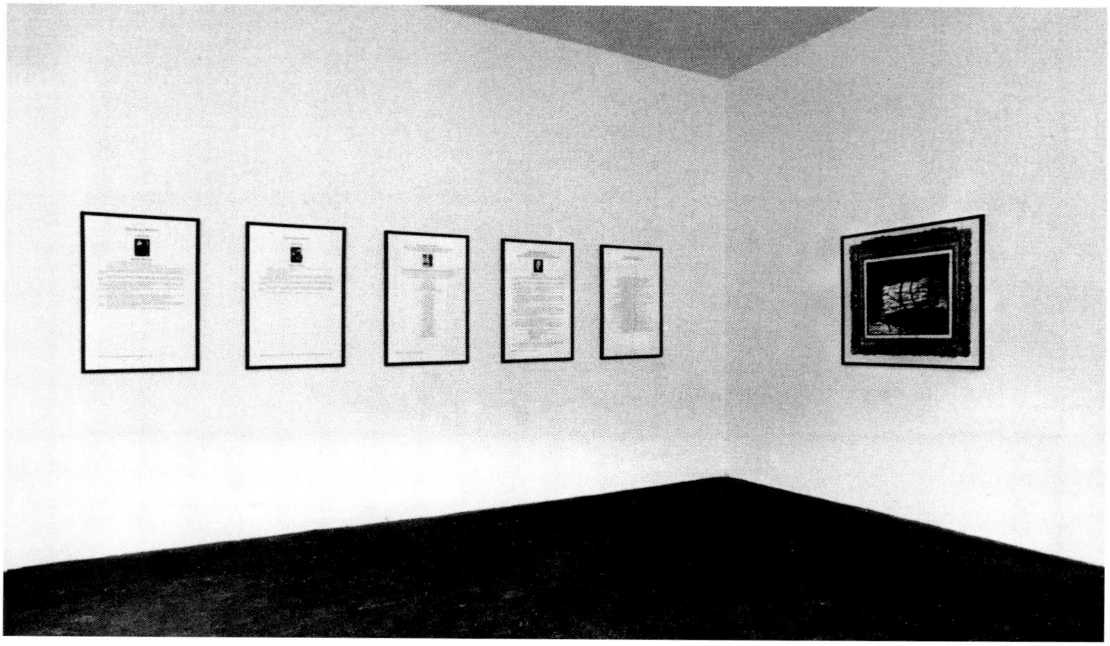

Fig. 1.
Hans Haacke (German, b. 1936).
Manet-PROJEKT '74 (detail), 1974, ten black-and-white panels and reproduction of Edouard Manet's *Bunch of Asparagus* (1880). Installation at Galerie Paul Maenz, Cologne, 1974.

in the long run.[3] This disavowal would be challenged by various trajectories of artistic practice, among them minimalism, postminimalism, conceptualism, and institutional critique, and finds elaboration in Daniel Buren's critique. As Buren argues, "the only value of an artwork is that assigned to it by the buyer.... In all cases, the high or low value of the work... depends first and foremost on the amount paid by the institution or collector... [and] the value of the work is given by people who are interested enough."[4]

The politics of such interest remains a long-standing preoccupation in the work of Hans Haacke. In 1974, Haacke was invited to participate in a group exhibition, *PROJEKT '74*, at the Wallraf-Richartz-Museum in Cologne, mounted on the occasion of the museum's centennial anniversary.[5] Several years earlier, in 1968, the museum had acquired Edouard Manet's *Bunch of Asparagus* (1880); at that time, Hermann J. Abs, a financier and chairman of the Wallraf-Richartz-Kuratorium (Friends o\f the museum) had been invited to preside over an event and deliver a lecture in front of the prized painting. A brochure that advertised the museum's acquisitions of the past few years was provided to Haacke during the commissioning process of *PROJEKT '74*; the brochure included within its pages a photograph of Abs in front of *Bunch of Asparagus* as well as a reproduction of the painting. In response to the institution's history of acquiring the painting, Haacke created a site-specific work, *Manet-PROJEKT '74*, which presented the results of his extensive research into the provenance of *Bunch of Asparagus* and the professional biographies of Abs and the painting's owners (fig. 1). *Manet-PROJEKT '74* examined the institutional circumstances surrounding the Manet's acquisition by the museum and its display in the exhibition. It did so by disclosing the painting's contingent value and economic support, including the price for which each buyer acquired the painting, the social and political milieu in which the painting was acquired, the buyers' financial circumstances and professional affiliations, and additional donors. Such information would ordinarily be excluded from a gallery viewer's consideration, due to the modernist rhetoric of autonomy in the display of contemporary art. However, in *Manet-PROJEKT '74*, the lineage of *Bunch of Asparagus*'s ownership was displayed on ten large paper panels, each representing one of the painting's owners, arranged in chronological order. Each panel had a headline announcing the price paid for the Manet upon a transfer in ownership, along with a photograph of the collector and a description of his professional biography—what Haacke calls the "C.V.s of the painting's owners"[6]—thus describing the inextricable binding of cultural objects to sociopolitical and personal histories. (Figure 2 shows the panel for Abs; translation opposite.) This use of biography, as Douglas Crimp observes, charted Abs's seamless professional transition from his active support of the Nazi regime in the 1930s and 1940s to his work on economic reconstruction during the postwar period, when he would downplay or omit mention of his work for the Reich altogether.[7] Because Haacke's piece enjoined the personal and the political, and because the panels offered explicit criticism of the venue and its patrons, *Manet-PROJEKT '74* was removed from the exhibition in advance of the opening. It was subsequently exhibited at the Paul Maenz gallery in Cologne (fig. 3).[8]

Justification for the censorship of *Manet-PROJEKT '74* was articulated in terms of the museum's division from its economic interests; as museum director Horst Keller wrote in a letter to Haacke, "a museum knows nothing about economic power; it does indeed, however, know something about spiritual power."[9] Keller also insisted that a work reached a "point of rest and finality embodied by a museum . . . one should discuss the price of the work to be acquired only up to the point of its acquisition."[10] Haacke's use of provenance challenged the autonomy of aesthetic experience that was frequently asserted in the conventions of visual display. Haacke incorporated the evidence of art's authentication processes—which legitimate its very right to be seen, its value as cultural property, and the propriety of historical politico-economic values—into the work of art. As Haacke argues: "The validation of certain products as contemporary high art, which, of course guides future production while feeding on the consensus of the past, obviously is not independent of art's economic base."[11] In his installation bringing together Manet's painting and its history of validation, Haacke positioned provenance within the same viewing space as the art object:

Das Spargel-Stilleben
erworben durch die Initiative des
Vorsitzenden des Wallraf-Richartz-Kuratoriums

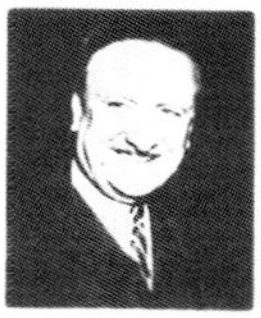

Hermann J. Abs

Geboren 1901 in Bonn. – Entstammt wohlhabender katholischer Familie. Vater Dr. Josef Abs, Rechtsanwalt und Justizrat, Mitinhaber der Hubertus Braunkohlen AG. Brüggen, Erft. Mutter Katharina Lückerath.

Abitur 1919 Realgymnasium Bonn. – Ein Sem. Jurastudium Universität Bonn. – Banklehre im Kölner Bankhaus Delbrück von der Heydt & Co. Erwirbt internationale Bankerfahrung in Amsterdam, London, Paris, USA.

Heiratet 1928 Inez Schnitzler. Ihr Vater mit Georg von Schnitzler vom Vorstand des IG. Farben-Konzerns verwandt. Tante verheiratet mit Baron Alfred Neven du Mont. Schwester verheiratet mit Georg Graf von der Goltz. – Geburt der Kinder Thomas und Marion Abs.

Mitglied der Zentrumspartei. – 1929 Prokura im Bankhaus Delbrück, Schickler & Co., Berlin. 1935-37 einer der 5 Teilhaber der Bank.

1937 im Vorstand und Aufsichtsrat der Deutschen Bank, Berlin. Leiter der Auslandsabteilung. – 1939 von Reichswirtschaftsminister Funk in den Beirat der Deutschen Reichsbank berufen. – Mitglied in Ausschüssen der Reichsbank, Reichsgruppe Industrie, Reichsgruppe Banken, Reichswirtschaftskammer und einem Arbeitskreis im Reichswirtschaftsministerium. – 1944 in über 50 Aufsichts- und Verwaltungsräten großer Unternehmen. Mitgliedschaft in Gesellschaften zur Wahrnehmung deutscher Wirtschaftsinteressen im Ausland.

1946 für 6 Wochen in britischer Haft. – Von der Alliierten Entnazifizierungsbehörde als entlastet (5) eingestuft.

1948 bei der Gründung der Kreditanstalt für Wiederaufbau. Maßgeblich an der Wirtschaftsplanung der Bundesregierung beteiligt. Wirtschaftsberater Konrad Adenauers. – Leiter der deutschen Delegation bei der Londoner Schuldenkonferenz 1951-53. Berater bei den Wiedergutmachungsverhandlungen mit Israel in Den Haag. 1954 Mitglied der CDU.

1952 im Aufsichtsrat der Süddeutschen Bank AG. – 1957-67 Vorstandssprecher der Deutschen Bank AG. Seit 1967 Vorsitzender des Aufsichtsrats.

Ehrenvorsitzender des Aufsichtsrats:
Deutsche Überseeische Bank, Hamburg – Pittler Maschinenfabrik AG, Langen (Hessen)
Vorsitzender des Aufsichtsrats:
Dahlbusch Verwaltungs-AG, Gelsenkirchen – Daimler Benz AG, Stuttgart-Untertürkheim –
Deutsche Bank AG, Frankfurt – Deutsche Lufthansa AG, Köln – Philipp Holzmann AG, Frankfurt –
Phoenix Gummiwerke AG, Hamburg-Harburg – RWE Elektrizitätswerk AG, Essen –
Vereinigte Glanzstoff AG, Wuppertal-Elberfeld – Zellstoff-Fabrik Waldhof AG, Mannheim
Ehrenvorsitzender:
Salamander AG, Kornwestheim – Gebr. Stumm GmbH, Brambauer (Westf.) –
Süddeutsche Zucker-AG, Mannheim
Stellvertr. Vors. des Aufsichtsrats:
Badische Anilin- und Sodafabrik AG, Ludwigshafen – Siemens AG, Berlin-München
Mitglied des Aufsichtsrats:
Metallgesellschaft AG, Frankfurt
Präsident des Verwaltungsrats:
Kreditanstalt für Wiederaufbau – Deutsche Bundesbahn

Großes Bundesverdienstkreuz mit Stern, Päpstl. Stern zum Komturkreuz, Großkreuz Isabella die Katholische von Spanien, Cruzeiro do Sul von Brasilien. – Ritter des Ordens vom Heiligen Grabe. – Dr. h.c. der Univ. Göttingen, Sofia, Tokio und der Wirtschaftshochschule Mannheim.

Lebt in Kronberg (Taunus) und auf dem Bentgerhof bei Remagen.

Photo aus Current Biography Yearbook 1970 New York

Fig. 2.
Hans Haacke (German, b. 1936).
Manet-PROJEKT '74,
(detail of fig. 1), 1974.
Excerpt, close-up of panel on Hermann J. Abs.

Translation of Figure 2

Bunch of Asparagus
Acquired through the initiative of Hermann J. Abs,
Chairman of the Wallraf-Richartz-Kuratorium
(Friends of the Museum)

Born 1901 in Bonn. Descendent of well-to-do Catholic family. Father, Dr. Josef Abs, attorney and judge, co-owner of Hubertus Braunkohlen AG [brown-coal mining company], Brüggen, Erft. Mother, Katharina Lückerath.

1919 graduates from Realgymnasium Bonn. Studies one semester law, University of Bonn. Trains as banker at Bankhaus Delbrück von der Heydt & Co., Cologne. Gains experience in international banking in Amsterdam, London, Paris, and the United States.

1928 marries Inez Schnitzler. Her father related to Georg von Schnitzler, member of executive committee of I.G. Farben group. Aunt married to Baron Alfred Neven du Mont. Sister married to Georg Graf von der Goltz. Birth of two children, Thomas and Marion Abs. Member of Zentrumspartei (Catholic Party). 1929 on staff at Bankhaus Delbrück, Schickler & Co., Berlin, with power of attorney. 1935–37 one of five partners of the bank.

1937 on board of directors and member of executive committee of Deutsche Bank in Berlin. Chief of its foreign division. 1939 appointed member of advisory council of Deutsche Reichsbank by Walther Funk, Minister of Economic Affairs of the Reich. Member of committees of the Reichsbank, Reichsgruppe Industrie, Reichsgruppe Banken, Reichswirtschaftskammer, and Arbeitskreis of the Minister of Economic Affairs. 1944, on more than fifty boards of directors. Membership in associations for the advancement of German economic interests abroad.

1946 imprisoned by British forces. Cleared by Allied denazification board and placed in category 5 (exonerated of active support of Nazi regime).

1948 participated in foundation of Kreditanstalt für Wiederaufbau (Credit Agency for Reconstruction). Extensive involvement in economic planning by West German government. Economic advisor to Chancellor Konrad Adenauer. 1951–53 head of German delegation to London conference negotiating German war debts. Advisory role during negotiations with Israel at Conference on Jewish Material Claims in The Hague. 1954 member of CDU (Christian Democratic Party).

1952 on board of directors of Süddeutsche Bank AG. 1957–67 president of Deutsche Bank AG. Since 1967 chairman of the board.

Honorary chairman of board of directors:
Deutsche Überseeische Bank, Hamburg; Pittler Maschinenfabrik AG, Langen (Hesse).
Chairman of board of directors:
Dahlbusch Verwaltungs-AG, Gelsenkirchen; Daimler Benz AG, Stuttgart-Untertürkheim; Deutsche Bank AG, Frankfurt; Deutsche Lufthansa AG, Köln, Philipp Holzmann AG, Frankfurt; Phoenix Gummiwerke AG, Hamburg-Harburg; RWE Elektrizitätswerk AG, Essen; Vereinigte Glanzstoff AG, Wuppertal-Elberfeld; Zellstoff-Fabrik Waldhof AG, Mannheim.

Honorary chairman:
Salamander AG, Kornwestheim; Gebr. Stumm GmbH, Brambauer (Westphalia); Süddeutsche Zucker-AG, Mannheim.
Vice-chairman of board of directors:
Badische Anilin- und Sodafabrik AG, Ludwigshafen; Siemens AG, Berlin-München.
Member of board of directors:
Metallgesellschaft AG, Frankfurt.
President of supervisory board:
Kreditanstalt für Wiederaufbau; Deutsche Bundesbahn.

Great Cross of the Order of Merit with Star of the Federal Republic of Germany, Papal Star with Cross of the Commander, Great Cross of Isabella the Catholic of Spain, Cruzeiro do Sul of Brazil, Knight of the Order of the Holy Sepulcher. Honorary doctorate degrees from universities of Göttingen, Sofia, Tokyo, and Wirtschaftshochschule Mannheim.

Lives in Kronberg (Taunus) and Bentgerhof near Remagen.

Photo from Current Biography Yearbook 1970, New York.

Translation provided by artist.

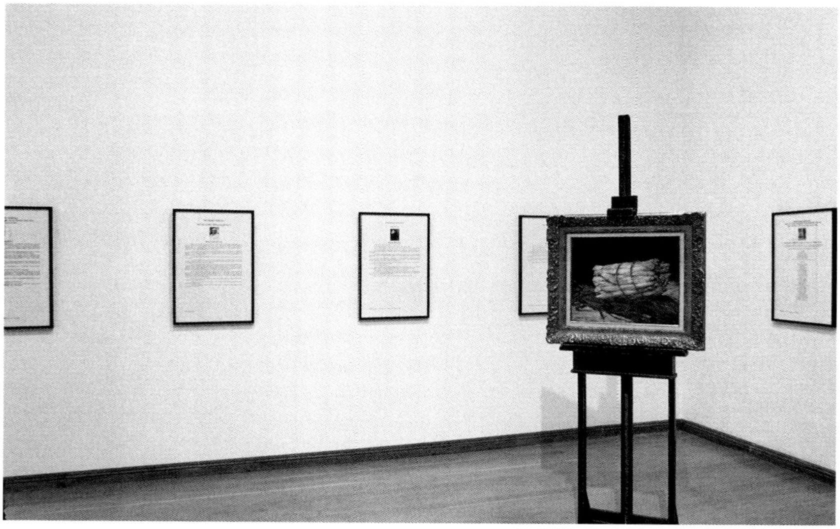

Fig. 3.
Hans Haacke (German, b. 1936).
Manet-PROJEKT '74 (detail), 1974, ten black-and-white panels and Edouard Manet's *Bunch of Asparagus* (1880). First exhibited at Galerie Paul Maenz, Cologne, 1974. Installation view at the exhibition *Deutschlandbilder,* Martin-Gropius-Bau, Berlin, 1997.

Manet-PROJEKT '74's accumulation of financial value occupied the frame of both phenomenological experience and art-historical interest, whose validity is inextricably bound to systems of validation.

While the collection and transference of art objects are generally constitutive of personal and political interests, Haacke's critique of institutions intervenes in the specific cultural condition of postwar Germany and the cultural mediation of the country's transition from the Third Reich to reconstruction.[12] In 1967, the "pathological inability to mourn" was a charge leveled at the Right's disabling refusal to understand its own complicity in the Holocaust, and its reluctance to accept collective guilt.[13] Benjamin Buchloh has described the time of *Manet-PROJEKT '74* as one in which "history would appear as a dialectical construct (rather than an openly accessible imaginary plenitude)."[14] Within such a dialectic of history, the artist's enactment of the historian's due diligence presented *Bunch of Asparagus* through its incremental legitimations of taste over the years. This shifts dramatically in the final panels, which cover the period when the painting was left in Switzerland following Nazi persecution of Max Liebermann and his widow, the painting's subsequent sale by their heirs, and its acquisition by a consortium in 1968. The consortium—headed by Abs—donated the painting to the Cologne museum. Ownership was recalibrated as debt: Haacke's work charts Abs's significant role in the "Aryannization" of Jewish property and the subsequent acquisition of the Manet—after a suspicious gap in *Bunch of Asparagus*'s provenance and after several of its previous owners were persecuted by the Nazis—and implicates the individuals operating behind the institutional façade that shielded them from questions about collection practices.[15]

In *Manet-PROJEKT '74*, provenance was mobilized toward counter-memory, as Haacke's work of research and information-gathering—described, by turns, as research, quasi-sociological inquiries, or investigative journalism[16]—critically applied the techniques of the historian to the purity of aesthetic experience, thus situating an elite German audience and institution as being necessarily complicit and manifestly historical subjects.[17] While Haacke has defended his works by citing their use of publicly available data and information, the contingency of his enterprise has not escaped the artist's attention. Haacke notes that "nothing can escape eventual absorption" by the culture industry.[18] The artist's use of public sources offers only temporary immunity—the project of counter-memory, while challenging certain forms of institutionalized forgetting and modeling a discursive turn in art practice, does not necessarily secure historical permanence.[19] Stephen Feinstein and James Young have suggested the difficulty of finding an appropriate visual language to convey memory with regard to the subject of the Holocaust, particularly in relation to monuments and memorials, and Young in particular traces the emphasis on topographies of destruction, ruins, and the rhetoric of redemption.[20] The use of provenance and its mode of research depart from the more dominant forms of memorialization and the various appeals to texture and trauma in the work of German artists such as Anselm Kiefer. More recent scholarship offers an alternative; for instance, Mark Godfrey's account of abstraction and the Holocaust considers how the work of artists such as Barnett Newman, Frank Stella, and Mel Bochner reorient abstraction's relation to history, to examine the relation between "work and mnemonic content" in the very structure of memory.[21] *Manet-PROJEKT '74* may be seen to elaborate such a project of signification and structure as a means to negotiate Holocaust memory, using research processes to pose a persistent critique of the signifying practices of artists, historians, curators, and institutions of art. While seeking knowledge is part of a commitment to declaring and discharging debts in contemporary moments of public mourning, the ongoing task and contingency of such work is clear; as inevitable gaps in a painting's provenance record appear, *Manet-PROJEKT '74* offers a picture of both information's importance and its inadequacy.[22]

By employing the informational sign of conceptual art and its use of magazines and journals, Haacke's provenance practice also includes the mechanisms of publicizing or recording a work of art; it excavates the past with an eye toward future dissemination.[23] The censorship of *Manet-PROJEKT '74* suppressed the piece by omitting it from the exhibition catalog. This situation was countered by Daniel Buren's attempt to rescue the work's content by pasting facsimiles of Haacke's panels on his own work in the exhibition and by creating a poster whose title, *Art Remains Politics,* references the exhibition's official slogan, "Art Remains Art." Over the past three decades, Haacke has reproduced the work's texts in their entirety, carefully sizing the texts and images to ensure their legibility and therefore the crucial meaning of his work.[24] Such a practice may be interpreted within the broader informational impulses of conceptual art, exemplified by Sol LeWitt's characterization of the conceptual artist as offering information through predetermined structures to withhold subjectivity, positioning the artist as "a clerk cataloguing the results of his premise."[25] This would subsequently be criticized by Benjamin Buchloh as the aesthetic of administration that did not "aspire to overcome the mere facticity" of artistic production's conditions but instead surrendered to the logic of advanced capitalism by mimicking the forms of its labor.[26] Against conceptual art's potential collusion with capitalism's administrative procedures, Buchloh's now-landmark essay offers a critique of institutions and cites the practices of Haacke, Buren, and Marcel Broodthaers as exemplary. For Buchloh, their use of bureaucratic structures and administrative procedures turned "the violence of that mimetic relationship back onto the ideological apparatus itself, using it to analyze and expose the social institutions from which the laws of positivist instrumentality and the logic of administration emanate," to question how artistic production is itself transformed "into a tool of ideological control and cultural legitimation."[27]

Buchloh's essay has since seen numerous responses and criticism. For one, as Thomas Crow points out, the "mimicry of bureaucratic information and classification that characterized Conceptualism in its early years," dismissed by Buchloh as an aesthetic of administration, remains a significant move within work of the 1960s and 1970s as well as more recent practices.[28] Crow cites Haacke's *Shapolsky et al., Manhattan Real Estate Holdings, a Real-Time Social System, as of May 1, 1971* (1971), in which Haacke exposed the complex web of dummy corporations that fronted a slumlord's real estate empire in New York, and argues that in the piece, "the artist operated entirely within the established systemic and serial logic that governed the advanced art of the moment."[29] However, in questioning a hard division between conceptualism and institutional critique, and in thinking about the place of information and seriality in relation to affect and visuality (in the work of artists such as Christopher Williams), Crow misses a crucial point in Buchloh's formulation: the artist of institutional critique is not outside of conceptualism's bureaucracy but operating fully within "*the violence of the mimetic relationship*" (emphasis my own) with the institution. Haacke's intensification of visual interest in the "C.V.s" of *Bunch of Asparagus*'s owners, their pedigree and affiliation, are executed fully within the logic of professional social capital, and *Manet-PROJEKT*'s installation required that Manet's *Bunch of Asparagus* be present as its foil.

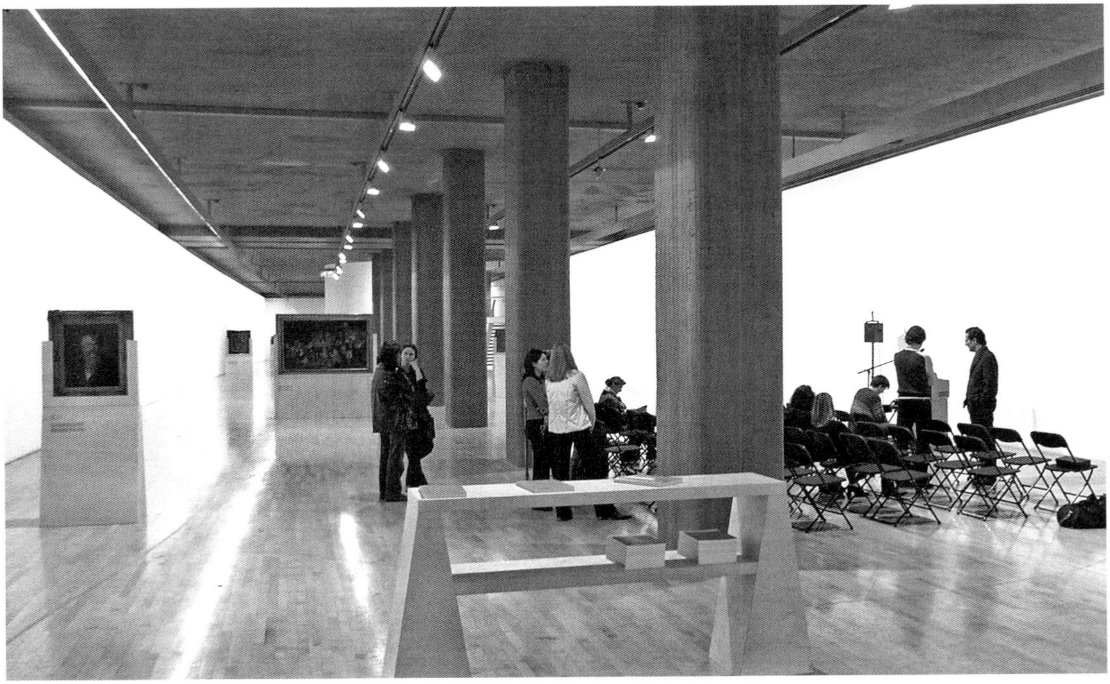

Fig. 4.
Maria Eichhorn (German, b. 1962).
Restitutionspolitik / Politics of Restitution, 2003, installation of sixteen paintings at the Städtische Galerie im Lenbachhaus München, mounted on freestanding displays, provenance research conducted on all paintings presented in an exhibition handbook, library, talks, and discussions held in the exhibition space.
Photographic detail: Audience prior to lecture by art historian Alexander Alberro, "On Provenance and Other Problematic Returns," held in the exhibition space on 3 February 2004.
Munich, Städtische Galerie im Lenbachhaus und Kunstbau.

Thirty years later, the politics of the art object's affect and institutional frame in relation to Holocaust restitution has shifted. Between 1998 and 2000, the United States, Germany, and numerous European states pledged to pursue provenance research to establish ownership of Nazi-looted art and settle post-war debts. Maria Eichhorn's *Politics of Restitution* (2003) was realized in the charged city of Munich, host to the Nazi-era *Grosse Deutsche Kunstausstellung* (Great German art) exhibitions and the first *Entartete Kunst* (Degenerate art) exhibition, and the historical collection point of Nazi-looted art.[30] Upon an invitation to realize a solo exhibition at the Städtische Galerie im Lenbachhaus in Munich, Eichhorn employed a historian, Anja Heuss, to research the provenance of a group of state-held "orphaned" paintings that were on permanent loan to the Lenbachhaus. The research was exhibited in a guide and exhibition catalog. The paintings, mounted on stand-alone displays designed to show both their front and back, were arranged at even intervals across the floor of the bunker-like exhibition space (fig. 4).

Folding the discursive institutional support of art history into the aesthetic experience of the paintings, the viewer was provided with an exhibition guide at the entrance of the exhibition. The guide includes photographs of each painting's front and back, formal descriptions, explanations of transport markings, scans of property cards, restitution contracts, and a glossary with both key terms and names of people. The content of this guide is similar to that of the exhibition catalog. Thus, the aesthetic experience was framed by and integrated with Heuss's research. As they passed through the exhibition, visitors had an opportunity to browse a miniature library that featured books on the Holocaust and on art restitution. During the course of the exhibition, a series of lectures, organized by Eichhorn as part of the work, was held amid the paintings. Extending the legacy of Haacke's interest in research and use of publications, Eichhorn's work employed the modern apparatus of the exhibition guide and catalog to collate historical research and documents for future dissemination. As a site-specific work dependent on the museum's collection—the piece has, at this point, not been purchased—*Politics of Restitution*'s record exists through its extensive catalog (itself nearly identical to the exhibition guide), sustained by its preemptive discursive siting.

Eichhorn's provenance research posed a significant intervention: when her piece was shown, Munich had suspended the budget for ongoing provenance research and was only responding to specific requests.[31] E. Randol Schoenberg notes that "outside the United States, the Washington Principles have been largely ignored. Most countries have undertaken only superficial or no research at all."[32] This neglect may be understood within a context that Rosalyn Deutsche previously cautioned against, the broader "forgetting of German fascist history, exposing and warning against the persistence of antidemocratic tendencies in the German cultural climate."[33] By employing Anja Heuss with funds from her exhibition budget, Eichhorn managed to produce provenance research on the paintings on loan from the state just when Munich has abdicated its responsibility; in so doing, Eichhorn produced provenance where hitherto there had been none.[34] One would be remiss to discharge politics completely from conceptualism's obsessive data-mining informational mode that opened post-studio and research-based art practices to the work of contemporary artists today. In Eichhorn's work, the informational mode was *activated* toward future recollections and deployments of politics against institutional and national forces of suppression and away from pious historicism.[35] Furthermore, the studies of taste produced by *Manet-PROJEKT '74*'s "C.V.s" and *Politics of Restitution*'s biographies of collection are important for postwar restitution, which hinges on understanding what types of art Hitler favored—as being representative of the German people, advancing his cultural ambition, and constructing his Pax Germania.[36] Knowledge of the period's politics of taste helps identify potentially looted art through the study of specific styles and themes because biography and taste do not follow or elaborate provenance research but are, in fact, often *preconditions* of provenance. In emphasizing the professional and cultural biographies of collectors, Haacke and Eichhorn map ownership as constituted by socioprofessional values, offering personal politics as necessarily constitutive of constructing historical provenance, and subjectivity as intrinsic to historical and art-historical study.[37]

Politics of Restitution focuses mainly on works considered "orphaned" and under the fosterhood of the state, and the provenance research by Heuss indicated that two works in the collection may have been looted; this information subtly brought into question the role of the state in adjudicating the cultural politics of art collection and ownership.[38] The exhibition's curatorial statement contends that by employing Heuss and by displaying both sides of the paintings, "nothing can be added or disguised." However, this rhetoric of transparency inoculates the museum's processes of collection maintenance against criticism of what continues to be inadequate archival information regarding the works in the collection, potentially displacing criticism onto the state while deflecting the gaze of those interested in the museum's operations and accountability.[39] Jacques Derrida once described the role of the archive as that of a "pledge, and like every pledge [gage], a token of the future.... Archival meaning is also and in advance codetermined by the structure that it archives."[40] As Mieke Bal warns: "Deceptively, collections, especially when publicly accessible, appear to 'reach out,' but through this complex and half-hidden aspect they in fact 'reach in.'"[41]

Yet, as Henrik Oleson polemically suggests, "the way out is the way in" for the legacy of conceptual art—with regard both to moving further into the histories of such art practices and to the contexts in which they are placed and complicit.[42] In the exhibition, Eichhorn included Max Slevogt's painting *Trotting Race in Ruhleben* (1920–21), a painting not on loan from the state but owned by the Lenbachhaus, as a reminder of the history of the Lenbachhaus's initial purchase of *Trotting Race;* previous research had revealed that the painting was looted. *Trotting Race* was restituted after considerable public attention—and subsequently repurchased by the museum.[43] While the museum's initial interest in Eichhorn's use of provenance as an artistic procedure could be read as a desire to repair its image, Eichhorn's insistence on featuring *Trotting Race* in the display of the state's "orphaned" paintings with Heuss's provenance research brings into question both the present and the previous claims to ownership, implicating the museum and state institutions in ongoing provenance restitution claims (fig. 5).

Eichhorn's work is also coterminous with an expanded definition of the sites of institutional critique. Alex Alberro has described the interventions of artists beyond the frame of art into other venues and structures, and into discursive sites beyond the walls and ideologies of the museum and gallery.[44] Eichhorn's work with provenance shuttles in between the two definitions of immanent critique and expanded institutionality. It includes the museum as a crucial site

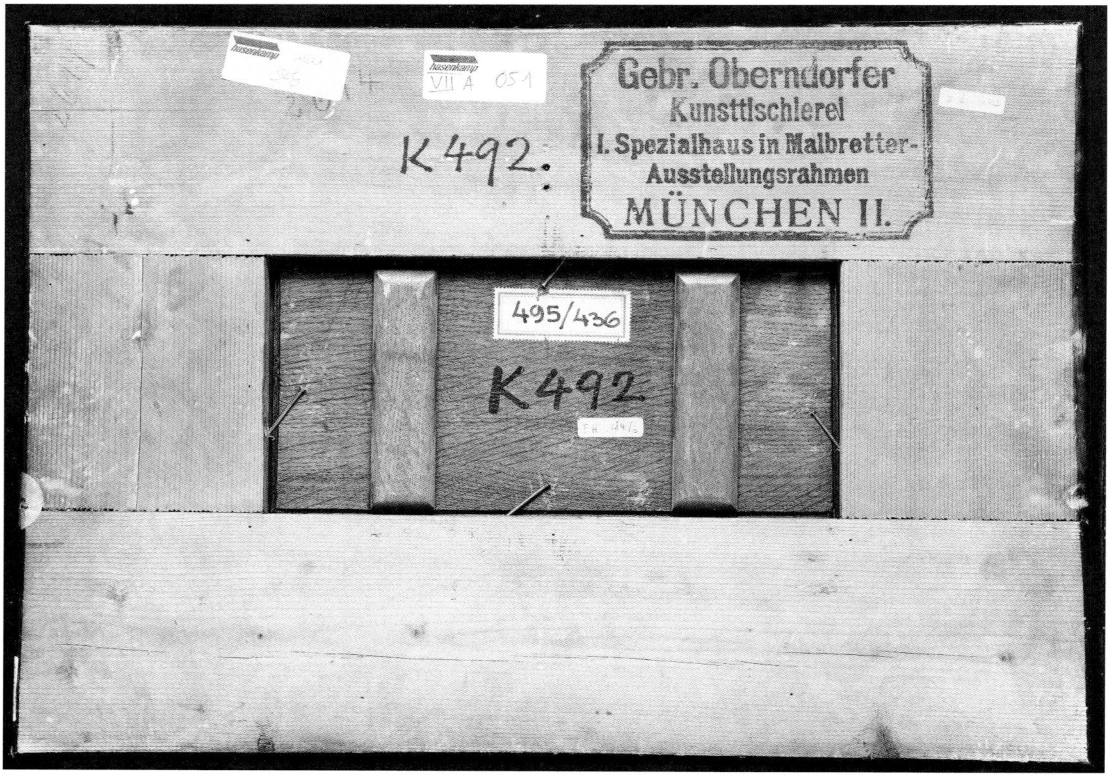

Fig. 5.
Maria Eichhorn (German, b. 1962).
Restitutionspolitik / Politics of Restitution, 2003, installation of sixteen paintings at the Städtische Galerie im Lenbachhaus München, mounted on freestanding displays, provenance research conducted on all paintings presented in an exhibition handbook, library, talks, and discussions held in the exhibition space.
Photographic detail: Reverse view of Robert Schleich (German, 1845–1934), *Foothill Landscape with Haymaking,* late 1800s, oil on wood, 12 × 26.8 cm (4¾ × 10⅝ in.).
Munich, Städtische Galerie im Lenbachhaus und Kunstbau.

of critique; however, the project also features an expanded definition of the cultural apparatus that highlights national and international policies and agreements as well as the state, federal administration, and transnational provenance research. It presents the research and public life of the museum, researcher, and artist as necessarily entangled within these broader circuits and forces of accountability and power.[45]

Preparing for Provenance

Yet, as Andrea Fraser astutely notes, a critique of institutions must always emerge from within them. While any agent is necessarily complicit within an institution, the maintenance of antagonisms in the field and the possibility of inappropriate gestures are crucial in expanding the target and range of critical subjects.[46] Reading Eichhorn's work now is also to engage with the art history of institutional critique and the response of artists to such an art history. According to Julia Bryan-Wilson, the introduction of institutional critique into the curricula of art requires a deeper consideration by scholars and artists, who should also attend to the avant-garde's relation to the market, the effects of which include the "institutionalization of the academy, the bureaucratization of curation, and the professionalization of art criticism."[47] We may read her argument in tandem with Fraser's insistence that the critique of "all the sites in which art is shown" should include "sites of production of art discourse" both commercial *and* educational, and, to quote Martha Rosler's 1979 essay, the "lookers, buyers, dealers and makers" themselves.[48] Emerging after the "project art" and KontextKunst (context art) of the 1990s, after the research practices of artists miming the ethnographer or historian in the 1990s and 2000s, and after work by artists such as Louise Lawler (who examined the effect of acquisition and collection upon the significance of the art object), Eichhorn's work considers "forms or media such as lectures, texts, statements . . . and events" to be "treated as commodities."[49] Haacke employs the visual aesthetics of data (and requests that photographic reproductions of his works in scholarship, including this essay, reproduce the images at sizes that allow for textual legibility) and is attentive to how art history frames and disseminates works of art; in contrast, Eichhorn deploys the informational mode while structuring the aesthetic encounter to incorporate the very processes and performances of art history's discursive operations.[50]

Elizabeth Ferrell rightly locates Eichhorn's work within "the critical assessment of Conceptual art that began in the late 1980s when she was studying at the Hochschule der Künste in Berlin"; that assessment evolved into sourcebooks and exhibitions of conceptual art in the 1990s and culminated, in the early 2000s, in an array of edited anthologies and scholarship on reformulating the premises of conceptual art and institutional critique. Eichhorn's intervention in the writing of conceptual art's history targets the landmark Artist's Reserved Rights Transfer and Sale Agreement (hereafter the Agreement), written in 1969 by curator Seth Siegelaub and lawyer Robert Projansky to protect artists' resale rights. Alexander Alberro's important study of conceptual art argues that the development of the contract required that the Agreement function as "a bill of sale" becoming "part of the work"; as a consequence, the contract revalorized the artist's signature as preserving exclusive ownership of the work. While ostensibly drafted to protect the rights of the artist and destabilize a calcified art industry, the Agreement nevertheless provided a concrete solution to the challenge of marketing ideas and dematerialized art, drawing conceptual art into what Lucy Lippard condemned as "the tyranny of a commodity status and market-orientation" and the insertion of conceptual art "into the art market as a pure commodity or bill of sale."[51]

Eichhorn's response to accounts of conceptual art's collusion with exchange value offers another view. While Alberro contends that "Siegelaub had solved his 'earlier queries of how to market ideas,'" Eichhorn maintains that "the reverse is true. The agreement removes all art from the market in that it is only under certain conditions that it does not exclude it from the market or keep it at a distance."[52] Eichhorn's research into the Agreement demonstrates its embattled usage, which generated thorny problems rather than pithy solutions. For a solo exhibition at the Salzburger Kunstverein (1998), Eichhorn produced a book and exhibition on the Agreement, presented Siegelaub's archive, and prepared an overview of resale royalty rights in Europe and international copyright laws.[53] Eichhorn interviewed various artists and gallerists associated with conceptual art—including Haacke—for their reflections on the Agreement and estimation of its meaning. More recently, as her contribution to the Berlin Bienniale (2008), Eichhorn organized a panel with Siegelaub and legal expert Daniel McClean on the Agreement, distributing copies of the Agreement at the event; she published her interviews with artists and gallerists on the Agreement as a book, *The Artist's Contract* (2009). That same year, the Contemporary Artists' Book Conference at MoMA PS1 in New York featured a keynote panel with presentations by Eichhorn, Haacke, Siegelaub, and MoMA curator Christophe Cherix discussing Eichhorn's recent publication.[54] Eichhorn's intervention may be viewed as both an intervention into the economics and institutional practices of art and an intervention into the institution of art history, offering up material for research and counterproposals for art's exchange value. To clarify Eichhorn's interest in the Agreement, I will now examine its major terms and assumptions regarding provenance—namely, the issues of the artwork's investment value and visibility.

The Agreement secures for the artist a percentage of future sales and control over sales and resale terms (*droit de suite*). It records future transfers and must be ratified by subsequent owners; a work's "price/value" and its "appreciated value" must be documented and available to the artist. For this to be viable, the Agreement includes a section on provenance, wherein the artist maintains a record of every transfer of the work, and collectors are legally bound to notify the artist of any exhibitions and subsequent sales so that the artist can validate the work's provenance, history, and authenticity. Thus, provenance secures for the artist both financial remuneration and control over the art object's circulation.[55] From the outset, artists in the Art Workers' Coalition—a group that formed in response to sculptor Takis's objection to the way his work was shown at the Museum of Modern Art in 1969—recognized the art object as intellectual property; they demanded the recognition of artists' rights as equivalent to the rights of producers working in the film and music industries, and strongly objected to the (mis)use of works for price speculation and manipulation.[56]

Paradoxically, the difficulties of implementing the Agreement have confined its use to those artists whose practices inherently complicate investment, secondary sales, and provenance. According to gallerist John Weber, a major problem for enforcing the contract has been the question of volume. For artists such as Haacke and Buren, whose site-specific works involve long periods of research—and whose general output remains low and saleable output even lower—the Agreement is ideal because it implicitly assumes a model of art making that does not target volume and speed. However, for artists who produce work more regularly, show prolifically, and succeed on the secondary market, tracking collectors and transactions can quickly become an onerous task.[57] By enforcing strict oversight procedures—since, according to Eichhorn, "the success of this Contract is also how it's policed, how it is controlled"—the Agreement reduces the rate of exchange and slows, even undermines, investment.[58] Haacke, perhaps the most active user of the Agreement, denies the privileging of resale remuneration while admitting its necessity, contending that artists should avoid depending on sales of their work as a sole source of income and that "artists who do sell well [should] insist on the Contract and thus make it socially acceptable."[59]

Tracking an object's future provenance bears a price. Informing an artist of subsequent resales increases the chance that the artist will intervene and assert his or her right to control the work's ownership and oversee proper maintenance, or *droit moral*, and many collectors are dissuaded by potential complications.[60] Buren's use of artists' contracts through his personal contract, called the *Avertissement* (the first version was produced with Michel Claura in 1968), allows Buren to track nearly all the locations of his work but also gave way to "a lot of fights and explanations, considerable loss of sales and a lot of disappointment—which explains very well why it's so difficult to use and so little used.... This raises interesting questions about selling and not; about opening some doors and closing others."[61] However, Eichhorn's research also points toward a possible shift in the Agreement's usage. Haacke's and Eichhorn's work mark two separate historical moments: Haacke's work was part of the early 1970s art world that birthed the neo-avant-garde practices of conceptual art and performance; its community of artists were relatively poor and their record of sales low. Eichhorn's work of the 2000s emerged during the peak of the art market's bubble, when artists such as Tino Seghal and Santiago Sierra were being represented by galleries able to sell their radically dematerialized work, and when reassessments of conceptualism and institutional critique were under way and their commercial and institutional absorption and enduring critical legacies for art practice were under debate.[62] Douglas Crimp contemporaneously described the art practices of institutional critique in the 1990s as "fitful, marginalized practices that struggle to exist at all" in an art landscape refigured by the consequences of policies advocating neoliberal markets and neoconservative politics, "more dedicated than ever before to commodity value."[63] A decade later, Paula Cooper noted the entrenchment of these circumstances in the art market of the 2000s, which briefly advocated contemporary art's investment value—a situation that "makes contracts dealing with related issues, such as speculation and the reselling of works at auction shortly after acquisition, entirely necessary."[64]

Since 1972, all collectors of Haacke's work must sign the Agreement, and the artist has vetoed sales to collectors he suspects of buying work to remove it from circulation.[65] Haacke underscores the vital importance determining "where and under what circumstances my works are exhibited"; consequently, he remains vigilant about the exhibition and provenance of his work, and readily invokes the Agreement's relevant clause to stop his work from being included in exhibitions he does not wish to be associated with.[66] At stake are the symbolic and cultural capital that the work of art and the artist lend to exhibitions, collectors, institutions, and funders—the work of art's circulation is, in Haacke's practice, deeply political. Although Siegelaub casts the Agreement in highly idealistic, emancipatory, and anti-institutional terms, he disavows the broader politics of the 1960s in forming the contract and attributes its birth to pragmatism. However, the politics Siegelaub disavows also laid the groundwork for artists' interest in the contract, not only to show and sell their work in more meaningful ways but also to withdraw their works from sale or exhibition. An example of the former would be the protests, by numerous artists based in New York and among Siegelaub's circle, against US interventions in Vietnam in the 1960s and '70s and Chile in 1970. These protests culminated in the artists' attempt to withdraw work from the US pavilion at the Venice Biennale of 1970, only to confront a lack of reasonable deadlines for the withdrawal of work, insufficient curatorial consultation, and no legal protections over their works' display.[67]

This is because exhibition—or lack of it—is fundamental to collecting because the custody of a work of art determines its visibility and consequent participation in public life. Institutions of ownership bring artists, historians, ideas, and objects into the public sphere. Conditions of ownership and display are crucial to the work of artists such as Haacke and Eichhorn, whose interventions require legal and institutional mechanisms to retain their voice in debates on restitution and research. While Eichhorn does not use the Agreement, her work frequently involves legal agreements that maintain her ownership and control over the transfers, longevity, and operations of her work. In the case of *Maria Eichhorn Aktiengesellschaft* (2002–), for example, Documenta 11 supported the founding of a self-contained public-limited company in the artist's name, which Eichhorn hopes to maintain in perpetuity through a legal agreement. (In 2007, the work was transferred into the collection of the Van

Abbemuseum.) The company holds, as shares, a portion of the exhibition budget amounting to 50,000 euros. According to Elizabeth Ferrell, by using the company's founding capital to buy back its stocks, the company "owns itself." The reacquisition withholds 50,000 euros from circulation, exchange value, and interest, and the gesture of reacquisition undermines the sovereignty of the public-limited company and its provisions for shareholders to "gain profit without risk, thus enabling the massive investment and accumulation of capital characteristic of late capitalism." The tautology of Eichhorn's use of acquisition and reacquisition, however, frustrates the production of surplus value, the possibility of speculation, and the creation of property.[68]

Maria Eichhorn Aktiengesellschaft undoes the relationship between an object's future history of collection and its secondary value—provenance could be written, quite literally, without the possibility of profit. Buren describes Eichhorn's interest in legal agreements and the art object's cultural and symbolic value as "working with a view to the future circulation of your work." [69] Or, as Eichhorn writes, "The status of artworks differs from ordinary private property because of the artwork's nature as a cultural product. Copyright laws, resale rights, uniqueness/originality, price, speculation potential, etc., qualify this status. Copyright laws and resale rights, the legislation, vary from country to country. All art works, regardless of whether they are unique objects, film, music, or literature, should be accessible publicly; they should not be withdrawn from the public sphere."[70]

Who would sign the Agreement? Weber—with reference to early collectors of Haacke's work—observes that collectors "enjoy signing the Contract because they have the same politics that Haacke does,"[71] and Eichhorn takes Sol LeWitt's position that a "collector would, in a sense, be the custodian of that art" to argue that the basis of the Agreement was that "a work of art should remain the artist's property."[72] Taken together, this imagines a different kind of collection practice: one where artistic property belongs to the artist, where collectors share commitments to Leftist politics, where art cannot be reduced or liquidated into pure commodity form for financial speculation, and where ownership is recalibrated as a space for participation in the public sphere.[73] Consequently, the Agreement does not distinguish between individual and institutional collecting—both are subject to the same terms—and thus implicates the personal experience and private phenomena of collecting as necessarily generating public consequences. The Agreement also functions in the gap between law and praxis: since the 1920s, artists' rights have been secured in France and Germany, a condition Haacke and Eichhorn would have been accustomed to as German citizens. However, in the United States, such rights did not exist during the 1960s and '70s, with the exception of California's Resale Royalties Act. While the Visual

Artists Rights Act (1990) in the United States now secures artists' rights over authorship of their work, it does not cover resale rights.[74]

The Agreement's necessity is also born of a failure on the part of arts, federal, and state institutions to support artists' rights; the Agreement operates within a nongovernmental *civil* space of praxis.[75] It is less a rejection of law than a supplement to the present limitations and deficiencies in legal processes. In spite of the protections afforded by federal art laws, international transactions within the global art market produce varying degrees of vulnerability for artists. When collectors and artists reside in different cities, it can be difficult to resolve legal matters because geographic jurisdictions will preempt attempts at litigation. Under these circumstances, civil practices and personal agreements become essential. The Agreement, with Haacke's modifications, vetoes any unregulated and unaccountable forms of sale that would prohibit the space of public debate, of which the artist is necessarily a part. Eichhorn's use of a legal agreement in *Maria Eichhorn Aktiengesellschaft* offers the possibility of art's circulation as governed by aspirations and procedures reflecting other kinds of social relations between artists, dealers, and collectors. In addition, it embraces a definition of ownership without property and the subsequent writing and production of provenance as primarily a matter of public, rather than profitable, interest.[76] Such an economy of acquisition would hold the financial and political transactions of art answerable to ethical and political questions in a global art system that could open up public debate or halt its traffic at the border.

Notes

My thanks to Hans Haacke and Maria Eichhorn for their assistance during the preparation of this essay.

1. Maria Eichhorn, "On the *Avertissement:* Interview with Daniel Buren," in *Institutional Critique and After,* ed. John Welchman (Zurich: JRP/Ringier, 2006), 85–121, esp. 115.
2. The classic polemic around which such debates rotated during the late 1960s and '70s is Michael Fried, "Art and Objecthood," *Artforum* 5, no. 10 (1967): 12–23. For a more sociological examination of artistic transcendence and for the general condition of the fine art object, see Pierre Bourdieu, "The Historical Genius of a Pure Aesthetic," in *The Field of Cultural Production: Essays on Art and Literature* (Cambridge, U.K.: Polity, 2004), 255.
3. Pierre Bourdieu, "The Production of Belief," in *The Field of Cultural Production: Essays on Art and Literature* (Cambridge, U.K.: Polity, 2004), 71, 81.
4. Eichhorn, "On the *Advertissement,*" 93–94.
5. Brian Wallis, ed., *Hans Haacke: Unfinished Business,* exh. cat. (Cambridge, Mass.: MIT Press, 1986), 118.
6. Yve-Alain Bois et al., "A Conversation with Hans Haacke," *October* 30 (1984): 23–48, esp. 37.

7. Bois et al., "A Conversation with Hans Haacke," 36–37. It should also be noted that Haacke's practice of researching and displaying biographies of his objects of interest, demonstrating the personal life of power, has extended through his art of the 1970s and '80s to include research on the museum trustees of the Guggenheim Museum in *Solomon R. Guggenheim Board of Trustees* (1974), corporations such as Mobil or Alcan Aluminium Ltd., e.g., *Voici Alcan* (1983), and business magnates such as Peter Ludwig in *Der Pralinemeister* (1982).
8. Carl Baldwin, "Haacke: Refuse in Cologne," *Art in America* 62, no. 6 (1974): 36–37.
9. Wallis, *Hans Haacke: Unfinished Business*, 118.
10. Baldwin, "Haacke," 37.
11. Hans Haacke, "The Constituency" (1976), in *Hans Haacke: For Real; Works, 1959–2006*, ed. Matthias Flügge and Robert Fleck, trans. Hans Haacke and Steven Lindberg (Düsseldorf: Richter, 2006), 266.
12. Bois et al., "A Conversation with Hans Haacke," 36.
13. Jeffrey K. Olick and Daniel Levy, "Collective Memory and Cultural Constraint: Holocaust Myth and Rationality in German Politics," *American Sociological Review* 62 (1997): 921–36, esp. 928, 930–31.
14. Benjamin Buchloh, "Hans Haacke: The Entwinement of Myth and Enlightenment," in Hans Haacke, Benjamin Buchloh, and Walter Grasskamp, *Hans Haacke: "Obra Social,"* exh. cat. (Barcelona: Fundació Antoni Tàpies, 1995), 45–60, esp. 51.
15. Matthias Flügge and Robert Fleck, eds., *Hans Haacke: For Real; Works, 1959–2006*, trans. Hans Haacke and Steven Lindberg (Düsseldorf: Richter, 2006), 120–21.
16. For Haacke, as a German artist living in the United States, showing frequently in Europe while a member of the Art Worker's Coalition in New York, we may think of *Manet-PROJEKT '74*'s use of the informational as emerging from a transatlantic field of concerns: while the piece targets the historical cultural condition of postwar Germany, Haacke's gathering of information predates this work, in examples such as *MoMA Poll* (1970); *Shapolsky et al. Manhattan Real Estate Holdings, a Real-Time Social System, as of May 1, 1971* (1971); and *Solomon R. Guggenheim Board of Trustees* (1974). These projects were informed by the Vietnam War–era interventions of artists into the North American communicative public sphere, where artists' informational polemics contested justifications for governmental colonial interventions into Vietnam and, subsequently, Central and South America.

    For a description of the research model of institutional critique, see James Meyer, *What Happened to the Institutional Critique?* (New York: American Fine Arts, 1993); for the limits of understanding Haacke's data acquisition in his early 1970s work, see responses of sociologists in Hans Haacke et al., *Framing and Being Framed: 7 Works, 1970–1975*, ed. Kasper König (Halifax: The Press of the Nova Scotia College of Art and Design, 1975); for an account of Haacke's work with information as a medium, approximating that of investigative journalism, see Julia Bryan-Wilson, "Hans Haacke's Paperwork," in *Art Workers: Radical Practice in the Vietnam War Era* (Berkeley: University of California Press, 2009), 173–214.
17. I borrow the term from Jonathan Crary's use of "counter-memory" to describe a possible antidote to the spectacle's colonization of everyday life, which he derives

from the alternative histories and geographies of the Situationists' use of surrealism's anthropological dimension. See Jonathan Crary, "Spectacle, Attention, Counter-Memory," *October* 50 (1989): 96–107.

18. Bois et al., "A Conversation with Hans Haacke," 48. Yve-Alain Bois praises "this quality of immediacy, of simply adding information," saying that it "is the way your work will always resist complete co-option," to which Douglas Crimp has responded: "Except insofar as one gets further away from what is referred to historically. After all, Heartfield can be recuperated now, even though his work includes real information," 48.
19. Andreas Huyssen has also noted, despite attempts at creating public spheres of "real" memory as antidotes to the politics of forgetting (by postdictatorship regimes, repressive silencing, and other forms of controlling national memory), "the fault line between mythic past and real past is not always easy to draw—which is one of the conundrums of any politics of memory anywhere." Andreas Huyssen, *Present Pasts: Urban Palimpsests and the Politics of Memory* (Stanford, Calif.: Stanford University Press, 2003), 16. While forms of information are certainly marshaled by Haacke and Eichhorn against a politics of forgetting, following Crimp, I would contend not that such practices posit a definitive, unassailable truth of the Holocaust but merely that their practices model a simultaneously historical and discursive turn, as a response to the transnational research practices of Holocaust cultural restitution.
20. See Young's distinction between monuments and memorials and his broader categorization of Holocaust memorials in James E. Young, *The Texture of Memory: Holocaust Memorials and Meaning* (New Haven, Conn.: Yale University Press, 1993), 2. See also Stephen Feinstein, *Witness and Legacy: Contemporary Art about the Holocaust* (Minneapolis: Lerner, 1995), 10. However, this is not to say that Haacke has not participated in the discourse of memorialization, as works such as *And You Were Victorious After All* (1988), in Graz, Austria, may be thought through a broader discourse of counter-memorialization, and alongside work by other artists such as Jochen Gerz's *Monument against Fascism* (1986) in a suburb of Hamburg, Germany. Also note Eric Michaud, *The Cult of Art in Nazi Germany*, trans. Janet Lloyd (Stanford, Calif.: Stanford University Press, 2004), 27. Also Buchloh, "Hans Haacke," 45–60.
21. Mark Godfrey, "Barnett Newman's Stations and the Memory of the Holocaust," *October* 108 (Spring 2004): 35–50, esp. 48.
22. Vered Maimon has posed a compelling critique of the equation of information with truth, rhetoric of unveiling, and dependence upon a sovereign artistic subject within Haacke's body of work and the art history that attends it—however, it should also be noted that, as suggested above, Haacke's admission of his work's contingency, and the provenance gaps within this particular project, may complicate an account of his work as a call for an undifferentiated and unassailable truth. Vered Maimon, "The Third Citizen: On Models of Criticality in Contemporary Artistic Practices," *October* 129 (2009): 85–112.
23. Bois et al., "A Conversation with Hans Haacke," 45.
24. See Haacke, *Framing and Being Framed;* Wallis, *Hans Haacke: Unfinished Business;* and Flügge and Fleck, *Hans Haacke*.

25. Sol LeWitt, "Serial Project #1, 1966," *Aspen Magazine,* no. 5–6 (1967), ed. Brian O'Doherty, n.p.
26. Benjamin Buchloh, "Conceptual Art, 1962–1969: From an Aesthetic of Administration to the Critique of Institutions," in *Conceptual Art: A Critical Anthology* (London: MIT Press, 1999), ed. Alexander Alberro and Blake Stimson, 531. The essay was originally published as "De l'esthétique d'administration á la critique institutionnelle/From the aesthetic of administration to institutional critique," in Claude Gintz et al., *L'Art conceptuel: Une perspective,* trans. Judith Aminoff et al., exh. cat. (Paris: Musée d'Art Moderne de la Ville, 1989): 29–31.
27. Buchloh, "Conceptual Art, 1962–1969," 533.
28. Thomas Crow, "Unwritten Histories of Conceptual Art," in *Art after Conceptual Art,* ed. Alexander Alberro and Sabeth Buchman (Vienna: Generali Foundation, 2006), 57.
29. Crow, "Unwritten Histories of Conceptual Art," 57.
30. Alexander Alberro, "Specters of Provenance: National Loans, the Königsplatz, and Maria Eichhorn's *Politics of Restitution,*" in Maria Eichhorn et al., *Maria Eichhorn: Restitutionspolitik / The Politics of Restitution,* exh. cat. (Cologne: Verlag der Buchhandlung Walther Konig, 2004), 53–67, esp. 57. Jonathan Petropoulos, *Art as Politics in the Third Reich* (Chapel Hill: University of North Carolina Press, 1996), 275. Stephen Feinstein, *Witness and Legacy: Contemporary Art about the Holocaust* (Minneapolis: Lerner, 1995), 9.
31. Maria Eichhorn et al., *Maria Eichhorn: Restitutionspolitik/The Politics of Restitution,* exh. cat. (Cologne: Verlag der Buchhandlung Walther Konig, 2004), 74, 264. On Washington Agreement violations, see Michael Franz, "Information, Transparency and Justice: International Provenance Research Colloquium (Washington, D.C., November 2004)," trans. Renate Gatzky, *International Journal of Cultural Property* 12 (2005): 503–8.
32. E. Randol Schoenberg, "The Unfinished Business of the Unfinished Business of World War II," in *Holocaust Restitution: Perspectives on the Litigation and its Legacy,* ed. Roger Alford and Michael J. Bazyler (New York: New York University Press, 2005), 288–314. Also note Alberro's footnote that if the Lenbachhaus wanted to hire a provenance researcher for this project, "the City of Munich would not have allowed public funds to be spent for this purpose." Alberro, "Specters of Provenance," 56n15.
33. Rosalyn Deutsche, "The Art of Not Being Governed Quite So Much," in *Hans Haacke: For Real; Works, 1959–2006,* ed. Matthias Flügge and Robert Fleck, trans. Hans Haacke and Steven Lindberg (Düsseldorf: Richter, 2006), 62–79, esp. 76.
34. In her writing on recent activist art, Carrie Lambert-Beatty advocates for what she terms an "art of the plausible" in Joep van Lieshout's designs for Women on Waves, asserting that "instead of symbolically promoting change, the project's method is to make it so." It is this effort, of performatively "making it so" and of information being produced and circulated, that is significant in the politics of Haacke's and Eichhorn's work. Carrie Lambert-Beatty, "Twelve Miles: Boundaries of the New Art/Activism," *Signs* 3, no. 22 (2008): 309–26.
35. Susanne Gaensheimer, "Politics of Restitution: An Exhibition by Maria Eichhorn at Städtische Galerie im Lenbachhaus und Kunstbau," in Maria Eichhorn et al.,

Maria Eichhorn: Restitutionspolitik / The Politics of Restitution, exh. cat. (Cologne: Verlag der Buchhandlung Walther Konig, 2004), 13. Note that in response to a question about the austerity of her work, Eichhorn replied that the piece's presentation was kept simple and bare, as there was no need to create a scandal with the work—that the present condition of restitution and provenance research was scandalous enough, one only had to show that. Maria Eichhorn, personal communication, August 2007.

36. Eric Michaud, *The Cult of Art in Nazi Germany,* trans. Janet Lloyd (Stanford, Calif.: Stanford University Press, 2004), 30, 34–36; on the relation of people, spirit, and art, see esp. 37. See also Jonathan Petropoulos, *Art as Politics: The Nazi Elite's Quest for the Political and Material Control of Art* (PhD diss., Harvard University, 1990), 357.
37. Note that Haacke and Eichhorn broaden the scope of biography from basic provenance recommendations. In Nancy Yeide et al., *The AAM Guide to Provenance Research* (Washington, D.C.: American Association of Museums, 2001): 9–32.
38. Maria Eichhorn, "Glossary," in Maria Eichhorn et al., *Maria Eichhorn: Restitutionspolitik / The Politics of Restitution,* exh. cat. (Cologne: Verlag der Buchhandlung Walther Konig, 2004), 278–79.
39. Eichhorn, *Maria Eichhorn: Restitutionspolitik / The Politics of Restitution,* 13.
40. Jacques Derrida, *Archive Fever: A Freudian Impression,* trans. Eric Prenowitz (Chicago: University of Chicago Press, 1996), 2.
41. Mieke Bal, "Telling Objects: A Narrative Perspective on Collecting," in idem, *A Mieke Bal Reader* (Chicago: University of Chicago Press, 2006): 269–88, esp. 277.
42. Henrik Oleson, "Pre Post: Speaking Backwards," in *Art after Conceptual Art,* ed. Alexander Alberro and Sabeth Buchman (Vienna: Generali Foundation, 2006), 213–32.
43. Eichhorn, *Maria Eichhorn: Restitutionspolitik / The Politics of Restitution*, 237–57.
44. Alexander Alberro, "Institutions, Critique, and Institutional Critique," in *Institutional Critique: An Anthology of Artists' Writings*, ed. Alexander Alberro and Blake Stimson (Cambridge, Mass.: MIT Press, 2009), 18.
45. Simon Sheikh, "The Trouble with Institutions, or Art and Its Publics," in Nina Möntmann, ed., *Art and Its Institutions: Current Conflicts, Critique and Collaborations* (London: Black Dog, 2006), 142. See also Bal, "Telling Objects," 269–88, esp. 276–77.
46. Andrea Fraser, "From the Critique of Institutions to an Institution of Critique," *ArtForum* 44, no. 1 (2005): 278–83.
47. Julia Bryan-Wilson, "A Curriculum for Institutional Critique, or the Professionalization of Conceptual Art," in *New Institutionalism,* ed. Jonas Ekeberg (Norway: Office of Contemporary Art, 2003), 105.
48. Fraser, "From the Critique of Institutions to an Institution of Critique," 281; Martha Rosler, "Lookers, Buyers, Dealers and Makers: Thoughts on Audience," in *Decoys and Disruptions: Selected Writings, 1975–2001* (Cambridge, Mass.: MIT Press, 2004), 9–52.
49. Mark Godfrey, "The Artist as Historian," *October* 120 (2007): 140–72, esp. 143; Maria Eichhorn, *Maria Eichhorn Aktiengesellschaft*, exh. cat. (Eindhoven, Netherlands: Van Abbemuseum, 2007), 27.

50. Jack Burnham, "Steps in the Formation of a Real-Time Political Art," in Hans Haacke et al., *Framing and Being Framed: 7 Works, 1970–1975,* ed. Kasper König (Halifax: The Press of the Nova Scotia College of Art and Design, 1986), 134.
51. Alexander Alberro, *Conceptual Art and the Politics of Publicity* (Cambridge, Mass.: MIT Press, 2003), 169.
52. Maria Eichhorn, *Maria Eichhorn: The Artist's Contract,* ed. Gerti Fietzek (Cologne: Verlag der Buchhandlung Walter König, 2009), 14, 170–71. This was based on the exhibition *The Artist's Reserved Rights Transfer and Sale Agreement by Seth Siegelaub and Bob Projansky*, Salzburger Kunstverein, 1998. Eichhorn's and Alberro's views may be more similar than Eichhorn sets out, as elsewhere Alberro argues "Siegelaub's contract ensured that one facet of the new art would not be so readily accessible—namely, the experience of ownership." Alberro, *Conceptual Art and the Politics of Publicity*, 169.
53. Elizabeth Ferrell, "The Lack of Interest in Maria Eichhorn's Work," in *Art after Conceptual Art,* ed. Alexander Alberro and Sabeth Buchmann (Vienna: Generali Foundation, 2006), 202.
54. Eichhorn, *Maria Eichhorn: The Artist's Contract.*
55. Eichhorn, *Maria Eichhorn: The Artist's Contract,* 349–50.
56. Andrea Fraser, "What's Intangible, Transitory, Mediating, Participatory, and Rendered in the Public Sphere? Part II," in *Museum Highlights: The Writings of Andrea Fraser*, ed. Alexander Alberro (Cambridge, Mass.: MIT Press, 2005), 60.
57. Eichhorn, *Maria Eichhorn: The Artist's Contract,* 170–71.
58. Eichhorn, *Maria Eichhorn: The Artist's Contract,* 69, 163
59. Eichhorn, *Maria Eichhorn: The Artist's Contract,* 74.
60. Catherine Moseley, *Conception: Conceptual Documents, 1968 to 1972,* exh. cat. (Norwich, U.K.: Norwich Gallery, 2001), 71.
61. Eichhorn, *Maria Eichhorn: The Artist's Contract,* 114–15. For reproductions of Buren's *Avertissement*, see Maria Eichhorn, "On the *Avertissement:* Interview with Daniel Buren (1998)," in *Institutional Critique and After,* ed. John Welchman (Zurich: JRP/Ringier, 2006), 85–123.
62. Eichhorn, *Maria Eichhorn: The Artist's Contract,* 254. For examples of this conversation, see Simon Leung, "Contemporary Returns to Conceptual Art: Renée Green, Silvia Kolbowski, and Stephen Prina," *Art Journal* 60, no. 2 (2001): 54–71; James Meyer, "The Strong and the Weak: Andrea Fraser and the Conceptual Legacy," *Grey Room,* no. 17 (2004): 82–107.
63. Douglas Crimp, "Redefining Site-Specificity," in *On the Museum's Ruins* (Cambridge, Mass.: MIT Press, 1993), 151–86, esp. 156. Also see Chin-Tao Wu, *Privatising Culture: Corporate Art Intervention Since the 1980s* (London: Verso, 2002).
64. Gertie Fietzek, "Editor's note," in Maria Eichhorn, *Maria Eichhorn: The Artist's Contract,* ed. Gerti Fietzek (Cologne: Verlag der Buchhandlung Walter König, 2009), 23–25.
65. Most famously in *Der Pralinenmeister (The Chocolate Master)* of 1981, Haacke researched chocolatier Peter Ludwig's professional biography and activities in relation to the various chocolate companies he owns. Ludwig wanted to purchase the work and Haacke refused, for fear that Ludwig was buying it to keep it out of

exhibitions and circulation. Previously, Ludwig also attempted to buy Haacke's *Manet-PROJEKT '74*—Ludwig's reluctance to sign the contract eventually led to Haacke's refusal to sell the work to him.

66. Eichhorn, *Maria Eichhorn: The Artist's Contract,* 74. See also Hans Haacke, "Museums, Managers of Consciousness," in *Hans Haacke: Unfinished Business,* ed. Brian Wallis (Cambridge, Mass.: MIT Press, 1986), 60–73.
67. Grace Glueck, "Artists to Withdraw Work at the Biennale," *New York Times,* 6 June 1970, 27.
68. Ferrell, "The Lack of Interest in Maria Eichhorn's Work," 197–98.
69. Eichhorn, "On the *Avertissement,*" 115.
70. Maria Eichhorn, *Between Artists: Maria Eichhorn, John Miller* (New York: A.R.T. Press, 2008), 77.
71. Quoted in Eichhorn, *Maria Eichhorn: The Artist's Contract,* 166.
72. Eichhorn, *Maria Eichhorn: The Artist's Contract,* 11.
73. Andrea Fraser, "What's Intangible, Transitory, Mediating, Participatory, and Rendered in the Public Sphere? Part II," 63. Fraser astutely notes that "the predominant orientation of conceptualism was not to refuse to sell an artwork, but to control it" and to "revolutionize the political economy of art by returning collectors to the more altruistic motives of patronage projected onto art's premarket past." See also Alexander Alberro, "Reconsidering Conceptual Art, 1966–1977," in *Conceptual Art: A Critical Anthology,* ed. Alexander Alberro and Blake Stimson (London: MIT Press, 1999), xxvi–xxvii, esp. xxiii.
74. According to Haacke and Weber, various institutions and organizations, such as the Museum of Modern Art and the Art Dealers Association, have lobbied against resale royalties' inclusion into federal law. Eichhorn, *Maria Eichhorn: The Artist's Contract,* 74.
75. Alberro, *Conceptual Art and the Politics of Publicity,* 168. Also, as Eichhorn notes in Eichhorn, *Maria Eichhorn: The Artist's Contract,* 15:

    > It recalls the law, without law, makes itself independent of legislatures. . . . In the Agreement, all clauses have the status of suggestions, which can be changed, replaced, or struck out. . . . [The Agreement] is an expression of the 1960s critique of social conditions applied to the example of art and the art trade; in the context of the civil rights movement, increasing political awareness, and the practice of negotiating contracts, as a reacquisition of rights based on a Marxist legal view.

76. Maria Eichhorn, *Maria Eichhorn Aktiengesellschaft* (Cologne: Walther König, 2007), 25; see also Eichhorn, *Maria Eichhorn: The Artist's Contract,* 176.

ANNE HIGONNET

AFTERWORD
The Social Life of Provenance

Provenance Lists

So many passions in such small spaces. So many epic tales compressed into such dry lists.

Provenances are posted right next to most of the art we see, though we might not notice them. They are a standard feature of the labels in museums, where we most often encounter real art (as opposed to reproductions of art). A label provenance is extremely abbreviated, with information grammatically compressed into a string of owners' names separated by semicolons. Yet even the provenances that are not printed on labels, for example, those in auction and collections catalogs, are not much more fleshed out, grammatically or conceptually. Researchers and art historians have devoted countless hours of skilled and meticulous research to tracking the ownership of art objects since they were made, only to leave us with husks. Provenance turns its research into dated lists of those who have legally owned objects called art, leaving out more than it includes. Sometimes the abbreviation excises entire swathes of history.

A remarkably extreme case can be found on the label of an ivory pendant mask from Benin in the New York Metropolitan Museum of Art (fig. 1). The Met, one of the most important museums in the world, urges its visitors to pay close attention to this label. The label is marked with three earphone icons that act, like the three stars in a Michelin guide, to designate an object that is among the greatest in the whole museum, not just in its department. On the left side of the label is the following information about the place and time the mask was made, as well as the material it is made of:

Pendant Mask
Nigeria, Kingdom of Benin
Edo Peoples
16th century
Ivory

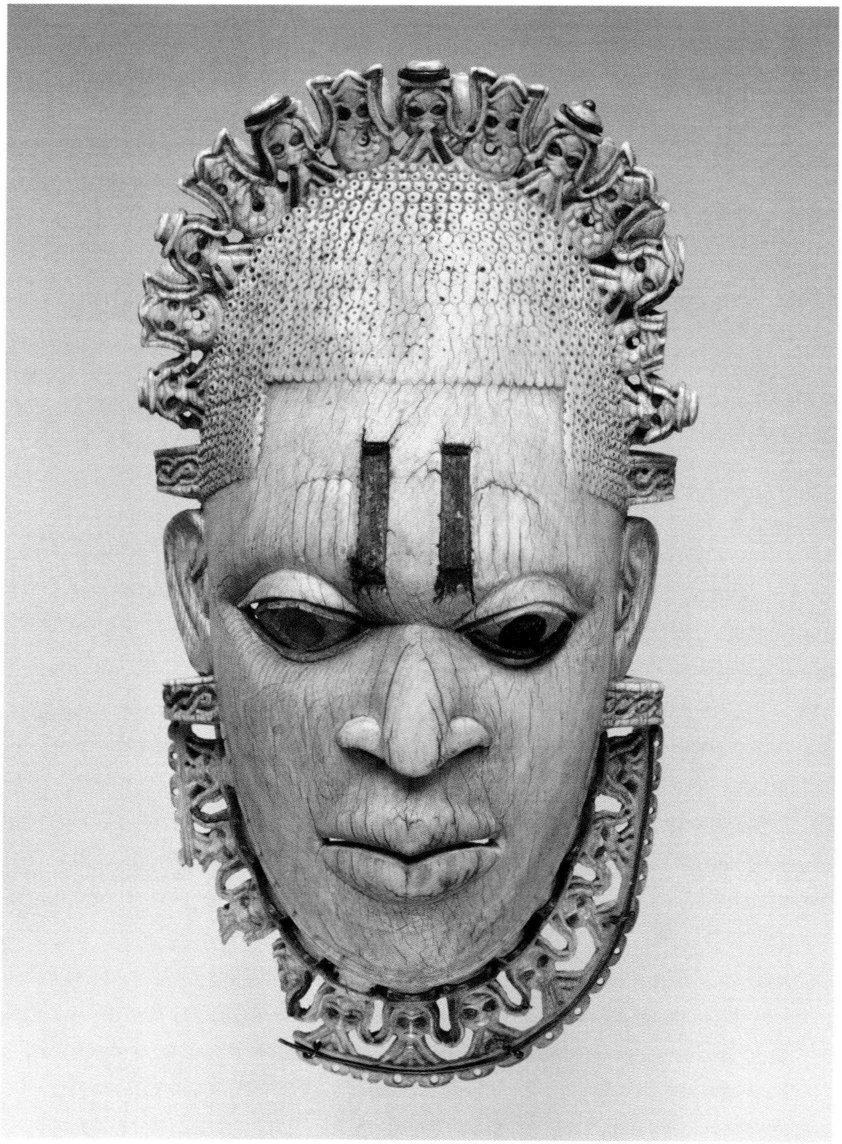

Fig. 1.
Pendant Mask: Iyoba.
16th century, Nigeria, Edo, Court of Benin, ivory, iron, copper (?), 23.8 × 12.7 × 8.3 cm (9⅜ × 5 × 3¼ in.). New York, The Metropolitan Museum of Art, The Michael C. Rockefeller Memorial Collection, Gift of Nelson A. Rockefeller, 1972, 1978.412.323.

The provenance of the object is printed below in a separate block of smaller type:

> Ex colls.: Ralph Moor; C. G. Seligman
> The Michael C. Rockefeller Memorial Collection
> Gift of Nelson A. Rockefeller, 1972

The typographic gap between origin and provenance, however, is nothing compared with the historical gap between the two. The little white space between the two lists on the wall label hides a huge leap across time and space. As if many decades never occurred and many miles never existed, an object made for a royal court in Africa suddenly appears in the collections of European and American art collectors and ends up in the Metropolitan Museum. In the gap are hidden the dramas of global power dynamics, military conquest, massive movements of wealth from one continent to another, and the tragedies of racism.

On second thought, the gap in the label may itself be the most eloquent part of the Benin mask's provenance. Some forms of ownership, apparently, have the power to obliterate others and alter history. Whoever wrote the label might have assumed that an object acquires a provenance only when it starts to be considered an art object. But perhaps that logic works the other way around: maybe provenance helps decide when and where an object becomes art. Is there a link between the power to hide and the power to create artistic status? Is artistic status withheld in order to make the history of the object less likely to be scrutinized?

Because it is so extreme, the case of the Metropolitan's Benin mask label reminds us that provenance can be a nasty business. In the best of cases, provenance implies some form of power, if only the power to make a generous gift. Provenance also, of course, records forms of power produced by random chance or direct inheritance. The avid acquisition that usually creates collections, however, is also likely to be enabled by less palatable sources of power, in the form of military or economic dominance, financial supremacy, theft, or pillage. No wonder we have been reluctant to confront those sources. In many cases, provenance does derive from some of humanity's worst behavior, whether on collective or individual scales. If we are determined to keep our art and its history apart from any greedy, elitist, ruthless, oppressive, or exploitive facts of ownership, then provenance will have to remain a parched, bleached domain of evasive erudition, one that allows current owners of art objects to commit sins of omission as needed. To separate an art object from the history of the passions it has aroused, both good and bad, denies the full range of the energy it has inspired. If we refuse to believe how badly art has made us behave, then we do not fully acknowledge its power. The history of collecting is the history of how we have cared about art, for better and, sad but true, very often for worse. Most provenances force us to find that passionate history only by reading between the lines.

The problem with provenance, however, is more fundamental than those sins of omission. It reaches into every aspect of art history, not only the obviously difficult political ones. In another provenance corner, we find the most socially neutral intellectual revolutions in taste condensed into lists that are just as reductive as the ones that conceal traumatic global events. Turning to standard museum catalog entries—the other ubiquitous location of provenance—we find, for instance, an entry like the one in a 2011 Tate Britain watercolor exhibition catalog:

> 36
> Francis Towne 1739–1816
> *The Source of the Arveyron* 1781
> Pen and ink and watercolour on paper 31 × 21.2 cm
> Tate. Purchased as part of the Oppé Collection with assistance from the National Lottery through the Heritage Lottery Fund 1996.[1]

The entry accounts for a watercolor by Francis Towne of a landscape, painted in 1781 (fig. 2). For the late eighteenth century, Towne's watercolor is extremely abstract. Such a watercolor was highly unlikely to have been collected by any public institution when it was made, let alone exhibited in order to set standards for its medium. In the 1780s, it might not have qualified as a finished work of art at all. The catalog entry does explain this discrepancy between late-eighteenth-century aesthetic standards and those of the Tate in 2011, but only between the lines. Provenance provides the key.

Further inquiry reveals that the watercolor had been collected by Paul Oppé, a man whose early-twentieth-century modernist vision allowed him to see qualities in eighteenth-century landscapes so radical they were still fresh in 1996, when the British state was able to acquire his entire collection, for reasons that had everything to do with national arts policy at the time.[2] This provenance story may be barely political and hardly controversial, but between the lines hovers a whole history of style—of how, when we change aesthetics, we can see old art in completely new ways.

Art historians like the meanings that cluster around an object at the moment it was created. Those are the meanings consciously or unconsciously intended by artists, along with the immediate reactions of audiences or critics. They may

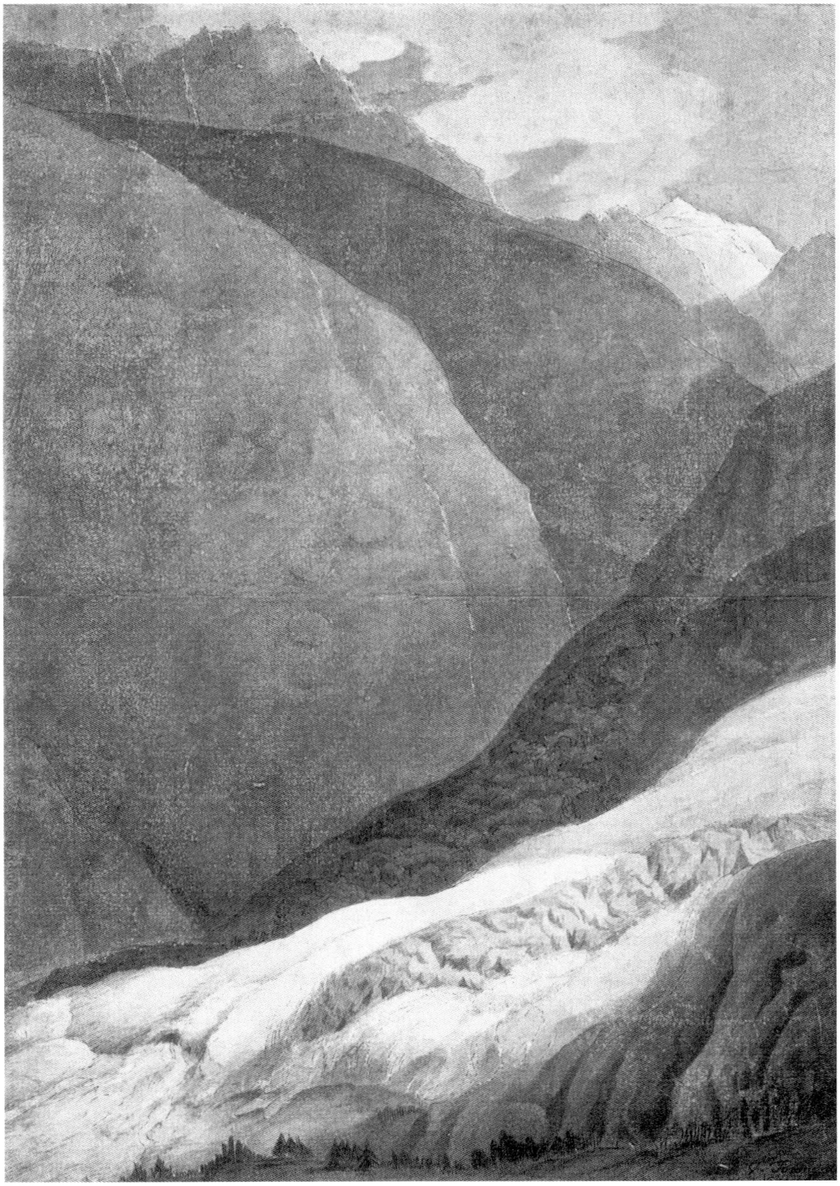

Fig. 2.
Francis Towne (English, 1739–1816).
The Source of the Arveyron, 1781, pen and ink and watercolor on paper, support: 31 × 21.2 cm ($12\frac{1}{4} \times 8\frac{3}{8}$ in.).
London, Tate, Purchased as part of the Oppé Collection with assistance from the National Lottery through the Heritage Lottery Fund 1996, T08147.

well be the single most important set of meanings in an object's history—but they are not the only ones. If we were taking into account meanings intended by patrons, for instance, we could be pushing an object's history back before the moment of its creation. Such provenance prequels, so to speak, create values for art through advance plans to possess, collect, or display an object not yet imagined by its author. And after an object is created, its meanings continue to change, until we receive them in all their complexity—or accept some while we refuse others. It will never be easy to tell a story in which meanings swirl in multiple helixes along a chronological line of history that rarely runs straight. If we have confined provenance to the lists we see, in their sparest form, on museum labels and in exhibition catalog entries, it is because we have not, as a discipline, been ready to confront the challenging ways in which meaning is transformed over time: flowing clearly and smoothly, wrapped, knotted, or tangled, while the forces of art criticism, art history, ownership, collection, and installation (among others) constantly create and compound new meanings that irrevocably alter all previous meanings.

Among the many forces continuously transforming meaning, none have more potential to push art historians further away from the creation moment than provenance. Because provenance examines where an object moves, and to whom, over time, it is by definition diachronic. And in the narrowest possible way, or perhaps I should say in the most latent possible way, the diachronic potential of provenance has been realized. Provenance, we all know, can dramatically increase price. Dealers and auction houses have therefore invested heavily in provenance research, either indirectly, through academia, or directly, as a part of their business. But this massive research effort, which sets the tone for all museum provenance work, has done as much to restrict our understanding of ownership as to enhance it, by producing a provenance in the image of the art market. Provenance as we have known it is only about transfers of ownership that allow buying and selling in art markets. Either the transfers are themselves sales or they are the inheritances and gifts that give the right to sell. This is why conventional provenances end with sales or gifts to museums. The museum, in theory, terminates an object's life in the art market.

Yet owning an art object could represent much more. Ownership expresses the energy of wealth, in all its myriad, and historically changeable, forms. Ownership also mobilizes expertise and the rhetorical articulation of expertise. Ownership controls the conditions according to which an object is seen; collection and display determine how we perceive art visually—in relation to other objects, in relation to institutional or personal space, and in relation to ourselves. We could begin to alter our understanding of ownership by calling it possession. If we were, however, to enlarge the scope of provenance by thinking of it as the history of possession, what model could help us manage that expansion?

Exchange Value in the Place of Punctuation

Many models might work. I chose the one I suggest here because it is based on transactions over time, which is to say because it is based on something like provenance. Let me start with Arjun Appadurai's *The Social Life of Things* and its idea of exchange value. *Provenance* could be renamed *the social life of art things*. According to Appadurai, value is produced by exchange: by the exchange of commodities. Long committed to the proposition that trade creates and sustains societies, anthropologists consider the exchange of things to be a social act, during which social values are negotiated and adjudicated, above and beyond the simple trade of things or currencies for each other. Appadurai defines what he calls a *commodity situation* as a "situation in the social life of any 'thing' . . . in which its exchangeability(past, present, or future) for some other thing is its socially relevant feature." He calls any given commodity situation a *regime of value*. Some exchanges, however, may involve intangible factors—a possibility Appadurai gingerly acknowledges by enclosing the word *thing* in quotation marks. Art objects, as Appadurai himself recognizes, may be among the subtlest commodities, the least like "things."[3] But after recognizing the problem of art, Appadurai sets it aside. So from this step forward, art historians are on their own.

At this step, art historians have, by and large, ceded the social life of art things to other fields. "The fields of anthropology, sociology, and economic history have traditionally been better equipped than art history to analyze the freight of significance embodied in such a gesture of marking," writes Gail Feigenbaum.[4] Has the social life of things perhaps also seemed too popularizing or too anecdotal? Some perceptive recent books about provenance have been written for general audiences, such as *The Hare with Amber Eyes* by Edmund de Waal, which tells the saga of a netsuke collection moving from one generation of his family to the next; or *Girl in a Green Gown* by Carola Hicks, which alternates chapters on the iconography of Jan van Eyck's *Arnolfini Portrait* with chapters on episodes of its ownership. I would argue that art history could and should reclaim the social life of art from its academic neighbors, because provenance is too tightly intertwined with form and visual meanings to be deprived of an art-historical skill set. The forms of art and the conditions of its technical making can generate its social life. In a reverse direction, the conditions of an art object's possession and display can alter most of its meanings, including whether or not it is considered art at all. Whom do we consider to be an object's maker? How and why do we remember it? What does it stand for? To whom should it belong? Where do we see it? The answers to all these questions may be determined by its provenance.

Usually, art objects are exchanged for some kind of wealth. In our modern era, we tend to equate wealth with money, which could be a mistake. It might be revealing to count how many of the transfers recorded in the provenances of all the objects in a major museum collection were money sales and how the pattern of those transfers has changed over time. My guess, which is only a guess, is that money sales become dominant sometime during the eighteenth century. In any case, rather than accepting the neutrality of any exchange, we could instead, thanks to Appadurai, consider how each time an object is exchanged, a link in a chain of transmission has been forged.[5] The simplicity of the punctuation marks that separate owners in classic provenances imply that objects just move from one owner to the next.[6] Those punctuation marks replace verbs, replace history, and replace meaning. It is in the place of those marks that the most crucial parts of provenance occur. Each punctuation mark signifies an exchange: an exchange of possession, which is always an exchange of some sort of value for another.

Nor is exchange always equitable, especially not when one kind of value is exchanged for a very different kind of value. In cases like those of the Metropolitan Museum's Benin mask, when provenance excludes some sorts of transfers—theft or looting, say—provenance actually hides imbalances of power among kinds of possession. Any form of possession includes the power to classify, to rank, to demote, to display or not; the power to tell a story or not, to tell one kind of story rather than another—the power, in short, to create meaning and also to suppress meaning. Provenance has often acted as an argument in favor of one kind of possession, possession due to money exchange, an argument that works by denying, through silence, other forms of possession. In cases like those of the Metropolitan's Benin mask, one can wonder if provenance represents not only the triumph of one kind of possession over another—Western money over Benin kingship—but also a broader historical triumph of one kind of exchange over another: Western money exchanges over Benin royal inheritance.

Lest my argument seem to be veering too much toward complaint, let me make it again with a second, much less fraught, example, the provenance of Tate Britain's Towne watercolor. When an exceptionally abstract (for its time) work of art enters a modernist collection, where it becomes part of a group whose dominant visual characteristics are purely formal, are not representational values being exchanged for formal ones? When those interpretive meanings leave a family collection, having been bought by a government for a national museum, are not private values being exchanged for public ones? Denunciation is by no means the only mode in which a new history of provenance could be written. The point is to analyze the history of art more fully, by taking into account more ways in which art has mattered to us. The point is to write essays like those in this volume. The essays in this collection make provenance an integral part of the history of art, each accomplishing a crucial task.

Should Provenance Emulate Provenience?

The value of art has always depended on relationships between objects, wealth, location, and knowledge. Those relationships have kept on changing in an ongoing history, a history that could be provenance. Which brings me to the central irony of Rosemary Joyce's comments on provenience and provenance. From my point of view, the irony is that *provenience,* which is denigrated by those outside the discipline of archaeology in favor of what has been called *provenance,* is what provenance could be and maybe should be. The debate tracked by Joyce over the difference between provenience and provenance seems, at first, to be a difference between one moment in the biography of an object and the entirety of its biography, between one findspot and a whole itinerary. And yet, the further Joyce delves into the debate, the more multidimensional provenience becomes, while provenance narrows. For some archaeologists, at least, the term *provenience* means not only the physical place where they discovered an object but also evidence about its use and value, which, in turn, implies how and why it got to the findspot. Archaeologists recognize that the findspot is a rupture in the circulation of the object, one that expresses and creates conditions of possibility for knowledge. Many art historians deem those forms of knowledge irrelevant, at least to their discipline, or believe formal stylistic analysis can be substituted for provenience. Hovering close to the surface of the provenience/provenance debate are the ethical issues of cultural property. Provenience exposes the conditions of ownership, while provenance accepts them. I imagine that every point on the itinerary of provenance could be a provenience. Together, those proveniences would constitute the social life of art things—extending from the conditions that brought objects into being all the way to present conditions of collection and exhibition (which might continue to change long after objects were acquired by a museum). Then—and here is where provenance would be transformed—could one not imagine a sort of provenience that extends from the find moment to the present? Could one not imagine those conditions of possibility prior to the find moment flowing right on past the find moment, constantly evolving or mutating, perhaps being interrupted, contradicted, distorted, or even replaced in an ongoing history of meanings? Surely the history of reception is one strand of such a history, and so is a historiography organized around art criticism. To these strands could be joined a renewed provenance.

Provenance Value

The art market has always put a value on some provenance exchanges. Uwe Fleckner reminds us that, for centuries, a famous or powerful owner—a prince, for instance, or a celebrity—added value to an art object, a value that could surpass the value of the original object itself.[7] The object was said to be "ennobled" by its previous possession. Elizabeth A. Pergam describes a particularly lucrative example. Sir Joseph Duveen earned the nickname "world's greatest salesman" by becoming perhaps the most successful dealer of the time (the turn of the nineteenth to twentieth centuries) at ennobling art objects. By cunningly putting history on hold during the Gilded Age, Duveen managed to exchange ancien régime noble status for capitalist gains. In the same complexly transitional moment, however, Pergam explains, an increasingly organized and professionalized field of art history perfected a discourse of formal style along with the discourse of individualized authorship, which together gradually supplanted the exchange value of aristocratic provenance.

What I want to emphasize here is the transformative power of exchange. In the dynamic moment of exchange, ennobling a work's provenance can turn an ordinary object into an extraordinary one, a moderately valuable object into a supremely valuable object. Roger E. Stoddard reminds us of an even more extreme type of transformative potential. When a copy of a book is bought for its prestigious or historically significant ownership, for an "amusing annotation" or a "presentation bookbinding," the copy is transformed into a unique object.[8]

Value Added or Subtracted

Because provenance values are produced by the dynamics of exchange, they are volatile, and they can be used arbitrarily. Fleckner provides us with a prime example of one type of provenance value being used simultaneously in two opposite ways, with "eloquent contradictions." Nazi confiscation of modernist art turned it into "degenerate" art. In their display of these objects, the Nazis made sure provenance would create a negative value. "In the exhibition, provenance information was usually displayed on the wall directly below the artworks and in arrestingly large type, so that the public could not fail to register which museum had bought a particular condemned work and how much it had paid." Yet when it came to selling such art abroad for foreign currency or keeping art for personal Nazi possession, all traces of its provenance were sedulously erased to conceal the mode of exchange through which it had most recently been acquired. In some cases of sales abroad, Fleckner tells us, the same kind of provenance information that had been displayed to create negative ideological value in German exhibitions was actually promoted to create positive financial value in the international art market.[9]

Positive or Negative Value—Objects as Functions of Provenance

The power of provenance to create either positive or negative value can sometimes become so great that the art object and its provenance reverse their usual roles. The Nazis used provenance to reinterpret objects, but though their interpretations could determine the fates of the objects to which they were attached, their newest exchange value remained a function of the objects and the histories those objects had accumulated. Dominique Poulot describes the way objects became a function of provenance during the French Revolution.

In an attempt to retroactively define creativity according to its Republican imperatives, revolutionaries selected art for exhibition according to their interpretation of the politics of all earlier makers or owners. "In this respect, the revolutionary museum might almost be defined as a collection of provenances through which one could effortlessly read a philosophical history of the political conditions required for the perfection of art."[10] Alternatively, revolutionaries posited the possibility of "freeing" art from the shackles of its provenance by replacing an unacceptable provenance with one that had been newly constructed according to revolutionary principles of natural individualism. "This principle is clearly illustrated in the policy of restoration, which theorizes a superior form of provenance: a primitive state deriving from the artist's independence and its recovery from the historical provenances subsequently layered over the work by its successive ownership and sales."[11] By passing into a public-museum domain constituted by the French Revolution, art objects acquired a singular new meaning. In such extreme cases, the power of one exchange value is demonstrated by its ability to become the sole criterion according to which art is evaluated.

Provenance Has a History

By taking the form of lists, classic provenances pretend to be neutral. Yet the enterprise of making provenance lists itself has a history, which proves to be far from neutral.

As Sophie Raux reminds us, Michel Foucault has made it impossible to ignore the thick and multiple quality of discourses and the discursive power of institutions.[12] Each of these discourses and institutions has a history and belongs to what Foucault called *epistemes* or what Appadurai called *regimes of value*. The discourses of provenances have always involved many factors. We can begin by considering the institutions of the gallery, the auction house, the personal collection, and the museum, as well as the forms of knowledge called *connoisseurship* and *art history*. It has been, at the very least, exchanges among the modalities of individual authorship, money, collecting, and professional expertise that have produced a modern regime of artistic value.

One crucial moment in the history of provenance occurred in the middle of the eighteenth century in France, when, as Poulot and Raux tell us, provenance became a self-consciously practiced activity.

Raux describes what she convincingly argues is the first modern moment in which provenance is consciously produced as a form of knowledge. Of course, objects were owned prior to the eighteenth century, and records kept. The concentration, acceleration, and above all public impact of the markers Raux provides us, however—1729: the so-called *Recueil Crozat;* 1748: the Angran de Fonspertuis catalog; 1755: Pierre Rémy's catalog of the Louis Pasquier sale; 1783: François-Charles Joullain's *Répertoire*—indicate a critical threshold in the discourse of art's value.

Consider the related issue of signatures. Raux points out that many paintings were signed. We assume that signatures are signs of authenticity, or at least that they are authentic until proven false. Yet in the period Raux describes, signatures were not used by the writers of catalogs as guarantees of authenticity. Poulot, furthermore, points out that the first book of artisan marks was published in 1750. This indicates that some kind of artisanal signature was considered to be relevant to the public domain of knowledge by that date; however, it also indicates that prior to 1750 such information was not considered worth publishing. Moreover, Poulot observes, the French word for "signature" was not commonly used until the nineteenth century. What this shows, I believe, is that no aspect or feature of an object functions as knowledge until it is mobilized and deployed as such, nor can any form of knowledge become valuable until it is exchanged. Can the production of provenance be isolated from the market it supposedly serves? Is it sufficient to place the expansion of a market for paintings and the production of provenance in a cause-and-effect relationship? I would argue that the discourse of provenance and the money value of paintings were in a dialectical relationship with each other, and neither the money value of paintings nor their ownership value could be created except through their exchange. The pace of paintings being sold was tied to the acceleration of exchange between forms of knowledge and wealth. Both provenance and money were currencies of artistic value, traded at the exchange rates Raux has demonstrated.

Provenance Becomes a Subject of Art

When artists began in earnest to take provenance as a subject for their work, another crucial moment in the history of provenance was reached. Although, as Gail Feigenbaum reminds us, Western objects have been inscribed with signs of their provenance (as, for example, when Abbot Suger "converted" a Muslim rock-crystal vessel to Christianity by mounting it and inscribing the mount),[13] and although, as Zaixin Hong recounts, Chinese paintings have for centuries routinely been inscribed with such signs of provenance, the moment located by Jeannine Tang in the mid-1970s, when the institutional-critique art movement began to build provenance into its very forms, was a point of no return.

By 1974, as Jeannine Tang argues convincingly in this volume, Hans Haacke, notably among others, had initiated a critique of provenance that took the form of visualized provenance. In his work on the history of Edouard Manet's *Bunch of Asparagus,* Haacke made us see a succession of exchange values, each framed just like the reproduction of Manet's painting that begins his sequence. By the early 2000s, Tang demonstrates, institutional critique had itself become institutionalized enough to be taught in colleges and universities. By 2003, Maria Eichhorn's *Politics of Restitution* built research about provenances occluded by Nazi confiscation into its mode of exhibition as well as into its content. The conscious production of provenance as a form of knowledge, begun at the moment Raux describes, was being challenged for not being conscious enough. Haacke and Eichhorn demanded, as it were, provenience. The traumas of twentieth-century German history, Tang shows, incited institutional critique's rupture of provenance's political and economic innocence. Art like Haacke's and Eichhorn's demands that we acknowledge the many forms of power at stake in provenance's transactions and also that we realize how a monetary price can conceal the consolidation of corporate power as well as the social networks of gift exchange.

More recently, we may have entered yet another phase in the history of provenance, one in which provenance is not only taken as the subject of art but even affirmed as a formal element of artwork. Institutional critique like that of Haacke and Eichhorn challenged provenance from the outside, from the position of critique. It dealt with provenance as a series of events originating in the existence of already-created art objects, events that could be organized into a serial history whose significance could be retroactively revealed and therefore corrected in the present.

Some art made in the last decade suggests that, in the twenty-first century at least, provenance generates art and art does not exist at all except within the meanings of its possession. An installation by Jan De Cock exhibited at the New York Museum of Modern Art in 2008 called *Denkmal 11* (also produced in a book version[14]) was constituted by floor-to-ceiling visual reiterations of its polysemous provenance. De Cock continued the legacy of institutional critique: in one framed panel on a MoMA wall, for instance (which was replicated as a book page layout), De Cock showed how art promoted by Tate Modern in London promotes UBS, the Union des Banques Suisses. Whereas Haacke proposed that the history of a canonical work of art (a painting by Manet) is the history of one mode of exchange value—its sales for money—De Cock proposed that the history of a canonical work of art (a sculpture by Umberto Boccioni) is the history of many kinds of exchange value, including the work's reproduction, art-historical analysis, and museum installation. De Cock's installation, furthermore, also included the conditions of its patronage and display by merging seamlessly into the hangings of the nearby permanent photography galleries. As De Cock said in an interview posted on the museum's website at the time, "I see the current works in the collection as a part of my exhibition, part of my wall. At the same time, 'Denkmal 11' is a part of the museum's history."[15] By including the name, and especially the exact location, of the museum in his full title—*Denkmal 11, Museum of Modern Art, 11 West 53rd Street, New York, 2008*—De Cock signals that the work and its provenance have become one and the same.

If provenance can become art, it surely can become art history.

Notes

1. Alison Smith, ed., *Watercolour,* exh. cat. (London: Tate Publishing, 2011).
2. Via the Internet, Tate Britain provides this information about the Oppé collection, which makes a transcendent value judgment about the collection without delving into the historical conditions of its quality:

   The Oppé Collection was formed by the distinguished scholar and collector Paul Oppé (1878–1957) during the first half of this century. After his death the collection remained in his family. It is one of the last major collections of British drawings and watercolours to have stayed in private hands and has long been regarded as being of national importance.

   The collection comprises some 3,000 individual works. It consists mainly of watercolours but also includes drawings, oil sketches on paper, sketchbooks, albums and prints. The overwhelming bias of the collection is towards landscape, reflecting the important development of the British watercolour school during what has become known as its Golden Age from 1750 to 1850.

The greatest strength of the collection is in late eighteenth-century landscape drawings, many produced by artists working in Switzerland and Italy in the era of the Grand Tour, for example, Richard Wilson, Francis Towne, JR Cozens, John (Warwick) Smith, John Downman, William Marlow, William Pars, and other less well-known contemporaries.

The acquisition of the Oppé Collection was made possible by grants from the National Lottery through the Heritage Lottery Fund and from the National Art Collections Fund. The cataloguing of the Oppé Collection has also been supported by the National Lottery through the Heritage Lottery Fund.

"The Prints and Drawings Rooms: Prints and Drawings Rooms Holdings," Tate Research, accessed 9 February 2012, http://www.tate.org.uk/research/researchservices/printrooms/holdings.shtm.

3. Arjun Appadurai, ed., *The Social Life of Things: Commodities in Cultural Perspective* (Cambridge: Cambridge University Press, 1986), 13, 15.
4. Gail Feigenbaum, "Manifest Provenance," this volume, 7, 25n6.
5. See Rosemary A. Joyce, "From Place to Place: Provenience, Provenance, and Archaeology," this volume, for more on this.
6. See Feigenbaum, "Manifest Provenance," this volume.
7. Uwe Fleckner, "Marketing the Defamed: On the Contradictory Use of Provenances in the Third Reich," this volume, 137.
8. Roger E. Stoddard, "Transfigured Books: Notes on Some Marks Left by Owners in Books of American Poetry Printed from 1610 to 1820," this volume, esp. 159–64 and 167–69.
9. Fleckner, "Marketing the Defamed," 141–42 and figs. 2, 3.
10. Dominique Poulot, "Provenance and Value: The Reception of Ancien Régime Works of Art under the French Revolution," this volume, 73.
11. Poulot, "Provenance and Value," 76.
12. See Sophie Raux, "From Mariette to Joullain: Provenance and Value in Eighteenth-Century French Auction Catalogs," this volume, 100–101, 103n37.
13. Feigenbaum, "Manifest Provenance," 23–25.
14. Jan De Cock, *Denkmal 11, Museum of Modern Art, 11 West 53rd Street, New York, 2008* (New York: Museum of Modern Art, 2008).
15. http://www.moma.org/interactives/exhibitions/2008/jandecock/interview.html.

BIOGRAPHICAL NOTES ON CONTRIBUTORS

GAIL FEIGENBAUM is associate director of the Getty Research Institute. She holds a doctorate in art history from Princeton University and has published extensively in the field of early modern European art. She worked at the National Gallery of Art in Washington, D.C., for many years and later headed the paintings department at the New Orleans Museum of Art. She has organized numerous exhibitions for which she has written and edited catalogs, including *Ludovico Carracci* (1994), *Degas and New Orleans: A French Impressionist in America* (1999), and *Jefferson's America and Napoleon's France: An Exhibition for the Louisiana Purchase Bicentennial* (2003); she recently coedited *Sacred Possessions: Collecting Italian Religious Art, 1500–1900* (2011), and she is coediting a book on the display of art in Roman palaces.

UWE FLECKNER is a professor of art history at Universität Hamburg, director of the Warburg-Haus Hamburg, and coeditor of the collected writings of Aby Warburg. He founded the Forschungsstelle "Entartete Kunst" (Research center on "degenerate art") and its ongoing publication series, seven volumes of which have appeared since 2007. Fleckner has authored numerous books and articles on eighteenth- to twenty-first-century art history, especially on French and German art and art theory, and political iconography.

ANNE HIGONNET works on eighteenth- and nineteenth-century art, childhood, and collecting. She received her PhD from Yale University in 1988. Higonnet once taught at Wellesley College and is now Ann Whitney Olin Professor of Art History at Barnard College. She has published five books and dozens of articles on topics ranging from impressionism to contemporary photography. Her many awards include Guggenheim, Getty, and Social Science Research Council fellowships, as well as grants from the Mellon, Howard, and Kress Foundations. Higonnet's most recent book is *A Museum of One's Own: Private Collecting, Public Gift* (2009).

ZAIXIN HONG received his PhD from China Art Academy in 1996 and is a professor of Chinese art history at the University of Puget Sound. His research interests focus on Song-Yüan (960–1368) and modern Chinese art. Hong has published widely on these subjects, often with an emphasis on global art collecting. He is working on a new book, *Shaking Hands with the Future: The Transformation of Chinese Painting through Overseas Collecting.*

ROSEMARY A. JOYCE received her PhD from the University of Illinois at Urbana-Champaign in 1985. She is currently Richard and Rhoda Goldman Distinguished Professor in the Social Sciences and professor of anthropology at the University of California, Berkeley. She moved to Berkeley in 1994 as associate professor of anthropology and director of the Phoebe A. Hearst Museum of Anthropology (1994–99). From 1985 to 1994, Joyce held appointments in the Department of Anthropology and the Peabody Museum of Archaeology and Ethnology at Harvard University.

ELIZABETH A. PERGAM received her MA in eighteenth-century French and British art from the Courtauld Institute of Art and her PhD from the Institute of Fine Arts, New York University, under Professor Robert Rosenblum. Her book *Manchester Art Treasures Exhibition of 1857: Entrepreneurs, Connoisseurs and the Public* (2011) is a study of the first blockbuster art exhibition and its role in the construction of an art-historical canon. She is currently editing a volume titled *Contemporaneity: Papers on Drawing in the 21st Century.* She teaches in the master's program at Sotheby's Institute of Art, New York. Her next project will be on the history of curatorial practice.

DOMINIQUE POULOT, professor at the Sorbonne (Université Paris 1), teaches art history and heritage studies. He was an invited professor at the Université de Genève, Laval University, and Columbia University in New York City. Poulot is the recipient of numerous fellowships, including a Getty Scholar grant (2009–10) and a New York University fellowship (2012). He is the author of *Musée, nation, patrimoine (1789–1815)* (1997), *Une histoire du patrimoine en Occident, XVIIIe–XXIe siècle: Du monument aux valeurs* (2006), the essay "Alexandre Lenoir and the Museum of French Monuments" in volume 4 of Pierre Nora, ed., *Rethinking France=Les lieux de mémoire* (2010), and the introduction to Antoine Quatremère de Quincy, *Letters to Miranda and Canova on the Abduction of Antiquities from Rome and Athens* (2012).

SOPHIE RAUX is associate professor of history of early modern art at the Université Lille (IRHiS-CNRS) in France. Her research focuses mostly on the circulation and consumption of pictures and art objects in the southern Low Countries and France during the ancien régime. From 2008 to 2012, she coordinated the Agence Nationale de la Recherche's international research program titled Art Markets in Europe, 1300–1800: Emergence, Developments, Networks.

INGE REIST received her PhD from Columbia University. She is director of the Center for the History of Collecting at the Frick Collection and Art Reference Library, where she is also chief of Research Collections and Programs. Her research has focused on Italian Renaissance and baroque art and on the history of collecting. She has published on topics ranging from issues surrounding looted art to analyses of turning points in collecting history and display such as the Orléans sale.

TILMANN VON STOCKHAUSEN studied history and the history of art at Munich, Manchester, and Hamburg universities. He received his MA in 1992 and a PhD in 1997. His thesis, *Gemäldegalerie Berlin: History of Its Acquisition Policies 1830 to 1904*, was published in 2000. He conducted postdoctoral research (1997–98) in conjunction with the Art Patronage research project at Freie Universität Berlin led by Thomas W. Gaehtgens and held a graduate internship at the Getty Research Institute, Los Angeles (1998–99). In 2008, after professional experience at Pommersfelden (near Bamberg), Dresden, and Potsdam, he was appointed director general of the Städtische Museen Freiburg in Breisgau and director of the Augustinermuseum in that city.

ROGER E. STODDARD retired from Harvard University in 2004 as curator of rare books in the Harvard College Library, senior curator in the Houghton Library, and senior lecturer in English. Since then, he has published bibliographies of Primo Levi (2006), Andrée Chedid (2006), and W. G. Sebald (2009); *Jacques-Charles Brunet, le grand bibliographe: A Guide to the Books He Wrote, Compiled, and Edited, and to the Book-Auction Catalogues He Expertised* (2007); *B. H. B. in Retrospect* (2007); *A Long Goodbye to Library Service* (2008); and, with David R. Whitesell, ed., *A Bibliographical Description of Books and Pamphlets of American Verse Printed from 1610 through 1820* (2012). He holds an appointment as associate in the Department of English and works from his carrel in the Harry Elkins Widener Memorial Library. His study of Joseph-Marie Quérard, "Un martyr de la bibliographie," will be published in *Bulletin du bibliophile* (Paris).

JEANNINE TANG is an art historian completing a dissertation at the Courtauld Institute of Art on conceptualism's media politics. She teaches contemporary art and curatorial history and is an academic adviser at the Center for Curatorial Studies, Bard College. Previously a fellow at the Smithsonian American Art Museum, she is also an alumna of the Whitney Independent Study Program and a contributor to publications including *Artforum*, *Afterimage*, *Journal of Visual Culture*, and *Theory, Culture, and Society*.

ILLUSTRATION CREDITS

Every effort has been made to identify and contact the copyright holders of images published in this book. Should you discover what you consider to be a photo by a known photographer, please contact the publisher. Photographs of items in the holdings of the Getty Research Institute are courtesy the Research Library. The following sources have granted additional permission to reproduce illustrations in this book:

Feigenbaum
Fig. 3. Réunion des Musées Nationaux / Art Resource, NY. Photo: Thierry Olivier
Fig. 4. bpk, Berlin / Gemäldegalerie, Staatliche Museen, Berlin / Joerg P. Anders / Art Resource, NY
Fig. 5. Image courtesy National Gallery of Art, Washington
Fig. 6. Réunion des Musées Nationaux / Art Resource, NY. Photo: Daniel Arnaudet

Hong
Figs. 1, 4, 6, 7. Image copyright © The Metropolitan Museum of Art
Fig. 2. Drawing by the author
Fig. 3. Image copyright © The Metropolitan Museum of Art / Art Resource, NY
Fig. 5. Courtesy of the National Palace Museum, Taipei

Poulot
Figs. 1, 4. © Réunion des musées nationaux (Château de Versailles) / Gérard Blot
Fig. 5. © Réunion des musées nationaux (Château de Versailles) / All rights reserved
Fig. 6. Photo: Courtesy Felicity Bodenstein
Fig. 7. © Versailles, Château de Versailles, distributed Réunion des musées nationaux / image Versailles, Château de Versailles

Raux
Table 1. Chart by the author
Fig. 2. © Dulwich Picture Gallery, London. Dist. RMN / By permission of the Trustees of Dulwich Picture Gallery
Figs. 6a, 6b. Bibliothèque nationale de France

Pergam
Fig. 1. Image © The Metropolitan Museum of Art / Art Resource, NY

Stockhausen
Fig. 1. bpk / Gemäldegalerie, SMB / Jörg P. Anders
Fig. 2. bpk / Gemäldegalerie, SMB

Fleckner
Fig. 1. © Berlin, Zentralarchiv der Staatlichen Museen zu Berlin—Preussischer Kulturbesitz
Fig. 2. © Berlin, Zentralarchiv der Staatlichen Museen zu Berlin—Preussischer Kulturbesitz. © VG Bild-Kunst, Bonn, 2011
Fig. 3. © Berlin, Zentralarchiv der Staatlichen Museen zu Berlin—Preussischer Kulturbesitz. © Fondation Oskar Kokoschka / VG Bild-Kunst, Bonn 2011. © VG Bild-Kunst, Bonn 2011
Fig. 4. Art © Munich, Stadtarchiv. Photo by Georg Schödl, © VG Bild-Kunst, Bonn 2011
Fig. 5. © Universität Hamburg, Kunsthistorisches Institut. © VG Bild-Kunst, Bonn 2011. © VG Bild-Kunst, Bonn 2011. Photo courtesy Kunsthistorische Institut.
Fig. 7. © Succession H. Matisse / VG Bild-Kunst, Bonn 2011

Stoddard
Figs. 1, 4. Courtesy of the Massachusetts Historical Society
Fig. 3. Boston Athenæum

Tang
Figs. 1, 2, 3. Photograph by Hans Haacke
Fig. 4. Städtische Galerie im Lenbachhaus und Kunstbau, Munich. Photograph by Ernst Jank. © VG Bild-Kunst, Bonn, and Maria Eichhorn, 2011
Fig. 5. The Federal Republic of Germany on permanent loan to the Städtische Galerie im Lenbachhaus und Kunstbau, Munich. Courtesy the Bundesamt für zentrale Dienste und offene Vermögensfragen (BADV). Photograph by Ernst Jank. © VG Bild-Kunst, Bonn, and Maria Eichhorn, 2011

Higonnet
Fig. 1. Image © The Metropolitan Museum of Art
Fig. 2. Image © Tate, London

INDEX

note: page references in *italics* refer to figures; those followed by "n" refer to notes, with note number.

Titles in the ISSUES & DEBATES series

Surrealism in Latin America: Vivísimo Muerto
Edited by Dawn Ades, Rita Eder, and Graciela Speranza
ISBN 978-1-60606-042-1 (paper)

Sacred Possessions: Collecting Italian Religious Art, 1500–1900
Edited by Gail Feigenbaum and Sybille Ebert-Schifferer
ISBN 978-1-60606-042-1 (paper)

Cultural Identity and the Ancient Mediterranean
Edited by Erich S. Gruen
ISBN 978-0-89236-969-0 (paper)

Bernard Picart and the First Global Vision of Religion
Edited by Lynn Hunt, Margaret Jacob, and Wijnand Mijnhardt
ISBN 978-0-89236-968-3 (paper)

Harry Smith: The Avant-Garde in the American Vernacular
Edited by Andrew Perchuk and Rani Singh
ISBN 978-0-89236-735-1 (paper)

Walls of Algiers: Narratives of the City through Text and Image
Edited by Zeynep Çelik, Julia Clancy-Smith, and Frances Terpak
ISBN 978-0-29598-868-9 (paper)

The Fragment: An Incomplete History
Edited by William Tronzo
ISBN 978-0-89236-926-3 (hardcover)

Rethinking Boucher
Edited by Melissa Hyde and Mark Ledbury
ISBN 978-0-89236-825-9 (paper)

Late Thoughts: Reflections on Artists and Composers at Work
Edited by Karen Painter and Thomas Crow
ISBN 978-0-89236-813-6 (paper)

Seeing Rothko
Edited by Glenn Phillips and Thomas Crow
ISBN 978-0-89236-734-4 (paper)

Situating El Lissitzky: Vitebsk, Berlin, Moscow
Edited by Nancy Perloff and Brian Reed
ISBN 978-0-89236-677-4 (paper)

Representing the Passions: Histories, Bodies, Visions
Edited by Richard Meyer
ISBN 978-0-89236-676-7 (paper)

The Archaeology of Colonialism
Edited by Claire L. Lyons and John K. Papadopoulos
ISBN 978-0-89236-635-4 (paper)

Looking for Los Angeles: Architecture, Film, Photography, and the Urban Landscape
Edited by Charles G. Salas and Michael S. Roth
ISBN 978-0-89236-616-3 (paper)

Dosso's Fate: Painting and Court Culture in Renaissance Italy
Edited by Luisa Ciammitti, Steven F. Ostrow, and Salvatore Settis
ISBN 978-0-89236-505-0 (paper)

Censorship and Silencing: Practices of Cultural Regulation
Edited by Robert C. Post
ISBN 978-0-89236-484-8 (paper)

Art in History/History in Art: Studies in Seventeenth-Century Dutch Culture
Edited by David Freedberg and Jan de Vries
ISBN 978-0-89236-201-1 (hardcover), ISBN 978-0-89236-200-4 (paper